Phillies
'93

Phillies
'93
An Incredible Season

Rich Westcott
Photographs by Alan Kravetz

 Temple University Press
Philadelphia, Pennsylvania

Temple University Press, Philadelphia, PA 19122
Copyright © 1994 by Temple University
All rights reserved
Published 1994

Printed in the United States of America

Library of Congress Cataloging-in-Publication Data

Westcott, Rich.
    Phillies '93 : an incredible season / Rich Westcott : photographs by Alan
Kravetz.
      p. cm.
    ISBN 1–56639–231–4
    1. Philadelphia Phillies (Baseball team)   I. Title.
GV875.P45W47   1994
796.357′64′0974811—dc20   94–5488

*To my son Chris Westcott for his constant help and
support and for his invaluable
technical assistance, without which this book
would not have been possible*

Contents

Foreword

During one of the first days of spring training, while the Phillies were still encamped at Carpenter Complex, Darren Daulton and I were having a short conversation about his personal expectations for the 1993 season.

The year before, Daulton had emerged from a long, uphill battle through a number of serious injuries and other setbacks to become the premier catcher in the National League. Not only had he led the league in RBI and set a club record for home runs by a catcher, Daulton had finally fulfilled his earlier promise and become an extremely capable defensive player.

When, on the late February day, he was asked to assess what he expected to achieve in the upcoming season, Daulton didn't hesitate with an answer. "I just want to do my part to help us win, and let the numbers take care of themselves," he said. "I'd like to do what I did last year, but I'd rather take less numbers and more wins. That would be a little more fun. I got some personal gratification from last year. But it still wasn't as much fun as having a winning unit could be."

Daulton's remarks were revealing. In an era when many major leaguers place personal glory above team success, the veteran catcher took just the opposite stance. And what he said would set the tone for the entire team during a season in which individual accomplishments took a secondary position to winning.

Indeed, the 1993 Phillies were a classic example of the old cliche, "There's no 'I' in team." This was a group that won as a team, that lost as a team and that shared the whole range of emotional experiences that surround a big league team. And what they accomplished as a team made for one of the most glowing success stories in Phillies history as well as in all of sports.

The following pages are intended to chronicle the people and the events that comprise that story. It is hoped that these pages will not only allow the reader to relive the wonderful, whacky season of 1993, but also to serve as a kind of documentary of that season.

Because of the impossibility of such a task in a book this size, this volume does not purport to cover every situation or discuss every personality. Nor is it intended as a compendium of funny one-liners or humorous incidents, many of which have been overemphasized elsewhere.

This team goes much deeper than comic relief, anyway. Had it been merely a team of comedians and beer-guzzling rogues, as it was so often portrayed, it would have more closely resembled Phillies teams of the 1920s, 1930s and early 1940s when a seventh place finish gave cause for a celebration.

This team had much more than that. It had heart. Guts. Desire. Talent. It was made up of a bunch of gamers with a never-give-up attitude. Sure, neither they nor their games were always pretty, but they never failed to be exciting and they never failed to put on a good show at the ball park.

Having covered the team from spring training through the World Series, I can say without hesitation that this was a team that was as enjoyable and as entertaining to watch as any Phillies team I've ever seen. And that covers a lot more Phillies teams—not to mention a few Philadelphia Athletics teams—than I care to admit I've seen.

When it comes to pleasurable viewing over the last 50 years, the '93 Phils rank right up there with the 1950 and 1980 Phillies, two teams that have a special place in the club's long and not terribly successful history. In vastly different ways, both had exhilarating teams and memorable seasons that took them to the World Series.

The 1993 Phillies were also an exhilarating team that staged a memorable season. They, too, have now earned a special place in Phillies history.

Rich Westcott

1

Gypsies, Tramps and Thieves

I n the 111-year history of the Philadelphia Phillies, it is entirely reasonable to suggest that the franchise never had a team quite like the one that carried its colors in 1993.

It was a team that exceeded the expectations of all but the wildest dreamers, vaulting all the way from last place the previous year to the World Series, where only four other Phillies teams had made an appearance since 1883. Only two other major league teams in the 20th century have made the leap from last to first.

The '93 Phils resided in first place in the National League's East Division for all but one day—a league record. And in finishing the regular season with 97 victories, the team had the third highest total of wins in club history.

In a pulsating League Championship Series, the Phillies, making their sixth appearance in a post-season playoff, achieved a stunning upset by defeating the powerful Atlanta Braves four games to two in a best-of-seven series. In the World Series that followed, the Phillies managed to stay close to the defending world champion Toronto Blue Jays but lost two games they could have won and wound up losing in six games.

It was, nonetheless, a memorable season, which was made that way, not only because of the marvelous record of the team, but also because of the special blend of athletes who comprised the team.

There were no nationally recognized superstars on the Phillies. To be sure, the Phils had some talent. But the team was basically a collection of hard-working, everyday players from vastly different backgrounds who had come together and learned—perhaps somewhat to their surprise— not only that they could play together, but also that they found immense pleasure in each other's company.

"We're really just a bunch of gypsies, tramps and thieves," said catcher Darren Daulton, the team's undisputed leader and the only player to have been with the Phillies before 1988.

Others had different names for the Phillies. Because of the distaste a few of them had for haircuts and the genteel art of shaving, they were portrayed as a grubby band of rogues. A few players seemed to have no objection to an extra meal now and then, which earned the team nicknames such as the Broad Street Bellies. Spitting, cursing, chewing tobacco and scratching various parts of the body also helped to build the team's image as a rough-and-tumble outfit that was really a throwback to an earlier era when the game of baseball was played by adult street urchins quite unlike the briefcase-laden robots who dominate today's game.

"We're a throwback, all right," first baseman John Kruk had said. "Thrown back by other organizations."

He was right, of course. Of the 25 players who played most of the year on the team, only five of them—Daulton, Ricky Jordan, Mickey Morandini, Kim Batiste and Kevin Stocker—had come up through the Phillies' farm system. The others had all been acquired through trades, drafted from other teams or signed as free agents.

Despite the persistence, especially of sportswriters, to portray the team in less than flattering terms—one wag even said they looked like "a prison softball team"—the image was largely distorted. The fact of the matter was, only a handful of players on the team really resembled what might be called a ragamuffin. Most of the players were trim, clean-cut fellows, who, unlike the dead-end kids they were cast as, more appropriately could have passed as the "boy next door."

True or not, the team's image did have an impact. Fans took to the '93 Phils like a hungry hound takes to a beefsteak. The Phillies were not only the darlings of the local citizenry—a group known in the past for its rough treatment of local teams and its willingness to criticize them at the drop of a pop fly—but they attracted a considerable amount of attention around the rest of the country.

The Phillies were often described as a "blue collar" team, and they attracted blue collar fans in droves. They also were the special favorites of legions of women who thought they were "cute" and children who idolized them, especially the likes of Lenny Dykstra, Kruk and Daulton.

Realistically, the Phillies were Everyman's Team. More so than any Phillies pennant winner since the endearing Whiz Kids of 1950, the '93 Phils could relate to the masses, especially the hard-bitten fans of the area who had spent a lifetime trying to embrace the Phillies but who in many cases were never quite able to do it.

So popular were the Phillies in all walks of life that the club drew a record home attendance of 3,137,674 in 80 dates at Veterans Stadium during the regular season. That was the first time the Phils exceeded three million spectators during a season, far surpassing the previous attendance record of 2,775,011 set in 1979.

The Phils were popular not only because of the scruffy, yet lovable image that set them apart from most ordinary teams and that evoked comparisons to the St. Louis Cardinals Gashouse Gang of the 1930s and the Oakland A's of the early 1970s. They also developed a following because of the special personality of the team.

They were known as a band of raucous, rollicking crazies; a gang of stand-up comics who could spit out hilarious one-liners as fast as they could down a pitcher of beer and who knew no boundaries when it came to having fun. But that was only off the field. When the Phils took to the diamond, they turned into an intense, highly motivated unit that was as serious as a police sergeant and that was hell-bent on winning.

"People look at this team and think we have a bunch of loose cannons," manager Jim Fregosi said. "But that's simply not true. This is an image that was built up in the press because we have a bunch of guys from different ballclubs. But we are a team, and no matter what happens we stay a team because the guys want to stay here and they want to win.

"If crazy is running out ground balls, playing hard and getting the uniform dirty," Fregosi said at another point, "then, yeah, they're crazy."

They were also determined. Few teams in this modern, laid-back time in professional sports played with the desire and determination with which they did in 1993. When the Phillies had to win, they usually did, as evidenced by key series during their regular season with the Cardinals and Montreal Expos and at both levels of post-season play when they came back after devastating losses. And no lead by an opposing team was ever safe. Throughout the season, the Phillies showed a relentless determination to never give up, rallying numerous times in the late innings to put out a victory that had seemingly been impossible.

"This was a team that never quit, that never died," said Dykstra, summarizing the way the Phillies played throughout the season.

It was also a team that had no shortage of arrogance, that could be difficult to get along with, especially with members of the press, who on more than one occasion were verbally assaulted for unflattering articles, and that was more than a little feisty. Whether it was an opposing pitcher throwing a ball close to the chin of a Phils batter, an umpire making a bad call or a sports writer asking what was considered to be a stupid question, the Phillies were never reluctant to show their disdain. Often it was accompanied by a spray of tobacco juice, an incredulous look or a loud disclaimer sprinkled with profanities and unflattering adjectives. On occasion, sneering was also a popular device.

But there was a warm side to the Phillies that was often hidden. The players cared deeply about each other. For the most part, they not only got along well with each other, but the season was marked with a glaring absence of team dissent. There were clubhouse cliques, of course. A cabal that included Daulton, Dykstra, Kruk, Dave Hollins, Mitch Williams and Pete Incaviglia roosted in the back of the clubhouse on what was often referred to as "Millionaires' Row," or by the residents themselves as "The Ghetto," and conspicuously and somewhat judgmentally set the tone for the whole team. But during the entire season, there was rarely any clubhouse bickering, and when it did occur, it was usually held in check and soon forgotten.

The Phillies were expert needlers, but when they razzed each other—which they did all the time—they did it in the spirit of fun. And having fun was certainly one of the major agendas of this team.

"This is the most fun I ever had playing baseball," said left fielder Incaviglia, who became one of the clubhouse leaders in his first season in Philadelphia. "I loved playing with these guys."

The Phillies' ability to laugh with and at each other was never more conspicuous than

Lenny Dykstra, sliding home against the Reds, led the National League in scoring with 143 runs.

on the first day of spring training. Outfielder Jim Eisenreich, one of the quietest players on the team and a victim of Tourette's Syndrome, was approached by Kruk, who jokingly requested some of the new player's medicine with the notation that he needed it to calm down. Later, when told about Eisenreich's affliction, pitcher Curt Schilling said, "Compared to what most of us have on this team, that's like having a common cold."

Such clubhouse banter was part of the spirited repartee that was the regular fare in the Phils' clubhouse. It was a clubhouse that also featured loud music blaring regularly from a boom box on top of Schilling's locker and players who after games frequently congregated over a few beers to discuss the battle just waged.

It was called chemistry by some, camaraderie by others. By any description, it was this one-for-all, all-for-one attitude and the players' uncanny ability to pick each other up that contributed as much as anything to the Phillies' 1993 success.

"One night somebody picks us up. The next night, somebody else picks us up. That's why we're on top," said third baseman Hollins.

In addition to getting along with each other and working well together, the most dominant characteristic of the 1993 Phillies was the unusual blend of colorful characters. This was a club that was filled with interesting and animated personalities.

There was Dykstra, the resourceful team catalyst with tobacco stains and infield dirt all vying for spots on his uniform; Daulton, the handsome heartthrob, team leader and consummate pro; Kruk, master of the one-liner, a character right out of a comic strip who could hit; Mitch Williams, the long-haired ulcer agent; fiercely intense Hollins; Tommy Greene, a quiet country boy with a loud and lively arm; the quietly elegant Eisenreich; the insightful Terry Mulholland; the talkative Schilling; the ebullient Wes Chamberlain; the raucous Incaviglia; the refreshing Mariano Duncan; the sometimes cantankerous Danny Jackson; the diligent Mickey Morandini; gentle Ben Rivera; wide-eyed, young, innocent Kevin Stocker; the articulate Milt Thompson; the hulking David West; team humorist Larry Andersen and the underutilized Ricky Jordan.

Each had his own set of special qualities, which when put together made the '93 Phillies a vastly more colorful—and appealing—team than most of the past entries of the franchise. The '93 Phils were certainly more colorful—and alive—than the often moody and highly mechanical 1980 team, which nonetheless rules as the best team in Phillies history by virtue of its winning the World Championship. Perhaps only the young and exciting 1950 team, which captured the attention of baseball fans throughout the nation with its fighting spirit and hustling style of play, rivaled the '93 Phils in the category of colorful teams.

And the '93 Phils had the nicknames to match. Dude (Dykstra), Bubba (Daulton), Jethro (Greene), Mikey (Hollins), Wild Thing (Williams), Jake (Kruk), Batty (Kim Batiste) and Schill, Mul, Stocks, Inky, Andy and Eisey all have carved a niche in Philadelphia legend.

It is a niche that hardly anyone but the players themselves thought possible when the squad convened for the '93 season. Most pre-season polls picked the Phillies to finish in the lower regions of the East Division, barely managing to squeeze in ahead of the expansion Florida Marlins. A few hardy souls thought the Phils might be able to inch as high as third or perhaps even second place, but the heavy favorite to win the division title was the Cardinals.

Why should anybody put much stock in the Phils anyway? Hadn't they finished a dismal last in 1992? And hadn't they placed last in three out of the five seasons prior to 1993? This was a team, the so-called experts concluded, that had a few good players and a lot of mediocre ones and that was going nowhere fast in a division that was regarded as the weakest in major league baseball.

The players and the team's management had different ideas. "We knew the guys could play," said general manager Lee Thomas, the architect who put together the club. "We really felt that we could win."

Daulton had similar feelings. "I went through spring training, and I thought we had a heckuva ball club," he said. "When I looked at the way we matched up with the other teams in the division, I thought that nobody got better and we did get better."

And they did. Bolstered by a flurry of off-season deals by Thomas, the Phillies had one of their best spring trainings in years, then began the season with the fastest start in club history. After falling out of first place for the only time all season on April 9, the Phils maintained a steady hold on the lead, stretching it to as many as $11\frac{1}{2}$ games—the high point of the season—by June 13.

By the All-Star Game, in which Daulton, Kruk and Mulholland were starters for the National League team and Hollins was a reserve, the Phillies' lead had slipped to five games. It dipped even lower a few days later when three straight losses at San Diego decreased the Phils' hold on the division to a scant three games. But a confidence-building three-game sweep of the Cardinals launched a successful home stand, and by mid-August the lead was back to nine games. It increased even more a little later before it slid backward again in September as the Expos threatened with a feverish second half finish. But regrouping, the Phils won 11 of 16 games over a critical stretch in mid-September, finally clinching the division title at Pittsburgh, 10–7, with the key blow being a grand slam home run by Duncan. Just five games remained in the season.

It was the team's sixth division title, joining the crowns in 1976, 1977, 1978, 1980 and 1983.

Almost no one expected the Phillies to stand a chance against the Braves in the League Championship Series. Atlanta was not only the National League champion in each of the previous two years, but in 1993 it had won the West Division title with a whopping 104 victories and with the third best second half in baseball history. Moreover, the Braves had the best pitching staff in baseball and a high-powered offense that made opposing pitchers run for cover. It would be no match, the experts all agreed.

Ah, but what did they know? After falling behind two games to one and getting battered in their two defeats, the Phillies roared back with three straight victories, clinching the National League pennant in the sixth game with a thrilling 6–3 victory that featured the pitching of Greene and the clutch hitting of Daulton, Hollins and Morandini.

Putting their names up with those of the 1915, 1950, 1980 and 1983 clubs, the Phillies had only their fifth pennant in club history.

It was on to the World Series where once again the Phillies were decided underdogs, this time to the American League champion Toronto Blue Jays, a team that had defeated the Braves in the World Series in 1992. Like the Braves, the Blue Jays were an awesome team with good pitching and a particularly devastating offense, led by hitters with the three highest batting averages in the American League during the regular season.

The Phillies waged a gallant fight. But in the fourth game, down two games to one, the Phils blew a five-run lead and wound up losing a disheartening 15–14 record-setting slugfest. Then, showing the toughness and resilience that had been a trademark of the club all season long, the Phillies came back with a riveting 2–0 victory on Schilling's five-hit masterpiece to force a sixth game back in Toronto. Once again, with victory within reach, reliever Mitch Williams, as he had done in Game Four, gave up the lead in the late innings. This time he did it by serving up a three-run home run to Joe Carter in the bottom of the ninth inning that gave the Blue Jays a series-clinching 8–6 triumph.

For the Phillies, Carter's blast put an end to what had been a marvelous season. A team in every sense of the word, the Phillies had attracted the attention and captured the hearts of the entire Philadelphia area and beyond by playing an exciting, animated brand of baseball that hadn't been seen in the area in years. They did it with a refreshing collection of players who were portrayed as misfits and crazies but who were really quite talented and who played the game the way it was meant to be played—hard, relentlessly and with unbending fervor.

It was a year of exceptional individual accomplishments, too. Dykstra became the first player in National League history to lead the league in at-bats and walks in the same season. He also led the league in hits, the 16th time a Phillies player has done that, and scored more runs (143) than any Phillies player since Chuck Klein crossed the plate 152 times in 1932. Dykstra, Hollins (104) and Kruk (100) gave the Phillies at least three players with 100 or more runs for the first time since 1932 and for only the fifth time in club history. And with Dykstra drawing 129 walks, Daulton 117 and Kruk 111, the Phillies became the first club in National League history to have three players walk 100 or more times in the same season.

While leading the league in runs, hits, doubles and walks, the Phillies had three players hit above .300—Eisenreich (.318), Kruk (.316) and Dykstra (.305)—the first time since 1976 that three regulars had done that. Seven players (Daulton, Incaviglia, Dykstra, Hollins, Kruk, Wes Chamberlain and Mariano Duncan) hit home runs in double figures—the first time that that many players had done it since 1987.

Pete Incaviglia (left) and Darren Daulton were the Phillies top home run hitters with 24 apiece.

All five Phillies starters—Greene, Schilling, Mulholland, Jackson and Rivera—won in double figures for only the second time in club history and the first time since 1932. Greene had the second best winning percentage (.800) in the league, while Greene, Mulholland and Schilling tied for second place in complete games with seven. David West tied for second in the league with 76 appearances, while Mitch Williams set a club record for most saves (43) in one season.

It was a marvelous year for a marvelous team. It was a team that would go down as one of the great sports franchises in Philadelphia history.

Wheeling and Dealing

The foundation for the 1993 Phillies was really laid on June 21, 1988, when club president Bill Giles announced the appointment of a new person to run the baseball operation of the team.

The Phillies had been without such a person since 1983 when then general manager Paul Owens moved down to the dugout to take over the manager's job after the mid-season dismissal of Pat Corrales. It was a fortuitous move for the Phillies because Owens guided the club to the National League pennant. But it effectively ended the widely respected Owens long tenure as the Phils' general manager, a position that would not be filled for five more years.

In the interim, Giles had run the club with the help of a group of the team's executives, who were somewhat derisively called by local pundits "The Gang of Six." It would not be one of the better periods in Phillies history.

One of the most visible functions of the Gang of Six was to evaluate talent and to recommend trades. It made a few good trades and a lot of bad ones. Meanwhile, the team headed downhill, slipping precipitously from the high levels the team had achieved as recently as 1983.

While small hordes of mediocre players came and went, managers and coaches came, saw and left, trailing a string of losses in their wake. The minor league system was in shambles, too, with much of the farm teams manned by stopgap players with hardly a bona fide major league prospect in sight. The scouting system was also weak, with a scarcity of strong draft picks, including those at the top, where Phils' selections each year seemed to be miserable failures.

Even with a second place finish in 1986, when they stumbled home a distant 21^1/$_2$ games behind the first place New York Mets, the Phillies were never remotely in contention, placing far down the ladder in the National League East standings. While a few good players such as Glenn Wilson, Juan Samuel, Steve Bedrosian, Von Hayes, Chris James and Kevin Gross adorned the Phillies' ranks, there was never enough of them. The result was that the Phillies went through one frustrating season after another, always opening the year full of promise and always ending it with disappointing outcomes.

Clearly, something had to be done to get the club that Giles had predicted would be the "Team of the 80s" back on track. And on June 21, 1988, Giles did it, naming a new general manager to run the team's baseball operation.

His name was Lee Thomas. A big, broad-backed, straight-shooter, Thomas had been a major league player himself with a nine-year career in the big leagues. Most notably he had been with the California Angels after being originally signed by the New York Yankees, with whom he broke into the majors in 1961. With the Angels, Thomas, whose nickname was Mad Dog, hit 50 home runs and collected 174 RBI over one two-year period, at one point lacing nine hits and driving in eight runs in a doubleheader. He was teammates with an offbeat bunch of characters that included Bo Belinsky, Dean Chance, Ryne Duren, Buck Rodgers, Rocky Bridges and a young and up-and-coming shortstop named Jim Fregosi.

Club president Bill Giles took charge of the organization in 1981.

After his playing days ended, Thomas went to work for the St. Louis Cardinals. In his 18 years with the organization, he served as a coach with the parent club, a minor league coach and manager, an assistant in sales and promotions, a traveling secretary and for the last seven years as director of the minor league system.

Thomas was a no-nonsense type, who occasionally demonstrated a fiery temper. He also had the guts of a bank robber, the nerve of a steeplejack and the courage of an NFL quarterback. In his carefully tailored suits, which he almost always wore around the office, Thomas did not project the image of a person who might harbor a secret ambition to be a high-wire artist. Nor would anyone ever have guessed that he could probably have earned a living washing windows on skyscrapers.

But as all who followed the Phillies came to realize, Thomas was really a closet daredevil, a riverboat gambler in corporate lawyer's clothing, a secret agent without a gun, a test pilot driving a four-door sedan.

Fearlessly, Thomas plunged into the business of righting a sinking ship. He revamped the farm system and the scouting department. He brought in new coaches and a new manager, and when his old friend from the Cardinals, Nick Leyva, didn't work out, he dumped him and hired another old friend, Fregosi.

Thomas used his biggest moves to rearrange the roster. Emphasizing that it was going to take five years for him to turn the club around, Thomas unleashed a flurry of player transactions, shipping players hither and yon and bringing in a slew of new players whom he thought could help. By the time the 1993 season arrived, Darren Daulton would be the only player still with the Phillies who was with the club when Thomas arrived. (Ricky Jordan came soon after Thomas.)

Some of Thomas's deals were outrageously one-sided in his favor. In fact, virtually every deal was a good one with only a few minor swaps turning out less than desirable. Always, Thomas traded with the idea of fitting the right player into the right place. He had a special talent for landing players whom he thought would get along with each other. Often when he traded, he made sure he would get a young pitcher in return, too.

"I'm not afraid to take the heat," Thomas said about his deals. "I've taken it before, and I can take it again. That's the fun of the job—knowing there's the heat out there.

"I like to win," Thomas added. "I don't like to lose. I think I know what you have to do to build a winner. You can't be impatient. Sometimes I am, and I know other people around here are, too. But if we're all patient, our time will come."

The first deal that would have a direct bearing on the 1993 Phillies was made on December 6, 1988, when Thomas sent veteran pitcher Kevin Gross to the Montreal Expos for pitchers Floyd

Through the 1993 season, Lee Thomas made 38 trades after becoming general manager.

Youmans, Jeff Parrett and Jeff Tabaka. Although the other two would contribute nothing to Phillies teams, Parrett had an outstanding season in 1989 and would later become a key part of a major swap with the Atlanta Braves.

But that was just the start for Thomas. Six months later, he made three blockbuster deals, including two on the same day that would have far-reaching implications for future Phillies teams. On June 2, 1989, Thomas sent outfielder Chris James to the San Diego Padres for outfielder John Kruk and infielder Randy Ready. Then on June 18, 1989, Thomas went way out on a limb by trading second baseman Juan Samuel to the New York Mets for center fielder Lenny Dykstra and pitchers Roger McDowell and Tom Edens. That same day, he also completed a deal with the San Francisco Giants in which he swapped Steve Bedrosian and minor leaguer Rick Parker for pitchers Terry Mulholland and Dennis Cook and third baseman Charlie Hayes.

All three trades were difficult to make because they sent away popular players who had enjoyed varying degrees of success in Philadelphia. But what Thomas got in return was the cornerstone for future Phillies teams and some talented players who would pump new life into a moribund franchise.

Kruk, a fine hitter, had slipped noticeably in San Diego and was badly in need of a change of scenery. The same was true of the irrepressible Dykstra, who had complained repeatedly about his lack of playing time in New York. In Mulholland and Cook, the Phillies were getting two young pitchers thought to be on the way up. Hayes gave the Phils a player they thought might be the third baseman of the future, while McDowell was a replacement for Bedrosian and Ready a valuable utilityman.

By the time the trades were consummated, the last vestiges of the golden era that extended from the mid-1970s to the early 1980s had also departed. In a teary farewell on May 30, future Hall of Famer Mike Schmidt announced his retirement. While Schmidt's exit left the Phillies temporarily without a marquee player, it also cleared the way for Thomas to mold a team completely to his own requirements. Thomas wanted players who would do anything to win and who would get along well together, and with his new players he had made some huge steps in that direction.

The general manager continued to make trades, but on December 4, 1989, he made a different kind of move that would turn into a big one for the Phillies. In the Rule 5 Draft, Thomas plucked an unheralded minor league third baseman away from the Padres, Dave Hollins. Within a few years, Hollins would be one of the premier young players in the National League.

The next major move by Thomas occurred on August 3, 1990, when he shipped Parrett and two minor leaguers with no chance of playing in Philadelphia, Jim Vatcher and Victor Rosario, to the Braves for outfielder Dale Murphy and pitcher Tommy Greene. It was hoped that the aging Murphy would supply some of the power lost by Schmidt's retirement, while Greene, a youngster with an incredibly lively arm, was seen as a future starter.

Later that same month, on August 30, the Phillies landed outfielders Wes Chamberlain, Tony Longmire and Julio Peguero from the Pittsburgh Pirates. The Bucs had inadvertently left Chamberlain and Longmire unprotected, and when the Phils put in a claim for them, Thomas had two more outfielders. To help ease the Pirates' embarrassment, the Phillies shipped outfielder Carmelo Martinez to Pittsburgh, getting Peguero in return.

Throughout the rest of 1990 and during 1991, Thomas made more trades, most of them involving fringe players. His next major deal came on April 7, 1991, when right before the season began, he acquired a much-needed relief pitcher, Mitch Williams, from the Chicago Cubs in exchange for young hurlers Bob Scanlan and Chuck McElroy, both with big league potential that had never quite been fulfilled in a Phillies uniform. In Williams, the Phillies finally got the closer they had lacked since Bedrosian's strong years in the late 1980s.

Shortly afterward, Thomas made another major move. This time, however, it did not involve a player. It involved a manager.

Thomas had been mildly criticized for hiring an unknown such as Leyva with no major league managing experience to run the Phillies after he dismissed popular Philadelphia native Lee Elia at the end of the 1988 season. But the general manager stuck by his good friend after the Phillies finished dead last in the National League East in 1989.

The Phillies' fortunes seemed to be on the upswing the following year when the club advanced to a tie for fourth place. But all was not well in the Phillies' inner sanctum. Thomas and Leyva were drifting apart. The split broke into a canyon early in the 1991 season when the Phillies got off to a slow start and seemed headed for nowhere. Thirteen games into the season, with the Phils having won just four games, Thomas abruptly fired Leyva and replaced him with Fregosi.

Thomas and Fregosi went way back together. They had been roommates as players with the Angels. When Fregosi needed a job after getting dismissed as manager of the Angels, Thomas hired him to pilot the Cardinals' Triple-A farm club at Louisville. Then after joining the Phillies, Thomas again summoned his old buddy, bringing Fregosi to Philadelphia originally in 1990 as a roving minor league pitching instructor and special assignments man, a position he held until named Phillies manager on April 23, 1991.

An outstanding shortstop during his playing days, Fregosi was a six-time All-Star who had hit .265 with 151 home runs and 706 RBI during a glittering 18-year career in the big leagues. The best days of his career had been spent with the Angels, but Fregosi also saw action with the New York Mets, Texas Rangers and Pittsburgh Pirates. He had landed with the Mets after being the main bait in a trade that sent Nolan Ryan to California.

Fregosi had become manager of the Angels at the end of his playing career and without benefit of minor league managing experience. He led the Angels from 1978 until his dismissal during the 1981 season, winning the American League West division title in 1979.

After being replaced by Gene Mauch in 1981, Fregosi didn't get back in the pilot's seat until landing in Louisville in 1983. In three and one-half seasons there, he won two division titles before getting the call to manage

Jim Fregosi was hired as manager early in the 1991 season.

the Chicago White Sox midway through the 1986 season. As skipper of the Pale Hose, Fregosi finished fifth in each of his two and one-half seasons.

Once he got to the Phillies, Fregosi quickly established himself as the man in charge. He got close to the players and developed a solid rapport with them, yet there was never any question about who was running the team. Fregosi ran a tight ship in many ways, but he gave the players plenty of leeway. The clubhouse, he said, belonged to the players and they were free to do whatever they wanted there.

"The job is to relate to the players, and get the best out of them," Fregosi said. "The day of managing where you say, 'This is how it's done and this is how it's going to be,' is all done with. That's the old style of managing, and it does not work in today's game.

"Players have to respect you and they have to trust you," he added. "If they don't do that, it's very difficult to manage. I don't have a lot of team meetings. But I do have a lot of meetings on an individual basis."

The players readily adapted to Fregosi's style of managing. He took to playing cards with them before games, laughing and joking with them in what is typically a rollicking clubhouse scene. He strived to keep the entire roster active, giving even reserve players playing time whenever possible.

And, most importantly, he communicated with his players, something several of his recent predecessors failed to do.

Fregosi also had an excellent coaching staff working under him. Grizzled pitching coach Johnny Podres, a World Series hero in 1955 when he won the deciding game for the Brooklyn Dodgers, was considered one of the best in the business. He was the dean of a talented staff that included hitting coach Denis Menke, third base coach Larry Bowa, dugout assistant John Vukovich, first base coach Mel Roberts and bullpen coach Mike Ryan. All except Roberts had long years of experience in the big leagues as players and coaches. Bowa, one of the great shortstops in Phillies history, had also been the manager of the San Diego Padres.

Fregosi could be gruff, especially with the media. He is supremely confident, egotistical and aggressive. He has a strong sense of humor and can trade wisecracks with the best of them. Fregosi refuses to criticize his players in public. Some of his critics say he is too stubborn, too reluctant to try things different ways, and that he's a better manager before the game than during it.

"I don't manage by the book," Fregosi said. "I manage according to the personnel I have. It's very easy to manage by the book because when you do that, everybody is thinking the same thing. I won't ask people to do certain things who don't have the ability to do those things. I try to keep my players in a realm where they can be successful, where they don't fail.

"What do I care about second-guessing? I can't worry about what other people say. I have to manage to get the most out of my players."

After driving the Phillies to a third place finish in 1991, Fregosi seemed to have the club poised to become a contender in 1992. Thomas pumped more help onto the roster that winter.

At the winter meetings in December, Thomas continued to build what would become the 1993 team when he drafted catcher Todd Pratt out of the Baltimore Orioles organization. The next day—on December 10—he signed free agent infielder Mariano Duncan, who as both a regular at second base and a roving utilityman would become an enormously valuable member of the Phillies lineup.

Perhaps two of the biggest outright heists pulled off by Thomas came early the following year. On April 2, 1992, the Phils' general manager swiped pitcher Curt Schilling from the Houston Astros for the meager price of unproductive pitcher Jason Grimsley. Then on May 28, he pilfered pitcher Ben Rivera from the pitching-rich Braves while giving up only minor league pitcher Donnie Elliott. In two deals in which he lost pitchers who were not in the club's immediate plans, Thomas landed not only two-fifths of the Phils' 1993 starting rotation, but a couple of strong righthanded hurlers who figured to be major forces on the Phils' pitching staff for many years.

Following a disastrous 1992 season in which injuries decimated the Phillies and the club tumbled back to last place, more lesser trades followed as Thomas continued to wheel and deal with the Phillies' roster. His next big acquisition came on November 17, 1992, when in a prearranged deal with the Florida Marlins, the Phillies got pitcher Danny Jackson, who had just been picked in the expansion draft from the Pirates, for minor league pitchers Matt Whisenant and Joel Adamson. Jackson would fill the bill, the Phillies hoped, as the fifth starting pitcher that the club so desperately needed.

Through much of the winter of 1992–1993, many hoped that the Phillies would land one or more of the many high-priced free agents who had entered the market. The fans urged it, the press urged it, but the Phillies ignored it, claiming that instead of spending a wagonload of money on a top-level player, they'd rather open their checkbook to several lesser but nonetheless useful players.

Available were pitchers such as Doug Drabek, John Smiley, Greg Swindell and David Cone, any one of whom, it was felt, the Phillies could dearly use. Numerous star-quality position players were also shopping for big money deals, including outfielders Kirby Puckett and Barry Bonds.

The Phillies did make a run at Puckett and Cone. But just as they had done the previous year when they went after outfielder Bobby Bonilla, the Phils' offers were rejected. It was back to the bargain levels of the free agent market.

There, the Phillies found some special bargains. For prices that collectively wouldn't have equalled the contract of one high-priced free agent, the Phillies signed outfielders Pete Incaviglia, Milt Thompson and Jim Eisenreich and relief pitcher Larry Andersen. They also ob-

Three of the Phillies off-season acquisitions before the 1993 campaign began were (from left) Pete Incaviglia, David West and Danny Jackson.

tained pitcher David West in a swap with the Minnesota Twins for pitcher Mike Hartley, who had come to the Phillies in a 1991 trade for Roger McDowell. All would become integral parts of the Phillies squad with the outfielders filling some gaping holes in the club's offense and Andersen and West playing major roles in the team's bullpen, a weak spot on the Phils for a number of years.

Those deals and a few other minor ones set the roster as the Phillies entered the 1993 season. Overall, the Phillies would acquire 13 of the players on their post-season roster by trades, two would be signed as draft choices and five would come to the club as free agents. Only five players—Daulton, Jordan, Mickey Morandini, Kevin Stocker and Kim Batiste—came up through the Phillies' farm system.

During the season, additional deals were made, extending Thomas's total since the 1992 season ended to 12 different transactions. Relief pitcher Roger Mason arrived on July 3 from San Diego in exchange for pitcher Tim Mauser; fireman Bobby Thigpen landed on August 10 from the Chicago White Sox in a swap for pitcher Jose DeLeon; and reliever Donn Pall was acquired on September 1 in another trade with the White Sox for minor league catcher Doug Lindsey in three moves designed to shore up the Phillies' sagging bullpen.

Others played during the season who had come through Thomas deals. Outfielder Ruben Amaro had come from the California Angels in the Von Hayes deal; shortstop Juan Bell came from the Baltimore Orioles, third baseman Jeff Manto and relief pitcher Mark Davis from the Braves and pitcher Kevin Foster from the Seattle Mariners.

Altogether, Thomas had made 38 different trades since his arrival in 1988 and had signed 20 free agents from other teams. It had taken him a little less than five years, but the club that he had fit together so deliberately was finally in place when 1993 arrived.

Hope Springs Eternal

Spring training is always a time when optimism comes in large doses. No matter what a team did the previous season, a new year brings renewed hope and a feeling that the forthcoming campaign will be better. Hope always springs eternal in baseball in the spring.

When the Phillies convened in February 1993 for spring training at Clearwater, Florida, there was, however, more than just the usual range of optimism. To a man, the Phillies were downright enthusiastic about their chances in the upcoming season.

After training at locations around the country as varied as New Braunfels, Texas; Birmingham, Alabama; Charleston, South Carolina and even Hershey, Pennsylvania; and Wilmington, Delaware—never staying too long at any one place—the Phillies had been holding their spring training at Clearwater since 1947. Then the town was a sleepy little village with a population of 15,000. It had grown over the years to a year-round population of 100,000—with an influx of nearly that many tourists each year.

Originally, the Phillies had trained at an old, wooden ball park that had previously been used by the Brooklyn Dodgers and the Cleveland Indians. But in 1955, the club moved into a brand new site across the street from the original field. Named after one of the town fathers, who had been a former major league pitcher of some note, Jack Russell Stadium was a compact, cozy little ball park that with revisions over the years had become one of the nicest places in Florida to watch a game.

Before setting up residence at Jack Russell Stadium each year, the Phillies always began their initial drills at the Carpenter Complex, an expansive layout which contained four separate baseball fields and assorted other facilities. Several miles from Jack Russell, Carpenter Complex was the brainchild of then farm director Paul Owens, having been opened in 1967. The Phillies used it for several weeks at the start of spring training, then would turn it over to their minor leaguers while heading down the street to Jack Russell.

The Carpenter Complex hummed with excitement as the Phillies converged on the site to begin their work for the 1993 season. There was a genuine feeling among the players that the Phillies fortunes were due to improve drastically and that the dismal results of the 1992 season were, if not a fluke, certainly something that wouldn't happen again.

The 1992 season, it was unanimously felt, was a nightmare that was best forgotten. And with good reason. Stymied by a club record 17 different players on the disabled list, including for long periods of time key players such as Tommy Greene, Jose DeJesus, Dale Murphy and Lenny Dykstra (Phillies players made 21 trips to the disabled list and missed a total of 1266 games), the club never even got out of the starting blocks.

Dykstra was hit by a pitch in his first at-bat of the season and, with the resultant broken arm and two other injuries that occurred later, made three visits to the disabled list and played in only 85 games all season. Out with a shoulder problem, Greene missed three and one-half months of the season, while DeJesus didn't pitch at all. Murphy appeared in a grand total of 18 games because of knee problems.

With these and an infirmary full of other ailments, manager Fregosi was forced into using 116 different batting orders as a club record 48 different players paraded through the clubhouse. Names such as Braulio Castillo, Dale Sveum, Julio Peguero, Jeff Grotewold, Greg Mathews, Don Robinson and Mickey Weston made appearances on Fregosi's lineup card in what was a steady stream of retreads, hasbeens, career minor leaguers and largely nondescript players who came out of nowhere and would probably never be heard from again.

It was not a very pretty sight, and the Phillies paid dearly. Although the Phillies scored more runs than any team in the National League except the Pittsburgh Pirates, a woeful pitching staff gave up more runs than any other staff in the league, and the club staggered home dead last in the National League East, 26 games behind the front-running Pirates. The Phils' 70–92 record was the club's worst since 1989 and gave it the third season of more than 90 losses in the last five.

But a new day was dawning in 1993. Or at least, so everyone on the Phillies hoped. General manager Lee Thomas had spent a busy winter acquiring players he thought not only would fit into the personality structure of the present team, but also would strengthen the club in areas that most needed help. Pitchers Danny Jackson as a starter and David West and Larry Andersen as relievers had been added with the hope that they would bolster a sagging pitching staff. And outfielders Pete Incaviglia, Milt Thompson and Jim Eisenreich had all been signed as free agents with the expectation that they would shore up the outfield and give the Phillies the kind of bench strength that they so sorely lacked in 1992.

In most pre-season polls, however, the Phillies were not projected as contenders. The national media still saw the club as a weak sister in what was caste as a weak division, and most forecasters picked the club for fourth or fifth place. One national magazine, noted for often missing the mark in its pre-season predictions, even suggested that the Phillies would be hard-pressed to finish ahead of the expansion Florida Marlins. Local writers saw the club a little differently, and many predicted that the Phils would contend with the St. Louis Cardinals and Montreal Expos for division honors before finishing second or third. A few fearless forecasters even had the team winning the division title.

Ageless Larry Andersen bolstered the Phillies bullpen after joining the club during the winter.

The players, themselves, were collectively more optimistic. Their optimism was evidenced not only by what they said, but by the fact that many of the position players arrived early from spring training, reporting to camp when only the pitchers and catchers were required to appear.

"I'm pretty excited about this year," said third baseman Dave Hollins, one of the early arrivals. "That's why I'm here early. I couldn't wait to get started."

Catcher Darren Daulton looked around a clubhouse bursting with the happy chatter of players and decided that the off-season additions of the Phillies were going to make a substantial difference between 1992 and 1993.

"We have a good group of major league players now," he said. "That's something we didn't have last year. There were times when you looked at our lineup, and you said, 'Who the hell are these guys?' Now, we have Jim and Milt and Pete. These are good, established big league players. That's what we need."

First baseman John Kruk concurred. The new players, it seemed apparent, would be vastly improved over the Stan Javiers, Jim Lindemans, Joe Millettes, Tom Marshes, Wally Backmans and assorted others who toiled in red pinstripes without much success the previous year.

"I like the looks of this team," Kruk proclaimed. "The new guys seem like good guys, and they have a good attitude. They want to play and win.

"I think one of the big differences will be in the middle of the batting order. Now, we have a good mix of right- and lefthanded hitters. Last year, we shuffled our third, fourth and fifth hitters. Hopefully, this year we can stay with a consistent lineup."

The offense was one part of the improved picture, but the changes on the pitching staff were equally significant. Thomas had landed another starting pitcher and two relievers, and it was felt that they would be more than adequate replacements for the likes of Bert Jones, Jay Baller, Danny Cox, Steve Searcy, Cliff Brantley and various others who came and went on the previous year's staff.

"What I like about this team is that we shouldn't run into problems of being short-handed because of injuries, like we did last year," said pitcher Terry Mulholland. "Now, we have guys who can fill the spots. Last year, the pitching situation got to the point where we had a lot of young kids whom we had to pitch. I'm not saying that they weren't ready for it. It's just that they hadn't had the experience of knowing what to expect. That makes a big difference. This year, I like what we have in reserve as opposed to what we had last year."

Despite the favorable outlook, there were still many question marks as the Phillies opened spring training. Two of the biggest ones concerned the unsettled situation at shortstop and the riddles still surrounding the pitching staff, particularly the bullpen.

In 1992, the Phillies had tried five different players—Kim Batiste, Mariano Duncan, Joe Millette, Mickey Morandini and Juan Bell—at shortstop. Each one had shortcomings, either offensively or defensively, and no one gained a foothold on the position until Bell was acquired on August 11 in a trade with the Baltimore Orioles for reserve second baseman Steve Scarsone.

Bell played the rest of the season as the regular shortstop, and although he hit an unbecoming .204 in 46 games, the Phillies touted him as their starting shortstop for 1993. With a career .182 major league batting average and failed tries with two other major league teams, plus a reputation as one of the less endearing players in the game, there were plenty of doubters. Bell, many people figured, would not be the Phils' shortstop for long.

While that prediction ultimately rang true, no one could get much of a handle on the full composition of the pitching staff. They were at least two openings in the bullpen, and uncertainties abounded in the starting rotation, where more question marks existed.

An army of pitchers were in camp vying for the open spots on the staff. Included were Pat Combs, a former starter and number one draft choice who had fallen victim to arm problems; Kyle Abbott, a starter through most of 1992 and owner of an embarrassing 1–14 record; Tyler Green, another former number one draft choice and one of the jewels of the farm system; late 1992 acquisition Jose DeLeon; reliever Bob Ayrault; young hurlers Mike Williams, Brantley and Brad Brink; and the still rehabilitating DeJesus and Ken Howell.

Missing from that group were two other pitchers, Andy Ashby and Keith Shepherd, who would have been in the thick of the competition had they not been drafted (along with Castillo) during the winter by the expansion Colorado Rockies.

The Phillies had the potential for an excellent starting rotation headed by Mulholland, who had emerged as one of the better moundsman in the league. But as camp got underway, no one knew for sure if Greene had fully recovered from the shoulder problems that sidelined him in 1992. The often-injured Jackson, who had made seven trips to the disabled list since mid-1989, was also an uncertainty, although he had gone through the whole 1992 season without an injury

One of the big question marks at Clearwater was whether or not Ben Rivera was as good as he appeared to be in 1992.

and had pitched effectively. One other nagging question persisted: Were Curt Schilling and Ben Rivera really as good as they showed in 1992?

There were other questions whose answers would not come easily. Who would be the backup catcher, a major concern should anything happen to Daulton? Where would the Phils play Duncan, whose highly productive bat demanded his presence in the lineup? Would the Phils be able to find room for the aging Murphy, a fading legend whose time was running out? Could Dykstra stay healthy for a full season after missing much of the last two years? And was there a place on the roster for Ruben Amaro and Jeff Manto, two popular Philadelphia-area natives, who if they both made the team would give the Phillies their first two local players on the same club since Del Ennis and Jack Meyer held roster spots in 1956.

After bidding in spring training to become the first two Philadelphia-area natives to play together on the Phillies since 1956, Ruben Amaro (left) and Jeff Manto later succeeded in playing with the Phils during the season.

Without question, it was going to be an intriguing spring. No one knew that better than the general manager who had carefully put the ingredients for this team together.

"We have some things to iron out," Lee Thomas said, "but I think we're a lot better off now than we were a year ago at this time. These guys have a great attitude, and we've got some guys who want to win. I really like what we've got in camp."

The Phillies wasted no time living up to their general manager's expectations. In their first game of the Grapefruit League season, they defeated the defending World Champion Toronto Blue Jays, 9–7, with veteran hurler Dan Gakeler getting the win in what would be a short-lived tryout with the Phillies and outfielder Wes Chamberlain slugging three hits, driving in two runs and scoring twice. A few days later, the Phils trashed the Blue Jays, 10–1, as Mulholland pitched three scoreless innings.

When the Phillies' record surged to 5–1 with a 4–3 victory over the Cardinals, the normally placid Fregosi found it hard to stifle his excitement.

"It's important to win games down here, especially after the last year we had," he said. "Now, we have a lot of veterans around here who feel like we have a winning club."

All, however, was not exactly perfect at the Phillies' Camp Harmony. In alarmingly rapid succession, Abbott came down with a strained ligament in his left elbow, Green was shut down because of pains in his shoulders and Combs struggled to refind his missing velocity. If that wasn't bad enough, problems with the pitching staff were compounded by the continuing struggles of Mitch Williams, a two-week bout with the flu by Rivera and most devastatingly, the revelation that Schilling was suffering from a stress fracture in his right leg. And along with these pitching woes, Kruk was hobbling around camp with a knee problem that required his flying back to Philadelphia for a diagnosis, which turned out to be less serious than was originally feared.

Amid these gloomy tidings, however, an odd ray of light beamed down on the Phillies' camp that not so subtly served as a portend of the coming season. In a March 21 game with the Cardinals, a bench-clearing brawl erupted. The Phils and Cards had traded hit batsmen earlier in the game and ill-will was running high, especially among the Phillies, who had led the league in 1992 in hit batters and had long ago stopped taking kindly to such acts of real or imagined malice. When Paul Kilgus hit Ricky Jordan with a pitch one batter after Duncan had slammed a home run, all hell broke loose. Jordan, followed closely by Hollins, Daulton and Incaviglia, charged the mound, and the battle was joined. Although it eventually ended with only Jordan's ejection, it not only solidified the Phillies' growing distaste for the Cardinals, a feeling that would last all season, it also knit the club into a closer unit while suggesting that this was a team that packed a fighting spirit that would not easily be quelled.

Six days later, another big game occurred when Greene pitched five strong innings while allowing just two hits as the Phils blanked Toronto, 1–0. It was clear by now that Greene was over the arm trouble that had sidelined him for much of the 1992 season, and that was good news to the Phillies.

In the closing days of spring training, the Phillies continued to search for extra help on the pitching staff, although Johnny Podres, coach of the moundsmen, seemed satisfied with the hand he had been dealt. In 1992, the Phillies had sent 24 different pitchers to the mound, 15 of them as starters. Podres did not wish for a repeat of that dismal procession.

"We've got some pretty good arms, that's for sure," he said. "When you send five guys [the starters] like we have out there, you've got a chance to win some ball games. We have some guys who can throw as well as anybody in the league. If we play good defense, they'll keep us in mostly every game."

By the end of March, the Phillies had won six of their last seven games, the latest coming on a 12–5 rout of the Minnesota Twins in a game in which Mickey Morandini had four hits, including two doubles. The Phillies went on to conclude the exhibition season with a 16–10 record, the best the club had done in many springs.

"Having a good spring was the plan of attack all along," Fregosi told reporters. "It was very important for us to do this after that disaster last year."

The exhibition season would prove to be revealing in other ways, too. The Phillies quickly became disenchanted with Bell at shortstop. Batiste got some playing time there, as did an unheralded youngster named Kevin Stocker, whom the club summoned briefly from the minor league camp to play a few games and show what he could do. Although Stocker—with less than two years of minor league experience—would play impressively, he was considered too inexperienced to make the big club.

The Phillies also gave brief looks during the exhibition season to some of their other top prospects: Tony Longmire, Mike Lieberthal, Ron Lockett, Jeff Jackson, Cary Williams, Andy Carter, Paul Fletcher and Steve Parris. But all wound up back at the Carpenter Complex after making limited appearances.

Fregosi gave the veterans most of the playing time during the Grapefruit season. Hollins (.380), Daulton (.378 with five home runs and 12 RBI), Thompson (.347), Morandini (.340), Bell (.333), Chamberlain (.321 with 13 RBI), Kruk (.302) and Incaviglia (four home runs, 15 RBI) all had outstanding springs at the plate, as did Jackson (4–1), Mulholland (3–0) and Greene (1.96 ERA) on the mound.

Before leaving Clearwater, Bell reclaimed the job at shortstop. Young Todd Pratt, showing he could handle big league pitching with the bat, although he needed more work defensively, won the job as the backup catcher. Murphy was released so he could sign with the Rockies; Amaro and Manto, as were Abbott, Combs and most of the other young pitchers, were assigned to the Phillies' Triple-A club at Scranton/Wilkes-Barre; Howell was released and DeJesus remained in Clearwater to continue his rehab work.

The exhibition season was marked by two other important developments. Injuries that had often plagued the Phillies in the past were relatively insignificant. And the Phils camp ran more smoothly and harmoniously than any the club had conducted in recent years.

There were no complaints, no feuds, no ill-feelings that had characterized Phillies teams of the past. No one sniped at the manager. And the players seemed genuinely to get along well with each other, with new players such as Incaviglia, Eisenreich, Thompson, West, Jackson and Andersen fitting in extremely well with the holdovers, as well as establishing themselves as valuable components of the team Thomas had put together.

It was clear that the Phillies were coming together as a team, and despite the varied backgrounds of the players, the club had a solid group of veterans who were determined to erase the blemishes of past years. There was a sense of purpose among team members; a singular goal, that of winning, seemed to envelop the team.

Before finishing training camp, the Phillies had one last important item of business. That was signing Daulton, the last of their unsigned veterans. Earlier in the year, the club had given Hollins a two-year contract, a meaningful gesture on the part of the Phils in terms of the young third baseman's self-esteem. They had also provided lucrative one-year pacts for Mulholland and Schilling. Finally, after a spring of negotiations, the Phils landed Daulton's name on a four-year contract calling for at least $18 million. Not only did that make Daulton the highest paid player in Phillies history, it served notice to all who cared to look that the Phillies were indeed serious about making long-term commitments to their players, a byproduct of which was a commitment to fielding a winning team.

Daulton was certainly the cornerstone of that commitment. The hard-hitting catcher had overcome a series of major injuries over his career to become the top man at his position in the National League. Daulton had finally achieved stardom in 1992, leading the league in RBI with 109, becoming

Veteran Ricky Jordan, who has had the second longest career with the Phillies of active club members, didn't crack the starting lineup, but he did get involved in a big fight in spring training.

only the fourth catcher in major league history (joining Roy Campanella, Johnny Bench and Gary Carter) to win an RBI title while hitting more home runs (27) than any backstop in Phillies history.

Along with his hitting, Daulton had also become a key player defensively. His strong arm and quick reflexes were tools of a superb receiver, and he handled the pitching staff with the skill seldom seen among those who go behind the plate today.

"There's no doubt in my mind that Daulton has become the premier catcher in baseball," Thomas said. "Defensively, calling games, producing with the bat, you name it, he does it for us. And our pitching staff really believes in him."

With matinee-idol good looks and a physique like a Greek god, Daulton had developed into one of the team's most popular players with the fans after a stormy relationship with them in the earlier years of his career. With maturity, he had also grown into a position as the team's unchallenged leader, a tough, hard-playing veteran, the team's primary spokesman with the press, a player who would speak out when necessary and whom the others on the team often sought for advice, guidance and either a boost to their self-confidence or a kick in the tail when needed. Clearly, the Phillies of 1993 were Daulton's team.

"It's all part of growing up," said the 31-year-old catcher. "I've achieved a lot more now than before. Naturally, people tend to notice you a little more when you have a little success. I think my teammates respect me, but I think it's because I respect them. I

Darren Daulton was rewarded as the National League's premier catcher with a huge contract.

work hard for them, for myself and for the team, and I think that shows. All I ask of my teammates is that they do the same."

They would heed that call in the months ahead. Ordinarily, the exhibition season is meaningless, except as a device to get the players in shape. But the Phillies took a special interest in working hard throughout spring training. The team developed a work ethic that seemed to know no boundaries and that became the envy of other teams. It was an attitude that would carry over into the regular season.

The Phillies left Clearwater feeling relaxed, confident and ready to start the regular season. Little could they have known, though, what lay ahead.

4

A Torrid Beginning

Although spring training results have never been accurate barometers of a team's performance during the regular season, the Phillies emerged from the 1993 Grapefruit League with high expectations. It was generally agreed that the team had a solid starting rotation, a strong offense and a bench with more than adequate depth. All were important ingredients for a team that hoped to be at least a contender in its division.

To be sure, the club still had some shortcomings. Overall, the defense was no more than mediocre. There remained some serious reservations about the bullpen. And there was the constant fear that injuries to key players—some of whom were especially vulnerable to such things—could destroy an entire season, as they had in the recent past.

The Phillies' opening day roster was made up primarily of veteran players with most of the key members being either slightly over or slightly under 30 years of age. Manager Jim Fregosi had elected to start with a roster that included just five outfielders and two catchers, along with seven infielders and 11 pitchers.

Lenny Dykstra, Wes Chamberlain and newcomers Pete Incaviglia, Milt Thompson and Jim Eisenreich were the outfielders. Darren Daulton and Todd Pratt were the catchers. The infielders were John Kruk, Ricky Jordan, Mickey Morandini, Mariano Duncan, Dave Hollins, Juan Bell and Kim Batiste. Terry Mulholland, Tommy Greene, Curt Schilling, Danny Jackson, Ben Rivera, Jose DeLeon, Mitch Williams, David West, Larry Andersen, Bob Ayrault and the only rookie, Tyler Green, were the pitchers.

With that squad in tow, the Phillies flew to Houston to open the 1993 season. In the years that it has fielded a baseball team in the National League, Houston has regularly been the site of important events involving the Phillies. Don Nottebart threw the team's first no-hitter there against the Phillies in 1963. That same year, Phils manager Gene Mauch staged his famous clubhouse tirade, upsetting a food table and heaving spare ribs around the locker room after a pint-sized rookie named Joe Morgan beat the Phillies with a hit in a late-season game. The Phillies also helped Houston christen the Astrodome, defeating the Astros, 2–0, in the first game there in 1965. Of course, the greatest post-season playoff of them all was decided in Houston when the Phillies defeated the Astros to capture the 1980 National League pennant.

In 1993, Houston would again play a role in Phillies history.

With Mulholland pitching a sparkling four-hitter, the Phillies defeated the Astros, 3–1, in the opener. It was the Phils' first opening day win since 1984.

The Phillies also won the next two games, beating the Astros, 5–3, as Schilling scattered six hits over eight innings and quieted fears that his injured leg would hamper his pitching, and winning the third game, 6–3, on Thompson's three-run double in the 10th inning. Not since

Terry Mulholland won the Phillies first opening day game since 1984 with a four-hitter at Houston.

The Phillies launched their home season with the largest opening day crowd in Philadelphia baseball history.

1970 had the Phils opened the season with three straight wins, and not since 1915 had they started the year with three wins in a row on the road.

The largest opening day crowd in Philadelphia baseball history—60,985—greeted the Phillies as they returned to Veterans Stadium. Before the game, a drama had unfolded in the clubhouse when Chamberlain overslept and arrived two hours and 11 minutes after players were required to report for duty. With just 1:14 to go before game time, the embarrassed outfielder hustled into the clubhouse, quickly changed into his uniform and rushed away from a horde of reporters waiting to hear his explanation. Fregosi erased his name from the starting lineup.

While some of the other Phillies privately grumbled about Chamberlain's mishap, also criticizing what they perceived to be the young outfielder's flamboyant behavior, the Phils went out and got themselves pasted by the Chicago Cubs, 11–7, in a 23-hit, eight-home-run slugfest in which Daulton drilled two homers and drove in five runs. Because of the loss, the Phillies fell out of first place for what would be the only time all season.

The Chamberlain affair seemed to be put to rest the following day when Wes stood up in the clubhouse and apologized to his teammates for his indiscretion. "It was my fault. I have no one to blame but myself," he told sports writers. "It's all over. Case closed," added Fregosi after meeting with the player. The rest of the team appeared to agree.

The incident would also have an effect on Chamberlain. The outgoing and sometimes erratic right fielder, a player many felt had fallen short of his enormous potential in his brief big league career, buckled down and played hard, problem-free baseball for the rest of the season, performing in a difficult platoon situation without complaint. Chamberlain, who had bounced back and forth between the Phillies and Scranton/Wilkes-Barre in his two full seasons with the organization, not only hit well, but was vastly improved on defense.

After the clubhouse meeting had cleared the air, the Phillies went out and defeated the Cubs, 5–4, as Kruk drove in four runs with three hits and Mulholland spread three hits over eight innings to get the win with relief help from Williams, who struck out the side in the ninth inning on 11 pitches. The victory vaulted the Phils back into first place, a spot they would not relinquish the rest of the season.

The Phillies followed that win with four more, blanking the Cubs, 3–0, on Schilling's four-hitter; blowing a 4–0 lead, then downing the Cincinnati Reds, 5–4, on Dykstra's game-winning homer in the seventh; beating the Reds, 4–1, behind Greene's first victory of the season; and clubbing Cinci, 9–2, with Chamberlain and Duncan each drilling three hits and Incaviglia collecting three RBI. It was the first time since 1968 that the Phils had swept the Reds in Philadelphia, and the five straight

After an early-season mishap, Wes Chamberlain caught fire, drilling three hits in one game and two home runs in another.

triumphs rocketed the Phillies to an 8–1 record, the club's best start after nine games since 1915.

Just before that last victory, the Phillies had made their first roster change. Hoping to bolster the team's relief corps, general manager Lee Thomas acquired former Phil Mark Davis from the Atlanta Braves in a trade for minor league hurler Brad Hassinger. Ineffective in recent years, Davis had bounced around after winning a Cy Young Award in 1989 with the San Diego Padres. Feeling the need for another lefthander in the bullpen, Thomas gambled that the veteran fireman might have something left. To make room on the roster for him, rookie Green was sent to Scranton/Wilkes-Barre.

Flushed by the success of their early showing, the Phillies returned to the road, but their winning streak was halted by the Cubs, 3–1, on a cold, windy April 16 day at Wrigley Field. Another loss followed before the Phils came back with a blustery 11–10 victory, won in the 11th inning on a three-run homer by Hollins in a wild game in which Kruk and Chamberlain each had two home runs.

Kruk, who had won the National League's Player of the Week award after the opening week of the season, homered again to give the Phillies a 14-inning 4–3 decision over the Padres back at the Vet. Three days later, Schilling fired a five-hit shutout, his second straight complete game shutout, to beat the Los Angeles Dodgers, 2–0. Jackson followed with his first April win since 1989 with a 7–3 victory over the Dodgers, and Greene completed the sweep of Los Angeles with a five-hit 5–2 triumph.

The next night—in their 18th game of the season—the Phillies went 10 games over .500 for the first time since 1986 with an astonishing 10-inning win over the San Francisco Giants. Trailing 8–0 after five and one-half innings and playing throughout the night in a steady rain, the Phils rallied to a 9–8 verdict in a wild affair in which Phils pitchers struck out 13 batters and issued 14 walks. Eisenreich, filling in at first base for Kruk, who had to leave the game with an injury and who would miss the next three games, was the batting hero with three hits, while Incaviglia drove in two runs to run his RBI total in the last three games to seven.

The one thing missing in the Phils' arsenal was the bat of Dykstra. The center fielder was mired in a 1-for-25 slump, and his batting average was .189. But Lenny was contributing to the club in a variety of other ways. He was still getting on base and scoring runs at a breakneck pace, and he was a superb defensive player, the anchor in an outfield that was not exactly noted for its smooth-fielding tendencies.

The pesky, extra-aggressive Dykstra, who was prone to giving clubhouse interviews while sitting at his locker with his back facing the interrogator, had a lot of street urchin in him. You could knock him down, but he'd quickly jump back up. With tobacco juice spilling from the corners of his mouth and dirt covering his uniform, Dykstra was a throwback to an earlier

Lenny Dykstra was the Phillies sparkplug, getting on base constantly so the big sluggers behind him could drive him home.

era when players didn't care what they looked like, only how they could help their teams win.

"He can hurt you in so many ways," said Fregosi admiringly. "All I want to do is put his name in the lineup as many times as possible. I can't think of another guy I'd rather have in the leadoff spot. He makes so much happen just being in there."

Dykstra had never been satisfied with his role as a platoon player with the New York Mets. But he had found a home in Philadelphia, and despite a string of untimely injuries, including one in 1990 when his car slid off a road and into a tree nearly killing himself and Daulton, the swaggering little man with the bulging muscles had become the foundation on which the Phillies' offense was built.

There were two things that Dykstra badly wanted when the 1993 season began: a batting title and a division pennant. "It's something I think I'm capable of doing," he said of the bat crown. "I think I have the right approach to hitting to do it."

As for his team's success, Dykstra thought the Phillies were also capable of doing it. "This is a good ballclub," he said. "It's got a good lineup. The starting pitching is much improved. And we've got good chemistry here. We came into this year believing we could win because we know we have a good team."

As the end of April approached, there was nothing to dispel that impression. Embarking on their first West Coast trip of the year, the Phillies suddenly got help from a different area. In the second game of their series at San Diego, the Phils won a 5–3 decision because of a spectacular catch by Thompson, who leaped high above the wall in left field to snare a drive by the Padres' Bob Geren with two outs and the bases loaded in the eighth inning. With a grand slam averted and victory preserved, the Phils then went to Los Angeles where another brilliant defensive play saved the day. This time, it was Morandini, who with no outs and the bases loaded in the bottom of the ninth inning, made a diving catch at second base on a line drive by Mike Sharperson, then tagged the bag to nail Mike Piazza to complete a rally-killing doubleplay. That saved a 7–6 victory and sent the Phillies into May in first place for the first time on that date since 1964. The Phillies' record for the month was 17–5, the best April record in franchise history.

The Phillies' blistering assault continued in May. By this time, St. Louis had moved ahead of Montreal in the standings after the Expos had held second place during most of April. To the Phils, it didn't seem to matter who was chasing them.

After losing to the Dodgers and Tom Candiotti, 5–1, on May 1 in a game in which Daulton and Fregosi were both ejected after ar-

Milt Thompson not only had three hits, he made a brilliant catch to save a win against the Padres.

Mickey Morandini is forced out at second in a game with the Cubs.

guing balls and strikes with home plate umpire Bill Hohn, the team exploded the next day with a six-run third inning that carried them to a 9–1 win over Los Angeles. One game later, the Phils won their fifth straight extra-inning game as Hollins blasted a two-run homer in the 12th to down the Giants, 4–3. Andersen got his second win of the season and Williams, who had switched his uniform number to 99 in recognition of his namesake, "The Wild Thing" in the movie *Major League,* his 11th save.

The Phillies oozed with confidence as they returned home to begin a three-game series May 7 with the Cardinals. Their lead had climbed to four and one-half games, and both players and their fans were beginning to think it was going to be a special year for the Phillies.

"We believe we can win. We expect to win every time we take the field," said Andersen, who had been with the Phillies' last pennant-winner in 1983 but who found no similarities between his past and present teams. "It's different here now," he added. "Before, I think some of the players weren't as focused. There wasn't a real good chemistry here. This group today is the best I've ever been associated with—bar none."

In support of that tribute, the Phillies swept the Cardinals with three one-run victories. Another two-run homer by Hollins gave Greene a 4–3 triumph in the first game. In the second game, Mulholland worked a career-high 10 innings to gain a 2–1 win on Jordan's pinch-hit single. Then an eighth inning grand slam by Duncan against Lee Smith with two outs and the Phils trailing 5–2 produced a 6–5 victory. The Phillies' lead was up to six and one-half games, and their 22–7 record was the club's best at that point since 1913.

Another grand slam the next day by Daulton gave the Phillies and Jackson a 5–1 win over the Pirates. At 23–7, the Phils now had the best start in club history and were not far off the major league record of 26–4 after 30 games, set in 1984 by the Detroit Tigers.

A lot of attention was focusing on the so-called chemistry of the team and the pleasure the players derived from playing with each other. The Phils displayed a refreshing brand of camaraderie with all factions seemingly getting along together. It was definitely fun to be a Phillie. So much fun, in fact, that some players had resurrected that ancient art of crushing pies in other people's faces. They used shaving cream instead of

Mariano Duncan (7) gets a royal welcome after hitting a grand slam home run off the Cardinals' Lee Smith.

pies, and hardly a soul was immune from an attack, including the nearly always impeccably dressed Thomas.

Before games, the Phillies' clubhouse often seemed more like a playpen with players rolling around the floor in mock wrestling matches, hamming it up with each other, practicing putting on an imaginary golf green or dancing to the beat of loud music blaring from a boom box. Playful ribbing was common, and the loud, often ribald comments filled the air at regular intervals. The Phillies had a one-for-all, all-for-one attitude that seemed to permeate the entire clubhouse.

"This is a team that picks each other up," said Hollins. "We have hitters picking up pitchers and pitchers picking up hitters."

Daulton, a late-season member of the '83 Phils, suggested that that club didn't start having fun until it got hot in September and made a successful run at the pennant. "When you come to the ball park now," he said, "you know it's going to be fun. Winning does that."

By this time, Fregosi had benched Bell for his weak-hitting and had inserted Duncan into the lineup at shortstop. Morandini was playing regularly at second base, and Incaviglia and Thompson platooned in left field, while Chamberlain and Eisenreich shared duties in right.

After a 4–1 win over the Pirates on May 12 when Greene notched his first complete game since 1991 and Kruk poled four hits, the Phillies' lead

In the course of the season, Dave Hollins hit five game-winning home runs, including this one against the Cardinals.

had stretched to seven games over the Expos, who had returned to second place where they would remain the rest of the month. But a trip to Atlanta proved to be ill-fated for the red-hot Phils. They were cooled off in the first two games with Mulholland coming down with a foot problem and lasting just two innings in his outing.

Fortunately, the Phils salvaged the getaway game as Morandini singled home the winning run to give Jackson a 5–4 victory. Better yet, the Phillies were headed to Florida where they would have their first meeting with the expansion Marlins. In a wacky first encounter, Kruk had five hits for the first time in his career to pace a 17-hit Phillies attack that led to a 10–3 verdict in a game in which the Marlins left 17 men on base. The next night, Greene struck out 10 and Daulton drilled his 10th home run of the season in a 6–0 Phillies win.

DeLeon got his first start of the season in the following game in place of the injured Mulholland. Despite a mammoth 440-foot home run by Incaviglia and a strong six innings by DeLeon, the Phils fell to the Marlins, 5–3. They returned home to confront the Expos with a six and one-half game lead.

While the Phillies were getting strong pitching from Schilling, Greene and Jackson in the starting rotation and excellent work from reliever West, one of the biggest guns in camp was Kruk, the hard-hitting first baseman. Although often kidded for his unathletic-looking physique and a scruffy appearance that featured long hair and an unshaven face, Kruk was probably the best natural hitter on the team.

By May 17, Kruk's batting average had soared to .382 and he ranked among the league leaders in that category. He hit to all fields, although not with as much power as he preferred, and his bat was as important to the Phillies as any single element on the team.

Kruk was one of the team's chief characters. At times the master of funny one-liners and sayings, he had perfected a country-boy image that, although only partly accurate, caught the fancy of fans as well as the media throughout the country and made him one of the team's most popular players.

The gum-chewing West Virginian, who confessed to stuffing as many as 20 sticks of gum in his mouth during the course of a tense game, could be surly and a man of few words, but more than anything else, he wanted desperately to play for a winner. "I don't care what happens [to his batting records] as long as we win," he said.

John Kruk had a torrid first half that ended with his being chosen to start in the All-Star Game.

Which, of course, was what the Phils had in mind as they returned to the Vet for a crucial four-game series with Montreal. It didn't work out quite as expected, though. Incaviglia's grand slam and five RBI powered Schilling and the Phils to a 9–3 win in the first battle, but the Expos came back with wins in the next two games with Duncan's three errors and a three-run ninth against Williams proving to be decisive in a 6–5 Montreal win on May 22. In the fourth game, the Phils returned to the win column with a 14–7 thrashing that featured Mulholland's return to the mound, three doubles by Dykstra, whose average had climbed over .250, four RBI by Daulton, who was among the league leaders in that category, and three errors by Bell, who was back at shortstop. The Expos left town with the same five and one-half game deficit with which they had arrived.

They were replaced at the Vet by the lowly Mets and their new manager, Dallas Green, the only skipper in Phillies history to win a World Series. Green's pathetic New Yorkers dropped two out of three games to the Phils with Chamberlain and Hollins carrying the big bats.

"We've got to play well against everybody," said Fregosi. "When you're in first place, everybody gets up to beat you."

From there, it was out on the road for the Phillies with the first stop in Colorado. There in their first meeting with the new Rockies, the Phils swept a three-game set, scoring 39 runs and collecting 47 hits in what players felt was a ludicrous Mile High Stadium in Denver. In the first tilt, the Phils banged out 20 hits to capture a 15–9 win. Mulholland blanked the Rockies, 6–0, in the second game. That win prompted Kruk to take a stand against the unpopular high Denver altitude: "I couldn't play here, I wouldn't breathe," he said. "And if I can't breathe, I'm

Pitching coach Johnny Podres (46), conferring here with Curt Schilling, played a major role in the success of the mound corps.

going to die. It's a nice city, but what the hell would you see of it when you're dead?"

In the third game, the Phillies cruised to an 18–1 decision, hitting six home runs, including three in one inning, and bashing 19 hits in the club's highest-scoring effort since 1986. Incaviglia had four hits and three RBI and Daulton had two home runs while taking the league lead in RBI to head the assault, while Greene hurled his fourth straight complete game to send his record to 7–0, good enough to earn him the National League's Pitcher of the Month award.

The Phillies ended May the following night with a 6–4 loss at Cincinnati. Fregosi, Daulton and pitching coach Johnny Podres were ejected by home plate umpire Bob Davidson, whose bad strike calls and a questionable balk call on Andersen angered the Phils. Despite the loss, the Phils ended the month with a 34–15 record and a seven-game lead over the Expos.

When June began, the Phils were in sole possession of first place at that date for the first time since 1981. The club wasted little time expanding its lead. After Eisenreich raised his average to .359 with a single that drove in the winning run in a 6–3 win over the Reds, Rivera hurled eight strong innings to get a 5–2 win in the series finale at Cincinnati. Back home on June 4, Mulholland struck out a career-high 14 but lost to the Rockies, 2–1, before Greene ran his record to 8–0 with a 6–2 complete game win over Colorado in what was the best start for a Phils pitcher since Steve Carlton in 1981.

Subbing at third base, Kim Batiste (right) had a home run and a two-run single to beat the Mets.

The following night, an 18-hit barrage, featuring four hits each by Dykstra and Duncan, buried the Rockies, 11–7. Duncan, summoned two nights earlier from the clubhouse where he nursed a flu-ridden stomach because he was needed to replace Batiste, who had gone down with a pulled hamstring, continued his hot hitting with three more hits—two of them triples—to up his three-game total to 9-for-12 and lead the Phillies to a 7–5 victory over the Astros in a June 7 game that pushed the club's lead to eight and one-half games.

Early June, though, was not to be without incident. Lackluster and mistake-riddled play finally convinced the Phillies to get rid of Bell. He was waived to the Milwaukee Brewers. Hollins, who had been having problems with his right hand, was diagnosed as having a broken bone and was placed on the disabled list. And Williams engaged in a shouting match with Fregosi behind closed doors in the manager's office after the pitcher had stomped off the mound and stormed into the clubhouse where he rearranged the furniture in an ugly incident that neither the manager nor the other Phillies felt too kindly about.

Still, the Phillies continued to roll along. After Mulholland's 8–0 shutout of the Astros on June 9 in a game that saw Eisenreich just miss hitting for the cycle by the absence of a single, the Phillies swept a four-game series with the Mets for the first time in New York since 1980. A home run and two-run single by Batiste, filling in at third for Hollins, aided one of the wins, and a six-hit shutout by Jackson produced another.

With an 11^1/$_2$-game lead—their largest of the season—the Phillies then moved to Montreal where they faced another critical

Manager Jim Fregosi never missed an opportunity to get his point across, even if it sometimes resulted in his ejection.

series with the Expos, who by now had dropped to third place behind the Cardinals. The Phils' arrival was accompanied by a small furor over a quote attributed to Mulholland in an article in a Montreal paper. "If that's what they [the Expos] have to offer, we should be able to hold them off," the pitcher supposedly said.

Naturally, the article wound up being pinned to a wall in the Expos' clubhouse. Mulholland denied that he had made the comment. "I don't appreciate what was written. I never said those words," he claimed.

In the midst of the uproar, Mulholland defeated the Expos, 10–3, for his eighth win of the season, getting a big hand from a grand slam homer by Eisenreich. It was the sixth win in a row for the Phillies and skyrocketed their record to 45–17, a mark unparalleled in Phillies history.

Plunked squarely in the middle of that mark was the unflappable Eisenreich, a consummate pro, who fit in beautifully on this team of boisterous characters, despite his own quiet demeanor. The first-year Phils right fielder, with the look and style of a 1930s player, was a skillful performer who was the most fundamentally sound player on the team. When they had signed him as a free agent during the winter, the Phillies had projected Eisenreich as being mostly a late-inning defensive replacement and a lefthanded pinch-hitter, but he had hit so well that they couldn't keep him out of the lineup.

Eisenreich was one of the great success stories in sports, a player who had missed nearly five full big league seasons because he had Tourette's Syndrome, a relatively rare neurological disorder that causes twitches, hyperventilating and vocal outbursts. The disease had gone undiagnosed for years, causing Eisenreich many instances of embarrassment and hardship, but it had finally been controlled by medication, allowing the player to return to baseball and to a normal life.

Throughout the first half of the season, Eisenreich's batting average had hovered in the .350 range, and the Phillies couldn't help but pat themselves on the back for their good fortune in signing the former American Leaguer whom no other team had pursued with much diligence.

"I didn't know until January whether I would even be playing," Eisenreich said. "But I never worried, I thought someone would want

Jim Eisenreich hit so well that the Phillies couldn't keep him out of the lineup.

In his first Phillies game of the 1993 season, Ruben Amaro had four hits and a game-winning homer to beat the Pirates.

me eventually. Teams need to fill needs.

"I'm just an average player," he added. "What I do doesn't get me excited. It's just a joy to be able to play."

The news that awaited the Phillies, though, wasn't so joyful. Eisenreich's running mate in right field, Chamberlain, pulled a hamstring running to first on June 15 and went on the disabled list, and the Phils and Greene parted company with their winning streak with an 8–4 loss to Montreal. A 4–3 defeat followed in 10 innings after Dykstra's two-out home run in the ninth had sent the game into overtime. The Phillies' lead was suddenly down to nine and one-half games.

"We don't need to be up by 14 or 15 games," said Duncan, one of the Phillies' most amiable players and an enormously valuable, although somewhat overlooked, member of the team. "Nine and one-half games is still a very good lead."

But it would decrease even further as the Phils returned home to face Florida and dropped the first game of the series. Three straight wins over the Marlins, however, the last one coming on a clutch three-run homer in the seventh by Kruk, got the Phils back into the proper frame of mind and readied them for a visit from the Braves.

Atlanta knocked out Schilling in the third inning and snapped a streak in which Dykstra had scored in 15 straight games as it won the first session, 8–1. But the Phillies came back to take the next two games, with Jackson getting the win and Incaviglia slugging a three-run homer for a 5–3 victory (the Braves' Francisco Cabera became only the 38th player in Vet history to drive a ball into the upper deck in left field) and Rivera notching the decision behind a six-run seventh for an 8–3 triumph.

Two days later at Pittsburgh, recently recalled Ruben Amaro, in his first start of 1993, slammed four hits, including a game-winning, two-run home run, to lead the Phillies to an 8–6 victory over the Pirates. The next night, the Bucs' Steve Cooke tossed the first complete game of the season against the Phillies in a 4–2 victory.

After another loss to Pittsburgh, the Phillies moved on to St. Louis where the rampaging Cardinals had won 17 of their last 21 games. The Phils got a much-needed lift when Hollins returned to the lineup after missing just two weeks with a broken hand that had required surgery.

"I talked with key players, my buddies and [coach] John Vukovich," Hollins said. "The reason I rushed back was more of a psychological lift for the team. We had gotten into a rut. I knew I wasn't capable of doing things I could before. But we were getting back our set lineup."

An extremely intense, aggressive player, Hollins was one of the toughest Phils, a no-nonsense figure who would rather win than breathe. The joke around the clubhouse was that no one ever was quite sure who would show up for a game—the likeable Dave or his evil twin Mikey.

Roger Mason was added to the bullpen in an early-July trade with the Padres.

Hollins rarely laughed and always seemed to be wearing his game face. On the diamond, he never gave an inch, especially when it came to dealing with his arch-enemies—opposing pitchers, a breed with whom he had had his share of fights.

His playing style was vintage yesteryear. He was probably the hardest slider on the club, and he was never reluctant to stick a part of his body in the way of a pitch if his team needed somebody on base. At third base, where he played with a rifle, albeit occasionally wild, arm, he readily knocked balls down with his body, which resembled that of a football linebacker.

"That's just the way I play the game," Hollins said. "I've never played any other way. It's the only way I can play to produce. I would love to have a blast, sing and be happy all the time. It doesn't work for me. When I relax, it seems I get kicked in the butt. This is the way I'll be until they don't put me in the lineup."

A switch-hitter who could hit with power from either side, Hollins was welcomed back to the lineup with open arms as the Phils began their show-down with St. Louis. Unfortunately, despite a monstrous, upper-deck home run by Incaviglia, the Phillies bowed, 3–1, in the opener. Then, after Rivera won his career-high eighth game, 13–10, the Phils dropped the next two with first Greene then Schilling getting shelled in 9–3 and 14–5 losses, respectively. The first loss ended the month of June with the Phillies' record at 52–25.

After the second rout, Daulton exploded in the clubhouse. "That was the most embarrassing game I've ever been a part of," the catcher and undisputed team leader proclaimed. "I've been on some bad teams, and I've been a very, very bad player. But that's the most embarrassed I've ever been.

"It's only July 1. I don't think there's any need for pressure," he added, warming up with a thinly veiled attack on Greene and Schilling. "But I think a couple of guys might have felt it. I would not think that four games against a con-tending team would cause guys to change the way they've been going about things, but maybe it has. And I'm not talking about everybody. We've got one guy who was 8–1 and in his last five decisions, except for maybe one game, he hasn't shown up. The other guy, I don't know if they're tired,

Both at bat and on the field, Dave Hollins always played the game with a high level of intensity.

nervous, scared, worried, feeling the pressure or what. I don't think this is the time for it."

With their tails somewhat between their legs and their lead reduced to five and one-half games, the Phillies returned home to face the Padres in what would be a historic homestand.

A doubleheader was scheduled for July 2. In the first game, scheduled to start at 4:35 P.M., three rain delays totaling five hours and 54 minutes pushed the conclusion of the Padres' 5–2 victory past 1 A.M. The second game began at 1:26 A.M., lasted 10 innings and finally ended when Mitch Williams, in his first at-bat of the season, singled home the winning run at 4:40 A.M., giving the Phillies a 6–5 victory.

It was the latest a major league game had ever finished, breaking the old record of 3:35 A.M. set in a July 4, 1985, game that ended with the Mets defeating the Braves, 16–13, in 19 innings at Atlanta. The Phillies twin-bill consumed 12 hours and five minutes. It began with 54,617 people in the stands. There

Mickey Morandini was a steady fielder at second, and he also beat the Giants with a grand slam homer and five RBI.

were only about 6000 left after the first game, but as the morning progressed, hundreds of people made their way to the Vet to witness history being made.

The players hardly had time to rest before they were due back at the Vet for another game. When they got there, Thomas had made another player move. The general manager shipped seldom-used and largely ineffective relief pitcher Tim Mauser to the Padres for reliever Roger Mason, a much-traveled hurler who it was felt could help the Phillies' continuing bullpen problems.

Mike Williams pitched six solid innings to get the win in the Phillies 20-inning victory over the Dodgers.

With Thompson falling just a home run short of hitting for the cycle and Rivera getting his ninth win, 8–4, the Phillies split their two remaining games with San Diego, then won two out of three from the Dodgers. Greene beat Los Angeles, 9–5, in the first game to become the first Phils pitcher since Jim Lonborg in 1976 to win at least 10 games before the All-Star break.

After the Phils lost the second game, Thomas bolted into Fregosi's office with some news for the manager. "You're getting a new shortstop," he stated. The general manager, who like his skipper had just received a contract extension from club president Bill Giles, had seen enough of bungled plays and balls that passed just out of the reach of his rangeless shortstops. It was time for a change, and Thomas had just the man for the job. It would be a move that would have a major impact on the Phillies for the rest of the season.

Kevin Stocker's first game as the Phils' new shortstop would be one he'd never forget. In their second marathon in less than one week, the Phillies went 20 innings to defeat the Dodgers, 7–6, on Dykstra's two-run double. Mike Williams, who had just joined the Phils a few days earlier from Scranton/Wilkes-Barre, pitched the final six innings to get the win in what tied (with a 1973 game with the Braves) for the longest game ever played at Veterans Stadium and for the second longest (after a 21-inning job in 1918) in Phillies history.

With that game finishing at 2:20 A.M., the Phillies had little left the next night. Despite Stocker's first major league home run, Barry Bonds walloped two round-trippers and drove in six runs to pace a 20-hit assault that gave the Giants a 13–2 victory. It got even worse the following night when the Giants bombed 23 hits, including four by ex-Phil Steve Scarsone, to bury the Phillies again, 15–8.

The Phillies regrouped behind Greene's 11th win to salvage an 8–3 victory that featured Morandini's grand slam and five RBI, but the series ended with another San Francisco rout, 10–2, with Scarsone again lacing four hits. In four games, the West Division-leading Giants had scored 46 runs and clubbed 68 hits, and those who foresaw a Phillies-Giants playoff at the end of the regular season could do little but shudder over what seemed to be the Phils' certain fate should such a series occur.

The All-Star break, however, was now at hand. As they scattered for a welcome rest, the Phillies took with them a 57–32 record and a five-game lead over the Cardinals. The club, it was unanimously agreed, still had a long way to go,

Darren Daulton got some last-minute batting tips from hitting coach Denis Menke before leaving for the All-Star Game where he was the National League's second highest vote getter.

and winning a division title wasn't going to be easy.

Four players and manager Fregosi as a coach trekked to the All-Star Game at the Baltimore Orioles' Camden Yards. Daulton—with the second highest number of votes in the National League and the first starting assignment in the game for a Phils catcher since Andy Seminick got the nod in 1949—and Kruk at first base were heavy favorites of the nation's fans in the voting for positions in the National League's starting lineup. Hollins was chosen as a reserve. Before the game, National League manager Bobby Cox, who had been roundly criticized for not selecting Dykstra to the team, named Mulholland as his team's starting pitcher.

In the American League's 9–3 victory, both Daulton and Kruk, who was tabbed as the cleanup hitter, went hitless in three trips to the plate. Kruk added some comic relief to the game after taking a pitch over his head by bailing out in a quick, strikeout by American League pitcher Randy Johnson of Seattle. Hollins had a double in his only at-bat while Mulholland gave up one run and one hit in two innings in the first All-Star start for a Phillies pitcher since Steve Carlton in 1980.

5

It's Finally Our Turn

Could the Phillies regroup and hold on to their lead in the National League East?

That was the big question on Phillies-watchers' minds as the club headed into the season's second half following the All Star break. An early July slump, coupled with a red-hot surge by the St. Louis Cardinals, had seen the Phils' once-staggering lead of $11\frac{1}{2}$ games fall dramatically to five. While no one expected the Phils to maintain their .700 pace of the first three months of the season, the team's showing in recent weeks had been particularly frustrating. And the vultures were starting to come out of the trees.

Montreal Expos pitcher John Wetteland had been quoted as saying, "Philadelphia will fold and take a skid. They're not the awesome power-house they're made out to be." That incensed the Phillies enough as it was, but Cardinals catcher Tom Pagnozzi shot his mouth into the breach by asserting that the Phils "were ripe for the taking." The Phillies would make a special mental note of both comments.

But there was genuine cause for concern. Leading up to the All-Star break, the Phils had won just six of 17 games. A general breakdown in hitting, pitching and defense had occurred. Of special concern was the untimely faltering of the starting rotation, especially Tommy Greene and Curt Schilling. To make matters worse, the team was mired in a hitting slump, and its defense was making far too many errors.

There was hardly any reason to panic, though. The club still had the second best record (behind the San Francisco Giants) in the major leagues.

Lenny Dykstra was on a hitting rampage, his average having climbed almost to the .300 level, and John Kruk and Jim Eisenreich were both hitting above .340. Moreover, new shortstop Kevin Stocker, who was summoned to Philadelphia primarily to provide defensive aid to a leaky infield, had astonished nearly everyone with his offense. After going 0-for-6 in his first game, the 23-year-old rookie, who was hitting just .233 at Scranton/Wilkes-Barre before getting called up, had gone 9-for-18.

Kevin Stocker helped to steady the Phillies infield after his arrival in early July.

The baby-faced Stocker was proving to be almost too good to be true. Not only was he hitting better than expected, his on-field demeanor had veterans shaking their heads. Manager Jim Fregosi, himself a former shortstop, praised Stocker for his "good field presence." The intense rookie, he said, had especially well-defined defensive instincts and "knows exactly how to position himself at the right place at the right time."

"He reminds me of a young Larry Bowa," said Phillies coach Larry Bowa, one of the club's all-time greats as a shortstop. "He makes all the right moves. I'm very impressed with him."

From his own vantage point, the refreshing youngster, who was the same age as Granny Hamner when he captained the Whiz Kids to a pennant in 1950, was waging a successful battle to keep his meteoric rise to the big leagues after less than two minor league seasons in the proper perspective.

"The guys around here have been real helpful, and I'm learning a lot," said the shortstop with a voice of innocence. "I try to pick things up as quickly as I can because I have such limited experience. I'm just trying to do my best."

While Stocker's best was plenty good, it still couldn't keep the Phillies from a rude jolt when they got to San Diego to open the second half with a West Coast trip. Lying in ambush, the lowly Padres treated the Phils to three straight losses. Several fielding misplays by Kruk helped the Padres to a win in the first game. In the second game, Darren Daulton hit two home runs, including his first one in 105 at-bats, but the Phils bowed again. After a third loss in which their lead skidded to three games, the Phillies finally salvaged a win in the getaway game as Schilling snapped a personal five-game losing streak in a 6–3 triumph.

Moving up the coast to Los Angeles, the Phillies continued to win, although it was not without a price. In the first game of a series with the Dodgers, scheduled starter Ben Rivera was hit on the right index finger during batting practice and was scratched from the lineup. Mike Williams took his place on the mound, pitched five innings, and the Phils won, 7–5, as Roger Mason got his first Phillies victory. The Phils won again the next night with a 15-hit assault, 8–4, although Stocker sprained his ankle at first base and would be out for one week. Injuries continued in the third game when Greene had to leave in the ninth with a strained groin, but not before pitching the Phillies to what would become a 7–0 win in a game that featured three hits and three RBI by Mariano Duncan and in which Dykstra would reach the .300 mark in batting for the first time all season. Greene would go on the 15-day disabled list, and Tyler Green would be recalled to Philadelphia.

The Phillies were back in stride, but not for long. They had another date with the dreaded Giants. Again, the results were disheartening. The Phillies dropped three out of four games, the only win coming in the second game of the series when Schilling took a 1–0 lead into the ninth, gave up a home run to Barry Bonds, then watched as the Phils pushed over a run in the 14th to win, 2–1, with David West getting the decision.

The Phillies returned home clinging to a four-game lead and facing a three-game series with the Cardinals. Injuries, also including ones to Kruk and Danny Jackson, were plaguing the club, and just a shadow of doubt was beginning to creep into the vocabulary of Phillies fans.

Third base coach Larry Bowa confers before a game with outfielder Milt Thompson.

"You know and I know there are going to be some down times," said general manager Lee Thomas with a stiff upper lip. "We've just had some off games. We're probably going to have a lot more before the year is over. But I have enough confidence in this club to know that it's a good club. I feel good about the second half."

If he didn't feel good when he said that, Thomas had to feel marvelous a few days later. All season long, the Phillies demonstrated the admirable

David West had a strong season while working in a career-high 76 games.

ability of being able to turn their level of play up a notch when necessary. The clichemeisters called it "rising to the occasion." By any description, the Phillies had the knack, and in the upcoming series with the Cardinals they would show what the terms meant.

In a series in which they were duty-bound to win, the Phillies swept the Cardinals in three games with a gaudy display of hitting that for all practical purposed wiped St. Louis out of the pennant race. In the first game, the Phils unloaded 18 hits, including five by Kruk—against five different pitchers, four of them lefthanded—to thump the Cards, 10–7. The following night, the Phils' offense rolled over Cards' pitching again, slamming 17 hits in an assault that featured Daulton's grand slam and six RBI, and overcoming Todd Zeile's first inning grand slam to win, 14–6. The Phillies completed the rout with a 6–4 win in the third game with help from a two-run homer by Wes Chamberlain. It was the first time the Phils had ever won all their home games in one season against the Cards.

It was unquestionably the Phillies' biggest series to date, and when it was over, they had climbed back to a seven-game lead. Two days later, after wasting Mickey Morandini's first pinch-hit home run of his career in a 4–2 loss to ex-Phil Bob Walk and the Pittsburgh Pirates, the Phillies ended July with a 10–2 victory over the Bucs in a game in which Jackson hurled his second complete game of the season, and Pete Incaviglia broke out of a prolonged 1-for-34 hitting draught with two home runs—one reaching the upper deck in left field—and four RBI. Not only did the Phillies reach the two million mark in attendance in that game for the 11th time and second fastest in club history, they ended July with a 66–39 record and a six and one-half game lead over the fading Cardinals.

Having won nine of 13 games since their flogging in San Diego, the Phillies roared into August with another spurt. Green got his first major league start on August 1, but after blanking the Pirates for the first three innings, he was lifted in the fifth after allowing nine hits and three runs. The Phillies won anyway as Todd Pratt, getting a rare start behind the plate, slugged two home runs and a double to spark his club to a 5–4 victory. It was a heated match in which the teams, both dressed in 1933 uniforms, had a near brawl and Fregosi was ejected for arguing with umpire Jeff Kellogg.

Just as hot was the bat of Incaviglia. The Phillies had signed the burly outfielder during the off-season with the hope that he could supply some right-handed power to an overloaded lefthanded lineup. Not only had he done that, Incaviglia had also become one of the most vocal members of the team, fitting right in in the often-bawdy Phils' clubhouse. What's more, he had also won the respect of his teammates with his aggressive, hard-working style of play, and although he

Getting a rare start, Todd Pratt homered twice to spark a Phils win over the Pirates.

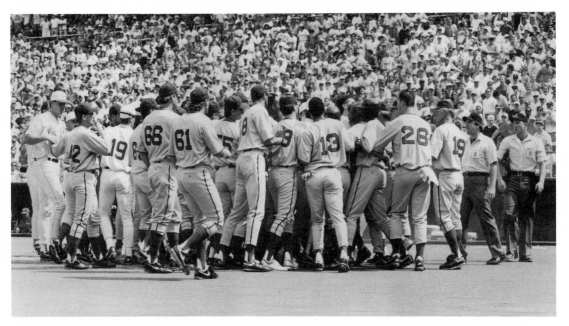

With the Phillies and Pirates dressed in 1933 uniforms, a typical baseball scuffle occurred with players mostly just standing around.

came with a reputation as a weak defensive player, he had performed well in the field, even to the point of making several spectacular catches.

"I'm very competitive. I like to go to battle," Incaviglia said in a moment of self-description. "Maybe it rubs off on everyone else. I'm vocal from the bench. I love the flavor of the game. I play the game hard—that's all I ever do. As long as I give everything I have every night, I can lay my head down and go to sleep. I can think, 'I did everything I could to help,' even if I had a bad day. That's the way I like to be perceived: 'He played as hard as he could. He gave people their money's worth.' "

In early August, Incaviglia was certainly giving the Phillies their money's worth. After hitting his third home run in two days in the 5–4 victory over the Pirates, he opened a road trip by walloping a three-run homer in a 5–3 win over the Braves. The next night, he had another three-run home run, although the Phillies bowed, 9–8, when West surrendered a three-run homer to Greg Olson in the eighth as Atlanta scored four times to overcome an 8–5 Phillies' lead.

On August 5 the occasional series of weird games resumed for the Phillies. This time, they overcame a 4–0 first inning deficit with Greg Maddux on the mound for the Braves, winning, 10–4, with Dave Hollins slashing three hits and driving in four runs and Dykstra scoring three times to run his major league-leading total to 101. The game was interrupted for 15 minutes when a power failure knocked out several banks of lights. Daulton was ejected for his comments to plate umpire Randy Marsh, and Rivera became the third Phillies pitcher to win in double figures.

In their next series, the Phils expected to fatten up against the Marlins, who had lost 32 of their previous 47 games. But they won only once in the three-game series, their lone victory coming on an 8–7 verdict in 10 innings after Green had been knocked out in his second start in one and two-thirds innings. For the fourth time this season, Daulton drilled two home runs while driving in five runs, while Mitch Williams got the win with the help of a line drive that was headed for a sure hit until it struck the Marlins' Gary Sheffield as he approached third base with what likely would have been the tying run in the bottom of the 10th. With the victory the Phils equaled their win total (70) of 1992.

With their lead at six and one-half games, the Phillies returned home for a crucial series with the Expos. The depth of the bullpen was still a concern, and in an effort to rectify that situation, Thomas made another deal before the first game of the series, sending seldom-used pitcher Jose DeLeon to the Chicago White Sox for reliever Bobby Thigpen, who had 57 saves and a 1.83 ERA in 1990, but who had been sliding downhill ever since then.

Pete Incaviglia carried a hot bat in early August with home runs in four straight games.

Like their crucial series in late July with the Cardinals, the Phillies once again demonstrated the ability to perform at their best in crises situations. In another extremely crucial series, the Phils swept third place Montreal in three games. Schilling pitched a sparkling five-hitter and Hollins drove in three runs to give the club a 5–2 victory in the first game. In the second

A familiar sight was Lenny Dykstra diving back into first base to avoid a pickoff attempt.

game, the Phillies got home runs by Incaviglia, Dykstra and Eisenreich, but it was a bouncer by Duncan against a drawn-up Expos infield that drove in the winning run in the bottom of the ninth for a 6–5 win. Greene came off the disabled list and started his first game since July 27 in the third contest that was won, 7–4, with Stocker singling home the winning run after making two errors, Mason getting his third Phillies win and Williams setting an all-time club record for a lefthander with his 31st save.

"I don't want to say they're out of it," said reliever Larry Andersen about the Expos."But we just made their climb a little more difficult."

By the time the Expos left town, the Phillies had opened an eight-game lead over the second place Cardinals. That would soon be stretched to nine games as the Phils took two out of three from the Mets in a series that was noteworthy because of the special contribution of Kim Batiste. Filling in, as he had done earlier in the season for Hollins, the rookie infielder stunned the Mets in the Friday the 13th opener with a ninth inning grand slam home run that overcame a 5–4 New York lead and powered the Phils to a 9–5 victory. Thigpen got the win in his first Phillies appearance. After the Mets whipped the Phils, 9–5, behind two doubles, two homers and four RBI by reserve second baseman Tim Bogar, Batiste resumed his heroics by driving in the winning run with a single that capped a four-run eighth inning rally and gave the Phillies a 5–4 win.

It was now mid-August, and the Phillies' lead had grown to nine games. The streaking Phils were headed to Denver for a date with the ever-beatable Rockies. Colorado proved to be an obliging host by dropping two out of three games. The biggest crowd (63,193) to watch the Phils all season saw Eisenreich's three hits and Stocker's three-run homer lead a 15-hit assault that landed a 10–7 Phils victory. That was followed by a 7–6 Phillies win that featured two home runs by Kruk, three RBI by Stocker and Thigpen's second win in relief. In the third game, with a series sweep close at hand, the Phils' bullpen coughed up a 5–1 lead by yielding five runs in the eighth that donated a 6–5 win to the Rockies.

On the next night, however, the Phils bounced back with a 6–4 victory over the Astros on Stocker's three-run, eighth inning triple that concluded an extremely tough at-bat in which the rookie shortstop fouled off four straight pitches from Xavier Hernandez with a full count. It was now apparent that the Phillies had turned the division race into a runaway. The club had won 21 of its last 30 games and with a nine-game lead in a division in which no one else seemed poised to rise above mediocrity, the Phillies' first title in a decade was moving closer to reality. With just 40 games left in the season, the Phils merely needed to win 17 more games to reach a victory total of 95, surely enough to claim a division title. No one was ready to order the champagne just yet, but that time didn't appear to be too far away.

Kim Batiste stunned the Mets with a grand slam home run in the ninth inning.

It was a lot farther away, though, than it looked, especially after the Phillies lost the next two games at Houston, then dropped their third straight in a 13-inning game against the Rockies. But they bounced back with two wins over Colorado as Jackson won, 4–2, and Schilling rode Pratt's two-run homer to an 8–5 verdict. Jackson's win made him the fifth Phils starter to win in double figures, a feat last accomplished by the club in 1932 when six troupers named Figety Phil Collins, Ray Benge, Ed Holley, Flint Rhem, Jumbo Jim Elliott and Snipe Hansen each corralled between 10 and 14 victories.

As for Schilling, the blond righthander had regained the form that in 1992 and early 1993 had brought him recognition as one of the league's toughest hurlers. A hard-working fellow who sunk a considerable amount of energy into both his on- and off-field endeavors, Schilling was the prototype major league pitcher, a big, strong, hard-throwing moundsman who always made opposing batters uncomfortable when he faced them.

Schilling was one of the Phillies' best bargains. He had come to Philadelphia after unsuccessful tenures in Baltimore and Houston as an ineffective relief pitcher for whom the Phils merely had to surrender Jason Grimsley, a pitcher who once was considered to be a fine major league prospect, but who was never quite able to overcome either control problems or a hot temper. After languishing in the bullpen during his early weeks in Philadelphia, Schilling got a shot at starting for the Phillies in May 1992, and suddenly his days as a reliever were over.

The Alaska-born son of a career Army man, Schilling always left a ticket for his deceased father whenever he pitched, saying it was his way of acknowledging his father for the profound influence he had on the hurler's life. As serious as he was about such things, though, the pitcher also had a fun-loving side. He was one of the club's characters, an extrovert who relished the publicity that followed him, and who delighted in slamming shaving cream pies in the faces of unsuspecting foils and whose high-decibel music boomed throughout the clubhouse before and after games.

Curt Schilling was a mainstay of the pitching staff, winning seven straight games after a mid-season slump.

"I wouldn't miss this year with these 25 guys for anything in the world," said Schilling in a statement that reflected the attitudes of most of his teammates. "These are the 25 most important guys in my life. A lot of times you see teams where guys can't wait to get away from one another at the end of the year. I don't think people here feel that way. This is as fun an atmosphere as I have ever been around."

Schilling's victory over the Rockies rocketed the Phillies' lead to 11 games. That, however, was followed by two losses to the Reds in games in which the bullpen caved in at the end. But the Phils won two of their next three games with shutouts. One was a 17-hit, 12–0 victory over Cincinnati in which Jackson scattered five hits over seven innings and Morandini and Chamberlain each drove in four runs. The second was a 7–0 whitewash of the Chicago Cubs in a game in which Rivera, angered about being passed over for his last start, took out his frustrations on the field by firing a spiffy, nine-strikeout, four-hitter. In between, the bullpen gave up another apparent victory when Rick Wilkins hammered an 11th inning grand slam to give the Cubs a come-from-behind 10–6 victory.

For Rivera, the sparkling performance he had just given was yet another indication of how good the giant hurler could be when he had all his stuff. Another one of the Phils' steals from the Braves, Rivera had not only one of the liveliest arms but was one of the hardest throwers on the staff. But the soft-spoken chucker suffered from control problems and a high ERA that hampered his work. Still, he was a key member of the starting rotation, and at just 24 years old was thought to have a bright future ahead of him.

Bobby Thigpen came to the Phillies in a mid-August trade with the White Sox and promptly won two games in relief.

The Phillies ended August with an 82–50 record and a 9½ game lead over Montreal, which had moved into second place ahead of the disappearing Cardinals. To aid in the stretch drive, the club acquired relief pitcher Donn Pall from the White Sox in a trade for minor league catcher Doug Lindsey, and recalled outfielders Tony Longmire and Ruben Amaro, infielder Jeff Manto and pitcher Kevin Foster from Scranton/Wilkes-Barre. Only Longmire, recalled one day before the September 1 cut-off, would be eligible for post-season play.

Terry Mulholland got the club's final month underway with his first victory since August 3 with a tidy six-hit, 4–1, victory over the Cubs. It was the seventh complete game of the season for the solid lefthander.

In previous seasons Mulholland had been the Phillies' top moundsman, winning 38 games over a two and one-half year period, including the club's only home no-hitter in the 20th century. The stylish southpaw had come to the Phillies in another one of Thomas's heists, and although he resisted the label, he had been the ace of the staff through the club's lean years.

Injuries, however, had plagued Mulholland off and on over the years, but they were particularly pronounced in 1993. Five days after he throttled Chicago, Mulholland faced just three batters before having to leave the mound with a strained hip. He would not pitch again until the last game of the season.

Meanwhile, the Phillies ripped into Cincinnati, 14–2, as Greene gave up just three hits, struck out 11 and slammed three hits, one a two-run homer. That and a 5–3 win by Schilling that was aided by Stocker's brilliant stop to start a key doubleplay surrounded a 6–5 loss to the Reds. That skirmish was mainly significant because it was the 151st consecutive game the Phillies had played without being shut out, a National League record previously held by the 1924–1925 Pirates.

Schilling's September 5 win put the Phillies lead at nine and one-half games. That was the last time during the season it was that high. The Phils would lose six of their next 10 games, including three straight to the Cubs. Two of those would be one-run defeats, a 7–6 loss in the game that Mulholland had to leave, and a 5–4 setback in which a late Phils rally that featured Duncan's pinch-hit home run fell short. The third was a devastating 8–5 drubbing that saw the Cubs overcome a 5–1 Phillies lead in the eighth inning by scoring seven runs with two outs.

Donn Pall was a big help in September after the Phils got him from the White Sox.

Jim Eisenreich (right) made a major contribution to the Phillies throughout the season.

The Phillies rebounded with a 10–8 win in their final game of the season with the Cubs with Dykstra socking two home runs and a single and collecting five RBI and Daulton smacking four hits and driving in three runs as the teams combined for 29 hits. A third inning brawl livened the encounter with Duncan charging Cubs pitcher Frank Castillo after a brushback pitch. Both players were ejected, and Duncan was later suspended for three days.

That game was followed by another Phillies win with Schilling's pitching and a two-hit, three-RBI outing by Incaviglia pacing a 6–2 decision over the Astros, although Schilling had to leave in the eighth after getting hit on the leg by a line drive off the bat of Ed Taubensee. But the Phillies, forced to start Mike Williams and Kevin Foster and use Brad Brink in long relief, then bowed 4–1 and 9–2 to Houston. Suddenly, the lead was down to five games.

The fact that the Phils had to throw three young pitchers in crucial games ably demonstrated the club's weakened condition on the mound. General manager Thomas had made a run one month earlier at Seattle Mariners pitcher Randy Johnson, but to no avail. In recent weeks, he had also tried to pry away upcoming free agent Mark Portugal from Houston but had backed off after the Astros demanded minor league reliever Ricky Bottalico as part of the proposed trade. With Mulholland sidelined, the Phils clearly needed help. But just as clearly, that help was not forthcoming, either from the club's farm system or in a deal with some other team.

Between August 25 and September 12 the Phillies lost six games off their lead. The slippage was hardly unnoticed, either by local fans or by the media. Quietly at first, but louder as the Phils' plunge continued, they began drawing comparison to the Great Collapse of 1964 when the Phillies blew a $6^{1/2}$-game lead with 12 games left to play. Would the 1993 Phillies emulate that most infamous collapse in baseball history? Was the club panicking?

"Nonsense," suggested team-leader Daulton. "The 1964 season has no bearing on us whatsoever. A lot of players on this team weren't even born then."

The Phillies did, however, have a history of collapses that included more than just the 1964 team. The 1950 team, for instance, had a $9^{1/2}$-game lead in late August and let it melt to one game by the end of the season when Dick Sisler hit a three-run homer in the 10th inning on the final day to give the Whiz Kids a 4–1 victory over the Brooklyn Dodgers and the pennant. The 1976 Phils let a $15^{1/2}$-game lead erode to three games before regrouping to win the division title by nine games.

It was time for the '93 Phillies to bite the bullet. Fortunately, they had a trip to New York on the schedule. A three-game series with the Mets was just the right tonic before the club embarked on a showdown meeting in Montreal with the red-hot Expos.

Greene took care of the first outing at Shea Stadium with a six-hit, 5–0, complete game victory. It was his seventh complete game and second shutout of the season and raised his record to a dazzling 14–3.

The easy-going North Carolinian, having overcome the groin injury that earlier had put him on the disabled list, was at this point pitching stronger than he had all season. Greene's fastball was crackling, and under the guidance of pitching coach Johnny Podres, he had developed his confidence as well as some of the finer points of pitching to the extent that he had become one of the league's premier hurlers. When he had command of all his pitches, which was most of the time, Greene was a dominating pitcher.

Greene was another one of Thomas's steals. He was traded in 1990 to the Phillies with Dale Murphy after being buried in the minors by the Braves' overloaded pitching staff. It didn't take Greene long to claim a spot in the Phillies' rotation, and by 1991 he was one of the club's top chuckers, even tossing a no-hitter that year.

"I don't look at it like the Braves made a mistake," Greene said. "I probably just took a little more time coming along than some other guys did. That's just the way things work out sometimes. Some people mature a little quicker than others. I was more of a late-bloomer as far as learning the things I had to learn and getting my confidence goes."

A power pitcher, Greene worked hard to come back from the tendinitis that idled him for much of the 1992 season. When he reported to spring training in 1993, it was obvious that he was in superb condition and primed for a banner season.

"The guy was hurt most of last year, but came to camp in unbelievable shape," said Daulton. "He did what he had to do to get back, and now you can see the results of his hard work."

Greene's work notwithstanding, the Phillies fell backward again in their next game with the Mets as a sixth inning error by Stocker led to three unearned runs and a 5–4 New York win. One night later, however, Stocker bounced back with two hits, two walks and three runs to lead the Phils and Schilling to a 6–3 triumph.

The Phillies went into Montreal with a five and one-half game lead and some pounding hearts in their chests. The moment of truth had arrived in what now appeared to be the most critical series of the season.

The Expos were hotter than an August day on a Texas desert, having fashioned a winning streak in which they had at one point won 17 of 20 games. What the Phillies feared most was an Expos sweep, which would have sliced the club's already precarious lead to a scant 2½ games.

The first game, played on September 17 before 45,757 manically screaming Cana-

One of the Phillies big winners was Tommy Greene, who won 16 of 20 decisions.

After he was called up, Kevin Stocker played well both offensively and defensively.

dians, was a bizarre affair in which both teams played like punch-drunk boxers. Phillies pitchers gave up 12 hits and 11 walks, and the game was marked generally by sloppy play with both teams frittering away opportunities to win. A seven-run sixth inning gave the Phillies a 7–4 lead, which Thigpen, hurt by a questionable two-out balk call that gave Rondell White a second-chance RBI single, couldn't hold. Eventually, the Expos prevailed with a 12-inning, 8–7 victory.

The howling snakepit of obnoxious Montreal fans grew worse in the second game, but the Phillies overcame that disadvantage to post a 5–4 win as Greene yielded just two hits over the first seven innings before getting knocked out in the eighth. Strong relief pitching by West and Mitch Williams saved the win, the Phillies' 90th of the season.

Breathing much easier now that they had avoided a dreaded sweep, the Phillies went into the rubber match looking for another win that would put the Expos away. All they got was another loss in the third one-run game of the series in a game they let get away. The Phils had a 5–2 lead, but with the margin cut to 5–4, Williams blew his second save of the series as Montreal pushed over two runs in the ninth with the help of a horrendously botched call at first base by umpire Charley Williams to win, 6–5.

Winging back to Philadelphia clinging to a slim four-game lead, the Phillies were greeted with even louder reminders of the 1964 collapse. But once again, those ever-helpful Marlins were about to enter the picture. In a three-game series that was just what the doctor ordered, the Phillies got a much-needed sweep. Kruk broke out of a prolonged 13-for-71 slump in the first game with a home run, two singles and three RBI to help Schilling win his seventh straight game, 7–1, with an 11-strikeout, seven-hitter. Fine stop-gap pitching by starter Mike Williams, three more hits by Kruk, strong relief pitching by Pall, who would be one of the club's most effective firemen in September, and some hustling base-running by Stocker, who raced home from first with the winning run on Amaro's sacrifice bunt and an error, gave the Phils a 5–3 win in the second game. In the third game, with the teams combining to leave 27 runners on base, Rivera allowed just five hits over eight innings and Hollins chased home pinch-runner Longmire with a bases-loaded, game-winning single in the 12th inning to produce a 2–1 victory.

The Phillies' lead was now back up to five and one-half games. Their magic number for clinching the division title was down to six. But the Expos' winning surge continued. And coming to town to face the Phils was—of all teams—the rampaging Braves, a club that had caught fire in the second half and was

Danny Jackson won 12 games but might have won four or five more with some better support.

on an unwavering mission to catch the faltering Giants in the National League West.

Pennant fever was in the air. The whole Philadelphia area was excited about the Phillies. Stores were selling Phillies paraphernalia almost as fast as they could order it. And people who had never given baseball a second thought before had suddenly become avid Phillies fans.

"It's exciting, no doubt about it," said Morandini, the slender second baseman who had started the season in the regular lineup but in the later days of the campaign had been unseated by the hot bat of Duncan. "This is what you play for. You want to be playing for something the last couple of weeks."

On September 24, Greene took the mound in the first game against Braves' ace Tom Glavine. Pitching the club's finest game during the regular season, he came up with a clutch, 3–0, victory, silencing the powerful Atlanta offense by scattering three hits over eight and one-third innings. Greene also chipped in with a two-run single, and Mitch Williams set an all-time club record by recording his 41st save, snapping the old mark of 40 set in 1987 by Steve Bedrosian.

The second game was in sharp contrast to the first. Ten pitchers gave up a total of 29 hits with the Phillies getting 15 of them, including three by Daulton. The Phillies made three key errors that led to three Atlanta runs. The seesaw battle was climaxed in the eighth when the Braves torched Mason for three runs, giving them a decision, 9–7.

For the third day in a row, the third game drew more than 57,000, sending the Phillies' home attendance for the season to a club record 3,137,674. But the Phils failed again as the Braves handed Schilling his first loss since July 11, a 7–2 defeat. Despite the two straight losses, the Phillies ended their home schedule with a five-game lead and with New York defeating Montreal, a magic number that was down to three games.

That number quickly shrank to one a day later when the Phillies clinched no worse than a tie for first with a 6–4 victory over the Pirates at Three Rivers Stadium. Facing a record-tying eight Pittsburgh pitchers, the Phillies got the win for Rivera as Hollins slammed four hits and Duncan poled a home run that launched a four-run fourth.

For Duncan, it was one more in a long line of key hits he had during the season. The outgoing infielder, who earlier in the month had an 18-game hitting streak, was often overlooked in the rush to shower attention on some of the bigger names on the club, but he had put together an extremely fine season in 1993.

Duncan had come to the Phillies the year before as a free agent, and although he had no regular position, he wound up playing in 142 games. His versatility was as much in evidence in 1993 as it was in 1992 when again he was seldom out of the lineup for much time. This season, he had filled in at shortstop when needed and had spent time at second. Midway through the year it had become apparent that his offense was too good to be kept out of the lineup, and manager Fregosi began playing him more and more frequently.

A native of San Pedro de Macoris, Dominican Republic, one of the most productive breeding places in baseball, he had responded admirably once he took over as the regular second baseman. His average, which had hovered in the low .200s in late May surged to the .280 range by late September, and Duncan played solidly, if not spectacularly, in the field. An extremely upbeat person, he was also influential in the clubhouse as a veteran player who got along well with everybody.

"I never forget where I come from," he said proudly. "I remember when I used to play ball in the Dominican. I didn't have real shoes, a real glove, a real baseball bat. For me to be able to play

Mariano Duncan hit one of the biggest home runs in Phillies history with his grand slam in the division title clincher.

on the major league level and have all this, I'm very proud of myself.

"I don't concern myself with saying I'm the everyday second baseman," he added. "I just play where the manager puts me. I've gotten used to shifting around. I'm the type of player who just wants to play."

Duncan's value to his team was never more conspicuous than on September 28 when the Phillies tangled again with the Pirates. The Phillies were trailing, 4–3, as they began the seventh inning of a game that Mike Williams had started. Daulton opened the inning with an infield single. Eisenreich followed with a single to center, then Milt Thompson dropped a bunt that Bucs' pitcher Rich Robertson fielded but threw late to third, trying to nail Daulton. Stocker then singled to right-center to chase home Daulton and tie the score. One out later, Dykstra walked to force home the lead run.

Up stepped Duncan. And out went a drive to deep left that didn't stop until it had cleared the fence for a grand slam home run, a club record eighth grand slam of the season and Duncan's second of the year. The blow culminated a six-run inning that gave the Phillies a 9–4 lead, and—a little while later when the game had ended, 10–7, in the Phils' favor—the team's first division title in 10 years.

The Phillies have benefitted from some other home runs of enormous significance: Sisler's dramatic home run against Brooklyn in 1950; Larry Christenson's title-clinching grand slam in 1977; Randy Lerch's two homers in the division clincher in 1978; and Mike Schmidt's 1980 blast that won the division crown. Duncan's swat ranks right with them on the list of the greatest home runs in Phillies history.

John Kruk is greeted at home after getting a key late-season home run in a game against the Marlins.

"That was the biggest hit of my life," Duncan said. "I was very excited. It's a great feeling."

The blow clinched for the Phillies what had been a long, long journey back from the pits of the National League standings. After Pall had retired the last Pirate—Dave Clark on a sharp grounder to Kruk—to preserve the decision for Thigpen, the Phillies erupted in a raucous post-game celebration that lasted far into the night.

"It's finally our turn," said a weary Kruk, hobbling around on legs battered by a long season. "You're used to going out there brain dead in September. For seven years, all I played on were bad teams. It got sickening, having to watch other people in baseball do this [celebrate]. You get so jealous. But not anymore."

No one was happier than Fregosi, the manager who had so marvelously kept together a team made up of such a vast array of characters.

"This is the most gratifying year I've ever spent in baseball," he said. "It's just great. There's nothing like it. I'm just so proud of these guys. They've been great all year long."

The Phillies won the title in the 157th game of the season, at the time moving to a six-game lead over the second place Expos. Ironically, the crown was claimed on the exact same date that the 1983 team won its division title. The title clinching also perpetuated another Phillies habit—that of never having won a division flag on the home soil.

It was, to say the least, suitable vindication for a team that had been much-maligned in recent years and that even as recently as a few weeks earlier had been cruelly and inaccurately compared to the infamous 1964 Phillies team.

As Chamberlain appropriately screeched during the champagne-splashed clubhouse party following the title-clincher, "It's 1993. It ain't 1964. Where are all those ghosts now?"

Throughout their history, the Phillies have had to chase away ghosts. They had to do it in 1950 after 35 years of futility; they had to do it in 1980 after the lingering effects of the 1964 collapse and the playoff failures of 1976, 1977 and 1978; and they had to do it again in 1993 after a decade of miserable, agonizing baseball teams.

"We rallied around each other," said the always-thoughtful and articulate Thompson, an extraordinarily valuable veteran who had a strong presence in the Phils' clubhouse, especially among the young and impressionable black players. "People say we have a bunch of strange characters on this team. But we played well together, and that's all that counts.

"At times, it's been like a roller-coaster," he added. "We've hit some bad spots and some people started to panic. But the team never panicked. We'd lose some tough games, but time after time we'd come back the next day and win. That's been the key for us all season. We've been able to rally back after tough defeats."

It mattered little that the Phillies won just one of their final five games of the season, the result of which placed their final record at 97–65 and their lead over Montreal at three games. Of minor significance during that final week was the fact that the Phils' National League record of not being shut out was finally ended after 174 consecutive games by the Pirates' Tim Wakefield, who blanked them, 5–0.

In the last game of the season, Mulholland got his first start since September 6 in what was hoped to be a tune-up for his return to full-time action in post-season play. He pitched four innings and gave up one hit in a 2–0 victory for the Cardinals. In that same game, Dykstra set a new club record with 129 walks in one season, breaking the old mark set in 1983 by Schmidt.

Afterward, the Phillies returned to Philadelphia to take a short rest and to get ready for the upcoming playoffs. The best was yet to come.

6

America's (New) Team

Having already established itself as a team with boundless amounts of determination, the Phillies entered the National League Championship Series (NLCS) faced with yet another test of their mettle. Standing ominously in the path in the Phils' sixth trip to the NLCS was the powerful Atlanta Braves, a team that was generally considered one of the two best clubs in baseball.

In a way, the Phillies were just happy to be in the playoffs. Winning the division title while becoming only the third team in the 20th century to go from last place the previous year to first provided ample satisfaction. Participating in the playoffs was just gravy, and if the Phils happened to lose, so what? They had already accomplished more than almost anybody with an ounce of sense could have expected.

That feeling, of course, was merely superficial, more an attitude of the fans and media than the players themselves. Deep down, the players maintained their season-long posture that they were capable of beating anybody.

"I don't think anybody suspected we were going to be as good as we are now," said Pete Incaviglia. "We felt after the first two or three weeks of spring training that we were going to be a lot better than people thought. We felt like we had a lot of talent, and that we were underrated as far as what people were predicting for us. Now, we have a chance to go to the World Series, That's what everybody who plays this game dreams about."

The odds of getting there, though, were decidedly not in the Phillies' favor. The Braves, after all, were the defending National League champions, had won the pennant two years in a row and were the first National League team since the 1970s Phillies to win three straight division titles. And after losing to the Minnesota Twins and Toronto Blue Jays in successive World Series, the Braves were determined to make amends in 1993.

Atlanta had been required to make a heroic stretch drive to win the National League West title. It trailed the red-hot San Francisco Giants throughout much of the season. In the second half, however, the Braves had caught fire. Although the Giants led by as much as $9^1/_2$ games in August, they started slowly to fade while the Braves came on with a torrid streak in which they won 38 of 54 games in July and August.

The Braves finally caught San Francisco in early September, taking sole possession of first place on September 4. From then on, the two clubs waged a furious fight to the finish. From August 1 until the end of the season, Atlanta won 41 of its last 56 games in what concluded the third best second half in baseball history.

Atlanta finally clinched the title on the last day of the season, edging the Giants by one game. The Braves set a franchise record with 104 wins.

There were no weak spots on the Braves, especially on what was billed as the best pitching staff in the majors. Atlanta's starting rotation featured 22-game winner Tom Glavine, the National League's first pitcher to win 20 games three straight years since Ferguson Jenkins did it for the Chicago Cubs six times in a row between 1967 and 1972; 1992 Cy Young winner, Greg Maddux, a free agent pickup who won 20 games and would go on to another Cy Young award in 1993; 18-game winner Steve Avery and 15-game winner John Smoltz.

While Maddux led the league in ERA, complete games and innings pitched, and Glavine in starts and wins (tied), the overall staff had the league's lowest ERA (3.14) and had given up the fewest number of hits.

Along with strong pitching, the Braves also packed a heavy wallop on offense. Outfielders Dave Justice and Ron Gant and first baseman Fred McGriff, who arrived at mid-season from the San Diego Padres, each finished with more than 100 RBI and 30 home runs apiece. Shortstop Jeff Blauser had enjoyed his finest season with a .305 average, steady third baseman Terry Pendleton was one of the game's best clutch hitters and center fielder Otis Nixon was a terror on the bases.

Twenty-two members of the Braves' roster had appeared in post-season games, while only seven Phillies (Larry Andersen, Mariano Duncan, Lenny Dykstra, Danny Jackson, Roger Mason, David West and Mitch Williams), had playoff experience. Moreover, there were six players on the Phillies who had played at least seven big league seasons without appearing in post-season play: Darren Daulton (nine years), Jim Eisenreich (eight), Incaviglia (eight), John Kruk (eight), Milt Thompson (eight) and Bobby Thigpen (seven).

Nevertheless, the matchup wasn't as one-sided as it appeared. The Phillies had won just seven fewer games during the season than the Braves in what was the club's third highest victory total in its history. And in head-to-head meetings, the Phillies had won six of the 12 games played with the Braves outscoring the Phillies in those games, 65–64.

You couldn't get much more even than that. And that was a characteristic that marked the rivalry between the two teams throughout the 20th century. Since 1900, the Braves, playing in Boston, Milwaukee and Atlanta, had won 904 games to the Phillies' 858.

While the Braves had led the National League in home runs in 1993 with 169, the Phils—with 156 homers—had led the circuit in runs scored, crossing the plate 877 times to Atlanta's 767. The Phillies also ranked second in batting average with a .274 mark to the Braves' ninth place figure of .262.

The Phillies may have been underdogs, but it was not likely that they would be left in the kennel when the series began. And no one was more anxious for the series to start than club president Bill Giles.

Since taking over the team after the 1981 season, Giles had desperately wanted a winner. But he got one only in 1983 when an aging coalition of holdovers from the great 1980 team and a group of faded free agent superstars mustered one last push to drive the Phillies to the National League pennant before falling in five games to the Baltimore Orioles in the World Series.

Giles, whose career as a baseball executive began in 1959 and who joined the Phillies in 1969, had

Pre-game festivities got the Vet ready for the first game of the LCS.

frequently been the target of fan criticism in recent years as the Phillies failed to come up with another winner. Although, by his own admission, he had made some mistakes, much of the criticism was either unfair or the result of unenlightened public opinion. Nobody wanted to win any more than Giles did, and nobody tried harder to make that happen.

"It's great to be a winner again," he had said after the division-clincher. "This is the most rewarding of all [Phillies titles] because we've been down for a few years. It's been a struggle to get back to where we want to be. But now I'm happy. This is going to be a joyful October."

Even before the League Championship Series had started, the joy had set in throughout the Philadelphia area. The interest level and excitement among fans was probably higher than any sports team had ever generated in the city. Few conversations were held without some discussion of the Phillies. Press coverage was at a frenzied pitch. Poems were written and songs were composed about the club. And Phillies red caps were a common sight on heads throughout the city and suburbs. Even Billy Penn, high atop City Hall, got into the act, donning a giant-size Phillies cap.

The rest of the country was warming up to the Phillies, too. Attracted by a group of appealing characters who were wholly unlike the boring robots who make up much of professional sports and by the team's image as a cast of outlandish free spirits, fans throughout the nation were jumping on the bandwagon. Suddenly, the Phillies were America's Team, embraced by a nation of baseball fans who longed for something new to root for and who demonstrated an almost universal distaste for the Ted Turner-owned Braves, who before the Phillies came along liked to fancy themselves as "America's Team."

"It's exciting, no doubt about it," said Mickey Morandini on the eve of the series opener. "I mean, this is why you play. You want to be playing for something the last couple weeks. It's exciting for everyone involved with this team."

While the city of Philadelphia geared up for an anticipated revenue of between $35 and $40 million, and Veterans Stadium was prepared for its first major sporting event in a decade, the Phillies got down to the business of trying to play what everyone perceived as the role of David versus Goliath. In somewhat of a surprise announcement, manager Jim Fregosi picked Curt Schilling to open the series on the mound for the Phillies. The League Championship Series would go like this:

GAME ONE—PHILLIES 4, BRAVES 3 (10 INNINGS)

In post-season play, it is often the most unlikely player who emerges as a hero. So it was with Kim Batiste in the first game of the League Championship Series at Veterans Stadium.

In the incredibly short space of one inning, the Phillies' utility infielder went from goat to hero in a high-tension game that summoned every possible ounce of drama.

Batiste's one out single drove home John Kruk from second to give the Phils a 4–3 victory over the Braves in 10 innings.

Just one inning earlier, with the Phillies leading 3–2, Batiste had thrown a potential doubleplay ball into right field to set up the Braves' tying run.

Batiste had entered the game in the ninth inning as a defensive replacement for Dave Hollins at third base.

"I was hoping I'd have a chance to redeem myself," Batiste said a few minutes after his jubilant teammates had carried him off the field. "I had a lot of encouragement from my teammates after the error. With the guys behind me like that, I couldn't let them down."

Batiste was far from the game's only headliner. He was joined by Schilling, who pitched superbly for eight innings before leaving against his will. Schilling struck out a Phillies playoff record 10 Braves, including five in a row to start the game, a League Championship Series record.

Schilling, who had spent the few days before the playoffs intently watching video tapes of the Braves, threw consistently in the mid-90-mph range. Daulton said it was the hardest he'd ever seen Schilling throw.

"I knew I had a good fastball," said Schilling. "I haven't pitched much better than that. Being in a game like this is the dream of my life."

The win was a big one for the Phillies, many of whom went into the series relishing their role as underdog.

"I definitely think it's important to get off on the right foot," said Fregosi.

The East Division champs got off on the right foot at the very be-

John Kruk scores in Game One on a wild pitch by Steve Avery (right).

ginning, taking a 1–0 lead in the first inning. Dykstra opened the frame with a line-drive double to left-center. Duncan followed with a liner to right-center for a single that sent Dykstra scampering to third. Dykstra scored when Kruk's grounder to second resulted in a force-out of Duncan.

Meanwhile, Schilling was sky high. He struck out Nixon, Blauser and Gant on swinging third strikes in the first inning. In the second, he fanned McGriff and Justice, looking before Pendleton broke the spell with a ground out to Kevin Stocker.

The Braves finally got to Schilling in the third. With two outs, pitcher Avery doubled down the left field line and scored on Nixon's double over the head of Incaviglia, who stumbled on both balls.

Atlanta added another run in the fourth on a walk to Gant, McGriff's single and a sacrifice fly to left by Justice.

Incaviglia tied the score in the fourth when he lined a 423-foot shot to the center field bleachers. The Phils then went ahead in the sixth. With one out, they loaded the bases on a walk to Kruk, a double to right by Hollins and an intentional walk to Daulton. Kruk romped home when Avery threw a pitch in the dirt that bounced away from catcher Damon Berryhill. The Phils had another scoring chance in the eighth, but pinch-runner Thompson was thrown out at home after Wes Chamberlain's double.

Pete Incaviglia crosses the plate after smacking a 423-foot home run.

Although he said he begged and pleaded not to be taken out, Schilling was lifted after eight innings. That led to the entry of Mitch Williams, who didn't disappoint his critics by walking Bill Pecota, the first batter he faced. Batiste then threw Mark Lemke's ground ball into right while going for the force at second. After a sacrifice bunt, Pecota scored on Nixon's grounder to short.

Thompson, inserted in left, saved a run in the 10th with a fielding play that went largely unheralded. With Pendleton on first with a single, Thompson cut off Greg Olson's double into the corner with a brilliant running stop that prevented a run from scoring.

The Phillies finally won in the 10th with the help of some hard base running by Kruk, who doubled with one out, then raced home to score on

Milt Thompson is tagged out by Damon Berryhill on a close play at the plate.

Batiste's single down the left field line. It might have been the fastest Kruk ran all year.

"Nothing's easy when you play these guys," Kruk said. "But we beat them the only way we can beat them—with hustle and a well-pitched game."

Atlanta manager Bobby Cox shared the same sentiment. "Both teams have great starting pitching, and I expect these will be the kinds of games you'll see the rest of the way," he said.

GAME TWO—BRAVES 14, PHILLIES 3

While it was often overlooked in the rush to fling bouquets at the Atlanta pitching staff, the power of the club's offense can be just as awesome.

The Braves left little doubt of that as the League Championship Series moved into the second game. Unleashing a mighty display of power, the Braves hammered Phillies pitchers for 16 hits, including four home runs, in a one-sided rout that had the fans leaving as early as the seventh inning.

It was simply no contest as the Braves battered Phils starter Tommy Greene, knocking him out in the third inning, and then continuing the assault against a string of hapless Phillies relievers en route to a 14–3 victory.

Phillies celebrate John Kruk's arrival at home with the winning run in Game One.

It was the most runs scored by one team in a League Championship Series and tied for the most home runs by one team.

"We just got the bleep kicked out of us tonight," said Daulton. "That's all there was to it."

In addition to the Braves' offense, which featured a mammoth 438-foot home run into the upper deck in right field by McGriff that was only the seventh ball hit to that area in Vet Stadium history, Atlanta also got its customary strong pitching. The Phillies could do little with Maddux, who struck out eight while scattering five hits in seven innings.

The only Phils batter to reach Maddux successfully was Hollins, who lashed a two-run homer in the fourth after Kruk had singled. The blow narrowed the Braves' lead at the time to 8–2 and temporarily gave the Phillies some hope. But it was merely false hope.

"You can't give Maddux that kind of lead," Hollins said. "He always has good stuff. He has that hard slider that he throws at your hip. Once he gets ahead of you, he's tough to catch."

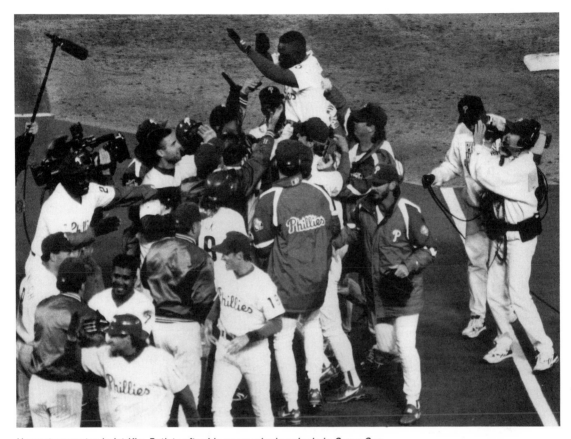

Happy teammates hoist Kim Batiste after his game-winning single in Game One.

The Braves got Maddux ahead quickly. McGriff became the first batter to drive a ball into the upper deck in right since Von Hayes did it in 1989 when he put a towering drive into orbit in the first with Nixon aboard. McGriff stood and watched as the ball soared majestically into the seats.

It was not Greene's night. After McGriff's home run, he surrendered five more runs in the third, one of them coming on Blauser's solo homer leading off the inning. With one out and two on, Thigpen relieved Greene and proceeded to issue a gopher ball to Berryhill that was planted in the right field stands for a three-run homer.

"He [Greene] didn't have good command of his fastball or his breaking stuff," Fregosi said afterward. "You get balls out over the plate, and you're going to get hit."

Greene refused to blame nervousness for his performance, even though pitching against his former teammates in his first post-season game gave him reason to be jittery.

"I wasn't nervous," he said. "I felt strong. Maybe I was too strong. I tried to keep the ball down, but I kept getting it up. They should have been hit, and they were hit."

The Braves also recorded a solo home run in the fifth by Pendleton off Ben Rivera, the Phils' fifth starter during the regular season whom Fregosi elected to stick in the bullpen in the League Championship Series. Rivera otherwise threw two respectable innings in relief against his former team.

Atlanta added four more runs in the eighth off West, who gave up four hits but wasn't helped by two bobbled grounders (one an error) by Stocker and a throwing error by Morandini.

Pendleton wound up driving in three runs, as did Gant and Berryhill.

Mickey Morandini slides into second with a stolen base in Game Two.

"This is a very explosive lineup," said Cox. "It's hard to hold our team down. I don't think Tommy (Greene) had his best location, and the ball was really jumping out of the park. McGriff's home run was the key hit for us. It got us started."

Other than Hollins' homer, the Phils managed to put only two men as far as second base against Maddux. Morandini singled and stole second in the first inning, and Stocker singled and went to second on a walk to pinch-hitter Ricky Jordan in the seventh.

The Phillies put two men on in the eighth against reliever Mike Stanton when Kruk singled and Hollins walked. But they couldn't score until the ninth when Dykstra slapped a home run to right in the midst of Mark Wohlers' striking out the side.

The two Phils' home runs combined with Atlanta's four to set a National League Championship Series record for most home runs in one game.

"It wasn't very pretty," said Fregosi. "But it's much easier to lose a game like this. If you're going to lose, I'll take what happened tonight."

GAME THREE—BRAVES 9, PHILLIES 4

As the League Championship Series shifted to Atlanta, the Phillies not only had to deal with the mighty Braves. They also had to face their fans and media.

"Keep the wife and kids off the streets, the Phillies are coming," blared one newspaper headline. Other accounts of the Phils' arrival pictured them as a wild bunch of barbarians. If you believed what you read, the Phillies had to be the most uncivilized visitors to Georgia since General Sherman marched his army across the state.

The Braves fans were hardly any better. With their incessant chanting and repulsive tomahawk chop, they turned a baseball game into a circus with watching it becoming only a secondary event. The only thing worse among the legions of pseudo fans who performed such acts was the obnoxious wave.

For the Phillies, on most occasions, it would not have been asking too much to call on Terry Mulholland to throw a blanket over the powerful Braves offense. But this time, it was different. This time, it was unrealistic to ask a pitcher who had worked in just five innings in the entire month of September to perform an assignment that would have been difficult even on normal days.

Mulholland did his best, though. For five innings, he pitched like the Terry Mulholland of old, the one who had been the Phillies' top pitcher for nearly three years.

After being shut out on five hits by Mulholland for five innings, the Braves erupted with five runs in the sixth. They added four more in the seventh, which gave them a total of 23 runs in successive games, a new League Championship Series record.

It turned out to be another ugly day for the Phillies and Mulholland.

"He just ran out of gas," said Fregosi.

Mulholland refused to blame his long layoff or the hip injury that had caused that layoff.

"I just kept throwing balls in the wrong spot," he said. "You can't let up on those guys. Make a mistake, and they're going to hit it."

With former President Jimmy Carter loyally cheering them on from the stands, the Braves wound up with 12 hits while again roughing up the Phillies' bullpen, which has been a glaring weakness since mid-season.

Although the Phillies had 10 hits themselves in a slight burst of offensive fireworks, it was really only Duncan, Kruk and Stocker who supplied the output. Kruk drove in three of the Phils' runs, while Stocker had three hits and Duncan two triples, the first time a player had poked two three-base hits in a League Championship Series game.

For most of the rest of the Phillies lineup, it was another futile day at the yard against the crafty pitching of the Braves' Glavine. In winning his first League Championship Series game after four losses, Glavine held the Phillies to two runs and six hits in seven innings.

"I decided to be more aggressive with them," Glavine said. "I really went after them. I figured if they're going to beat me, it has to be with my best stuff."

Glavine retired the first seven Phils in order before yielding a hit in the third when Stocker punched a double down the right field line. Then the Phils broke on top in the fourth, snapping a scoreless tie when Duncan and Kruk hit back-to-back triples with none out. Kruk, however, died at third as the heart of the Phils order again failed to deliver.

Wes Chamberlain slugged three doubles during the LCS.

The Phillies even took a 2–0 lead in the top of the sixth on an opposite field home run by Kruk. Ever-so-briefly, it looked like the Phils might be on the road to victory.

The Braves quickly dispelled that notion in the bottom of the sixth. Blauser bounced a hard grounder off Mulholland's glove for a single. A walk to Gant and singles by McGriff and Pendleton followed to give the Braves two runs. Justice made it 4–2 with a double to left-center, his first hit of the series.

That kayoed Mulholland and led to Roger Mason. One more run scored when Duncan bobbled Lemke's grounder with his throw reaching the plate a fraction too late to get Justice.

The ugliness continued in the seventh as the Braves battered Andersen and West for four more runs on three hits and two walks. Lemke's three-run double to right-center was the big blow.

To their credit, the Phils refused to fold. Duncan got his second triple in the eighth and scored on Kruk's ground out to short. In the ninth, Chamberlain doubled to the gap in left-center, went to third on a single up the middle by Stocker and scored when pinch-hitter Jim Eisenreich hustled his way into a ground ball double to right-center.

The next day, a headline in Philadelphia's morning paper read: "Phillies appear dead in the water."

Right.

GAME FOUR—PHILLIES 2, BRAVES 1

There was never any doubt in Danny Jackson's mind what he had to do when he went to the mound in the fourth game of the League Championship Series. Jackson had some things to prove.

He had to prove to the fans and to the media who had maligned him that he was a far better pitcher than he'd been given credit for. He had to prove to himself that his awful performance in the 1992 League Championship Series when he was battered in one and two-thirds innings by the Braves while pitching for the Pittsburgh Pirates was a fluke.

And, of course, he had to restore some lost dignity to the Phillies pitching staff and get the club back in the hunt in a playoff series in which the Phils were down two games to one and on the verge of falling completely out of the picture.

On a crisp evening in Atlanta with another heavy dose of Braves fans from the lunatic fringe performing their assorted inanities, Jackson accomplished all these items and more as he pitched and batted the Phillies to a pulsating 2–1 victory.

Jackson not only drove in the winning run with a single, he also pitched seven and two-thirds of the grittiest innings imaginable, holding the potent Braves' scoring machine that had scored a record 23 runs in the last two games to a meager one run and 10 hits.

"Nobody gave me a chance," said a somewhat testy Jackson afterward. "All I heard [from the media] was I had no chance. I wanted to go out and stick it up your rear ends. When you hear time and time again that you're no good, it kind of puts you off. But I believed in myself and my teammates believed in me. I am more than happy with the way I pitched."

Said Atlanta manager Bobby Cox, "That was the best I've seen Jackson pitch since he was with Kansas City."

Although he had to pitch out of several jams in which the Braves stranded five men in scoring position, Jackson used a crackling fastball and an excellent slider to get the outs when needed.

Like the turnaround Jackson gave the Phillies pitching staff, the club also enjoyed a defensive rejuvenation. Thompson made the defensive play of the series when he saved the game with a leaping catch against the wall in left on Lemke's two-out drive with two men on base in the eighth. At the time, Mitch Williams had just entered the game.

"I knew I had the ball," Thompson said. "The main thing was holding on to it when I hit the wall."

Williams was also the beneficiary of fine fielding plays by Batiste and Morandini that got him out of trouble in the ninth. After giving up a lead-off single to pinch-hitter Pecota, Williams tried to barehand Nixon's bunt and dropped the ball, allowing the batter to reach first safely. Blauser then dropped another bunt. Williams raced off the mound to his right, fielded the ball, but threw wide to third. Batiste made a lunging stab of the ball with his foot still on the base to get a force-out.

A moment later, Gant hit a hard grounder to Morandini, who gobbled up the ball, touched second and threw to first while getting dumped by a hard slide by Blauser to complete a game-ending doubleplay.

Morandini had also made a diving catch of Blauser's blooper behind first in the first inning.

Lenny Dykstra scores one of his team-leading five runs in the series.

"For a team that's not supposed to play defense very well, we came up with some big plays," Morandini said.

Records continued to fall in the series. The 26 men left on base (15 by the Phillies) was a new National League Championship Series mark. So were the four strikeouts in one game by Kruk and the four walks in one game by Daulton. And Braves starter Smoltz grabbed first place in career National League Championship Series strikeouts (40) by fanning 10 Phils. The Phillies' 15 whiffs in the game tied a National League Championship Series record.

The Phillies left men on base in every inning but the eighth, including eight in scoring position.

Atlanta took an early lead in the second on singles by McGriff and Justice and a double by Lemke.

The Phils came back to take the lead in the fourth. Lemke booted Daulton's grounder. Thompson followed one out later with a double down the right field line. Stocker then lifted a fly to left that scored Daulton from third. Jackson chased home Thompson with a single up the middle, his first hit in the League Championship Series.

That was it for the scoring. The Phillies clung to their precarious lead through five more nerve-racking innings. In the seventh, Fregosi decided not to lift the lefthanded-hitting Thompson for a pinch-hitter when southpaw Kent Mercker entered in relief for the Braves. An inning later, Thompson made his game-saving catch.

"I never take my defense out when we're ahead in a game," Fregosi said.

The Phillies were outhit, 10–8. But with sparkling defense and the strong pitching—and batting—of Jackson, the Phillies won a game they had to have.

GAME FIVE—PHILLIES 4, BRAVES 3 (10 INNINGS)

Combine strong pitching, sparkling defense and timely hitting, and the result should be an easy victory.

The Phillies got all three, but the victory didn't come easily as the series concluded its stay in Atlanta. It took all kinds of heroics before the Phils suddenly found themselves leading a series they weren't supposed to win, three games to two.

For the Phillies, their ultra-dramatic, 4–3 victory in 10 innings was a game filled with spectacular contributors.

Mariano Duncan nails Braves Fred McGriff on a force-out at second base.

There were the late-inning heroics of Dykstra and Daulton. There was the superb pitching of Schilling and Andersen. And there was brilliant defense by Chamberlain and Incaviglia.

It was Dykstra's 10th inning home run that won for the Phillies, who took a 3–0 lead and a four-hitter by Schilling into the bottom of the ninth, only to watch the Braves storm back with three runs to send the game into overtime.

"I told my wife this morning that I hope I get in a situation where I can do something big to help us win," Dykstra said afterward. "I just like to play in these situations. Some people want to be out there. Some people are scared to be out there."

As big as Dykstra's home run was, the homer by Daulton was almost as big. Coming in the top of the ninth, it gave the Phils a run without which they would have lost the game in regulation.

Up to that point, Schilling had hurled his second masterful game of the playoffs. He threw eight strong innings, issuing just four hits, including only one after the second inning.

Schilling finally came out in the ninth after giving up a leadoff walk to Blauser and a made-to-order doubleplay grounder that Batiste lost the handle on. The exit and the shaky relief by Williams that followed deprived Schilling of what should have been a well-deserved win.

"After the seventh inning, I had pretty much given it all I had," said Schilling, who pitched the last two frames on guts alone. He finished with nine strikeouts, giving him 19 for the series.

Schilling got brilliant defensive support from Incaviglia and Chamberlain, two outfielders whose defense has often been criticized.

"If they don't make those plays, we don't win the game," Schilling said.

Incaviglia made a diving catch of a Pendleton liner to left in the second inning. Chamberlain tied a League Championship Series record with two assists, one in the first when he fielded McGriff's drive high off the right field wall, and threw to Stocker, who fired home to nail Blauser at the plate, and one in the third when he threw out Berryhill trying to stretch a single into a double.

Dykstra, Kruk and Hollins also made sparkling defensive plays during the game as the Phillies came up with one big fielding play after another.

"There has been a lot said about our club, that we weren't supposed to be on the same field with these guys," Fregosi said. "But we're a solid club, a good club. I couldn't be prouder of these guys."

Dave Hollins is greeted at the plate after hitting a two-run homer in the sixth game.

The Phillies took an early lead with one run in the first on a single by Duncan and a double by Kruk. Although they didn't get another hit until the sixth, the Phils added another run in the fourth after Incaviglia hit a high drive off the left field wall that Gant failed to jump for (and was charged with a three-base error) and scored on a sacrifice fly by Chamberlain.

All the while, Schilling and the Braves' Avery were locked in a fierce pitching duel. Avery finally departed after seven innings. In the ninth, Daulton led off the inning with a home run to right for his first RBI of the series.

After Schilling left in the ninth with two on and none out, Williams again failed to hold the lead. Singles by McGriff, Pendleton and Berryhill and a sacrifice fly by Justice gave Atlanta three runs and goat horns were being ordered for Batiste and Williams.

With men on first and third, a drive by Lemke just curved foul down the left field line before Williams struck him out. He then retired pinch-hitter Pecota on a fly to Dykstra.

In the top of the 10th with one out, Dykstra became the hero with a towering drive to the right field seats on a 3–2 pitch from fireballing Wohlers.

"I got a pitch that I could handle," said Dykstra of the nearly 100-mph fastball that he belted out.

Andersen came on in the bottom of the 10th and was brilliant. He got Nixon on a lazy fly to center, then struck out Blauser and Gant to end the game with a flourish and sent the Phillies back to Philadelphia with a series lead that no one thought possible.

The Phillie Phanatic fired up a whole stadium in Game Six, except perhaps this somber member of the Phillies' finest.

"We've been perceived as underdogs all year," said Incaviglia. "Everybody wants to look at our long hair, bellies and beer. But we thrive on that. We thrive on people saying we can't do this or we can't do that."

GAME SIX—PHILLIES 6, BRAVES 3

Riding the arm of Tommy Greene, the glove of Mickey Morandini and three of the most timely hits in club history, the Phillies rocketed to the National League pennant with a magnificently exciting victory over the defending champion Braves.

It was the Phils' third straight win of the League Championship Series, but again it didn't come easily. Playing before a wildly ecstatic, almost frenzied home crowd at Veterans Stadium, the Phillies needed a myriad of big plays and stellar performances in a game that had heroes galore.

The Phillies got three key hits—a two-run double by Daulton in the third, a two-run home run by Hollins in the fifth and a two-run triple by Morandini in the sixth.

They also got terrific relief pitching from West and Williams, each retiring the three batters he faced. Williams ended a rare one-two-three inning in the ninth by striking out pinch-hitter Pecota, touching off a wild celebration that extended from the clubhouse to all corners of the Vet and beyond.

"I'm just so damn excited I'm out of breath," said Fregosi.

Mitch Williams leaps with joy after getting the final out in Game Six.

He was hardly alone in that regard. Some 62,502 breathless spectators, fueled by the antics of the hard-working Phillie Phanatic and roaring "Whoot, There It Is" in what had become Phillies fans latest battle cry, sat on the edges of their seats for most of the game as Greene outdueled Maddux on a highly charged evening. No one was more determined to get the win than Greene, the big righthander who had been knocked out in the third inning of Game Two.

"He was stronger and more aggressive out there tonight," said Fregosi. "He felt terrible about his last start. This game meant a lot to him. This is the type of game that can be tremendous for a young man in terms of what it can do for his career."

"This is what we worked for. This is all that matters," said Greene, who shook off the effects of Game Two and slammed the door on the Braves by yielding five hits and three runs in seven innings. Prudently, Greene walked McGriff three times in an excellent piece of strategy of taking the bat out of the dangerous slugger's hands.

"I was not going to let him hurt me," Greene said.

Greene was aided by a spectacular leaping catch by Morandini in the second inning off a drive by Justice and another fine stop by the second baseman on a hard grounder by Justice in the fourth. Morandini also started a crucial inning-ending doubleplay in the second.

"Mickey has been a great defensive performer for us all year long," Fregosi said. "I thought he just played great. He's an integral part of the club."

Morandini may have helped the Phillies in another way when he lined a hard shot off the leg of Maddux in the first inning. Although Maddux stayed in the game, his effectiveness may have diminished after the injury.

Nevertheless, it still took the Phillies until the third inning to get on the scoreboard. Greene walked, Dykstra singled and Hollins walked to load the bases with two outs. Then Daulton drilled a line drive that was just fair by inches down the right field line, the ball bouncing into the stands for a ground-rule double as two runs scored.

The scoreboard tells the story after the Phillies beat the Braves, 6–3, in the final game.

The Braves scored once in the top of the fifth on two walks, a passed ball and Blauser's single. But the Phillies came back in the bottom half when Morandini reached first on Lemke's error and one out later Hollins axed a drive into the center field bleachers 422 feet away to give the Phils a 4–1 lead.

"We needed guys to step up when they had to," Hollins said. "That's what's getting us to the World Series."

The Phillies' advantage went to 6–1 in the sixth when Morandini tripled into the right field corner after a single by Thompson and an intentional walk to Dykstra. But the lead was comfortable for only a short time. Just as the fans were starting to relax and savor the idea of going to the World Series, Blauser followed a single by Nixon with a home run to left field. Greene got out of the inning without further damage, but by his own admission he was exhausted.

As policemen line the field, the Phillies start a victory celebration near the pitching mound.

West came in and threw bullets to retire the Braves in order in the eighth. Williams did likewise in the ninth, striking out Berryhill, getting Lemke to fly weakly to center and fanning Pecota.

"I've just been kind of teasing people all year," Williams kidded. "I saved my best for the last game."

As the stadium exploded in massive roar, the final out sent the Phillies leaping ecstatically into an unforgettable pileup on the field.

"I never had a feeling like that on a baseball field," said Daulton. "I went crazy out there. I just never had that kind of emotion before. I saw the house rocking. To know that something has happened that means so much to three or four million people, it was just an unbelievable feeling.

"This is something special. You can look in the mirror and say, 'Now, we really did this.'"

* * *

In the joyous clubhouse following the final out, with players hugging and dousing each other with beer and champagne, the Phillies celebrated the team's fifth National League pennant and talked about the long journey that had taken them from the dregs of the league to the top.

"This may sound strange," said Mulholland, "but in the back of my mind in spring training, I felt that with the way we played and what we meant to each other, I knew that there was something special going on."

And so there was. It was called heart, desire, determination. By any name, the Phillies had it.

"People said the Braves were better on paper," said Daulton. "I don't think you can put desire on paper."

To that, club president Bill Giles added: "I think the Braves have the best talent I've seen since 1980. They're the best team I've ever seen on paper. But there's a difference between stats and rising to the occasion. We beat them with heart."

Schilling was named the Most Valuable Player of the series. Although winless in his two starts, the hard-throwing right-hander gave up just 11 hits and four runs in 16 innings while striking out 19 and walking five. Both of his outings were brilliantly pitched, and both resulted in Phillies wins.

Darren Daulton exhalts in Phillies victory with manager Jim Fregosi.

"I thought I pitched well enough to win a couple of games," Schilling understated. "Luckily, the outcomes came out all right. You have to take your hats off to Atlanta. They are a bunch of classy guys. Everyone said that we would have to outslug them to win, but I really thought we would have to outpitch them."

The Phillies were outhit by the Braves, .274-.227, and outscored, 33–23, and the pitching staff had a 4.75 ERA to the Braves' 3.15. Yet, the Phillies played as though they were possessed by demons.

"We never quit. We never died all year," proclaimed Dykstra. "Everybody thought we were down when they blew us out two games, but we answered right back. We got great pitching performances from Jackson and Schilling and another from Greene tonight. We got some big hits and we had a total team effort.

"Sometimes, you can't control what's meant to be," Dykstra added. "And this has been meant to be since spring training."

Lee Thomas, the general manager who put the championship team together after coming to the Phillies a little more than five years before, agreed.

"When you do something, and things don't work out, it's kind of disheartening," he said. "But this year, we knew the guys could play. We really felt that they could win. They stayed healthy and they proved us right."

For the Phillies, the 1993 pennant joined previous flags won by the club in 1915, 1950, 1980 and 1983. Unlike the others, though, this pennant came after a feisty group of players, much maligned in the nation's press and painted as comic strip characters in baseball uniforms, banded together with a never-say-die attitude.

"We sent a message to a lot of people," said Duncan. "A lot of people were wrong."

Added Eisenreich: "We're a bunch of loose guys. In the clubhouse, we kid around. But when we step on the field, we're all business."

It's hugs and pats for all as happy Phils stage a joyful gathering on the field.

"I figure it took until tonight for people to realize we have a good ball club," Hollins said. "We've played hard all year, and tonight we beat a powerhouse team. They didn't expect us to be in the same ballpark. We're the only ones who knew we belonged and that we can play with them. We felt we hadn't gotten any respect, but maybe after tonight we will."

Much was made of the Phillies' special characters, but when it came down to crunch time, this was a team of highly talented players.

"Whatever it took to win, that's what type of team we are," said Greene. "Everybody picked each other up. It was a team effort. We're not a bunch of individuals. We're a team, and that's why we won."

"Mickey Morandini, Wes Chamberlain, Todd Pratt, the bullpen, one through 25, you cannot win unless you have somebody making an impact," added Daulton. "And that's what we had. Somebody was always making an impact."

In the final analysis, the Phillies outpitched the highly rated Atlanta starting rotation when it counted. The Phils got key hits and the Braves didn't. The Phillies made one big play after another on defense. And even the often-ridiculed Phils bullpen came through when it was needed the most.

"This is something you dream about when you're a little kid," Kruk said. "And tonight it came true."

"It feels so great to do this at home in front of all these people," added Chamberlain. "All I ever did was dream about this, and now my dream is a reality."

Game Four hero Danny Jackson has his own way of celebrating as he "pumps it up" on the field.

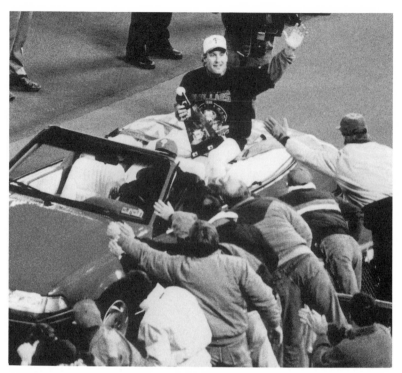

Series MVP Curt Schilling takes a victory ride in the car he just won.

Roger Mason (left) and Tommy Greene hoist the championship banner.

LEAGUE CHAMPIONSHIP SERIES BOX SCORES

Game One   October 6—Phillies 4, Braves 3 (10)

Atlanta	AB	R	H	RBI
Nixon, cf	4	0	2	2
Blauser, ss	4	0	0	0
Gant, lf	4	1	1	0
McMichael, p	0	0	0	0
McGriff, 1b	5	0	1	0
Justice, rf	4	0	0	1
Pendleton, 3b	5	0	1	0
Berryhill, c	3	0	0	0
Pecota, ph	0	1	0	0
Olson, c	1	0	1	0
Lemke, 2b	4	0	1	0
Tarasco, pr, lf	1	0	0	0
Avery, p	2	1	2	0
Sanders, ph	1	0	0	0
Mercker, p	0	0	0	0
Belliard, ph, 2b	0	0	0	0
Totals	**38**	**3**	**9**	**3**

PHILLIES	AB	R	H	RBI
Dykstra, cf	4	1	1	0
Duncan, 2b	5	0	1	0
Kruk, 1b	4	2	1	1
Hollins, 3b	4	0	1	0
Batiste, 3b	1	0	1	1
Daulton, c	3	0	0	0
Incaviglia, lf	4	1	2	1
Thompson, lf	0	0	0	0
Chamberlain, rf	3	0	2	0
Williams, p	0	0	0	0
Stocker, ss	3	0	0	0
Schilling, p	3	0	0	0
Eisenreich, rf	1	0	0	0
Totals	**35**	**4**	**9**	**3**

```
Atlanta      001  100  001  0 – 3
PHILLIES     100  101  000  1 – 4
```

One out when winning run scored. E—Batiste (1). DP—Atlanta 1. LOB—Atlanta 11, PHILLIES 8. 2B—Nixon (1), Olson (1), Avery (1), Dykstra (1), Kruk (1), Hollins (1), Chamberlain 2 (2). HR—Incaviglia (1). S—Belliard. SF—Justice.

Atlanta	IP	H	R	ER	BB	SO
Avery	6	5	3	3	4	5
Mercker	2	2	0	0	1	2
McMichael (L, 0–1)	1⅓	2	1	1	0	0

PHILLIES	IP	H	R	ER	BB	SO
Schilling	8	7	2	2	2	10
Williams (W, 1–0)	2	2	1	0	2	2

WP—Avery. Time—3:33. Attendance—62,012.

Game Two   October 7—Braves 14, Phillies 3

Atlanta	AB	R	H	RBI
Nixon, cf	4	2	3	2
Wohlers, p	0	0	0	0
Blauser, ss	5	1	2	1
Belliard, ss	1	1	0	0
Gant, lf	5	1	2	3
McGriff, 1b	5	2	3	2
Stanton, p	0	0	0	0
Tarasco, rf	0	0	0	0
Justice, rf	3	1	0	0
Sanders, cf	0	0	0	0
Pendleton, 3b	5	2	3	3
Berryhill, c	5	1	1	3
Lemke, 2b	5	1	0	0
Maddux, p	4	1	1	0
Bream, 1b	1	1	1	0
Totals	**43**	**14**	**16**	**14**

PHILLIES	AB	R	H	RBI
Dykstra, cf	4	1	1	1
Morandini, 2b	5	0	1	0
Kruk, 1b	3	1	2	0
Hollins, 3b	3	1	1	2
Daulton, c	4	0	1	0
Andersen, p	0	0	0	0
Eisenreich, rf	4	0	0	0
Thompson, lf	4	0	0	0
Stocker, ss	4	0	1	0
Greene, p	0	0	0	0
Thigpen, p	0	0	0	0
Longmire, ph	1	0	0	0
Rivera, p	0	0	0	0
Chamberlain, ph	1	0	0	0
Mason, p	0	0	0	0
Jordan, ph	0	0	0	0
West, p	0	0	0	0
Pratt, c	1	0	0	0
Totals	**34**	**3**	**7**	**3**

Atlanta	206	010	041 – 14
PHILLIES	000	200	001 – 3

E—Morandini (1), Stocker (1). LOB—Atlanta 6, PHILLIES 8. 2B—Nixon (2), Gant 2 (2). HR—Blauser (1), McGriff (1), Pendleton (1), Berryhill (1), Dykstra (1), Hollins (1). SB—Morandini (1). CS—Nixon (1).

Atlanta	IP	H	R	ER	BB	SO
Maddux (W, 1–0)	7	5	2	2	3	8
Stanton	1	1	0	0	1	0
Wohlers	1	1	1	1	0	3

PHILLIES	IP	H	R	ER	BB	SO
Greene (L, 0–1)	2$\frac{1}{3}$	7	7	7	2	2
Thigpen	$\frac{2}{3}$	1	1	1	0	1
Rivera	2	1	1	1	1	2
Mason	2	1	0	0	0	1
West	1	4	4	3	1	2
Andersen	1	2	1	1	0	1

PB—Daulton. Time—3:14. Attendance—62,436.

Game Three   October 9—Braves 9, Phillies 4

PHILLIES	AB	R	H	RBI	Atlanta	AB	R	H	RBI
Dykstra, cf	5	0	1	0	Nixon, cf	5	0	1	0
Duncan, 2b	5	2	2	0	Blauser, ss	4	2	2	0
Kruk, 1b	4	1	2	3	Gant, lf	4	1	1	0
Hollins, 3b	3	0	0	0	McGriff, 1b	4	2	2	1
Daulton, c	4	0	0	0	Pendleton, 3b	4	2	2	2
Incaviglia, lf	4	0	0	0	Justice, rf	4	1	1	2
Chamberlain, rf	4	1	1	0	Berryhill, c	3	1	1	0
Stocker, ss	4	0	3	0	Lemke, 2b	4	0	2	3
Mulholland, p	2	0	0	0	Glavine, p	3	0	0	0
Mason, p	0	0	0	0	Cabrera, ph	1	0	0	0
Thompson, ph	1	0	0	0	Mercker, p	0	0	0	0
Andersen, p	0	0	0	0	McMichael, p	0	0	0	0
West, p	0	0	0	0					
Thigpen, p	0	0	0	0					
Eisenreich, ph	1	0	1	1					
Totals	**37**	**4**	**10**	**4**	**Totals**	**36**	**9**	**12**	**8**

```
PHILLIES        000  101  011 – 4
Atlanta         000  005  40x – 9
```

E—Duncan (1). LOB—PHILLIES 7, Atlanta 7. 2B—Chamberlain (3), Stocker (1), Eisenreich (1), Blauser (1), Gant (3), McGriff (1), Justice (1), Lemke (1). 3B—Duncan 2 (2), Kruk (1). HR—Kruk (1). SB—Hollins (1). CS—Nixon (2).

PHILLIES	IP	H	R	ER	BB	SO
Mulholland (L, 0–1)	5	9	5	4	1	2
Mason	1	0	0	0	0	1
Andersen	$1/3$	2	3	3	1	0
West	$2/3$	1	1	1	1	2
Thigpen	1	0	0	0	1	2

Atlanta	IP	H	R	ER	BB	SO
Glavine (W, 1–0)	7	6	2	2	0	5
Mercker	1	1	1	1	1	0
McMichael	1	3	1	1	0	1

Mulholland pitched to 5 batters in the 6th.
Time—2:44. Attendance—52,032.

Game Four   October 10—Phillies 2, Braves 1

PHILLIES	AB	R	H	RBI
Dykstra, cf	3	0	2	0
Morandini, 2b	5	0	2	0
Kruk, 1b	5	0	0	0
Hollins, 3b	4	0	1	0
Batiste, 3b	0	0	0	0
Daulton, c	1	1	0	0
Eisenreich, rf	5	0	1	0
Thompson, lf	4	1	1	0
Stocker, ss	4	0	0	1
Jackson, p	4	0	1	1
Williams, p	0	0	0	0
Totals	**35**	**2**	**8**	**2**

Atlanta	AB	R	H	RBI
Nixon, cf	3	0	1	0
Blauser, ss	4	0	0	0
Gant, lf	5	0	0	0
McGriff, 1b	4	1	2	0
Pendleton, 3b	4	0	1	0
Justice, rf	4	0	2	0
Olson, c	2	0	0	0
Berryhill, c	1	0	1	0
Lemke, 2b	4	0	1	1
Smoltz, p	1	0	0	0
Mercker, p	0	0	0	0
Cabrera, ph	1	0	1	0
Sanders, pr	0	0	0	0
Wohlers, p	0	0	0	0
Pecota, ph	1	0	1	0
Totals	**34**	**1**	**10**	**1**

```
PHILLIES     000  200  000 – 2
Atlanta      010  000  000 – 1
```

E—Williams (1), Lemke (1). DP—PHILLIES 1. LOB—PHILLIES 15, Atlanta 11. 2B—Thompson (1), McGriff (2), Pendleton (1), Lemke (2). CS—Gant (1). S—Nixon 2. SF—Stocker.

PHILLIES	IP	H	R	ER	BB	SO
Jackson (W, 1–0)	7²/₃	9	1	1	2	6
Williams (S, 1)	1¹/₃	1	0	0	0	0

Atlanta	IP	H	R	ER	BB	SO
Smoltz (L, 0–1)	6¹/₃	8	2	0	5	10
Mercker	²/₃	0	0	0	0	0
Wohlers	2	0	0	0	3	5

HBP—Olson by Jackson. WP—Wohlers.
Time—3:33. Attendance—52,032.

Game Five   October 11—Phillies 4, Braves 3 (10)

PHILLIES	AB	R	H	RBI
Dykstra, cf	5	1	1	1
Duncan, 2b	5	1	1	0
Andersen, p	0	0	0	0
Kruk, 1b	4	0	1	1
Hollins, 3b	4	0	0	0
Batiste, 3b	0	0	0	0
Daulton, c	3	1	2	1
Incaviglia, lf	4	1	0	0
Thompson, lf	0	0	0	0
Chamberlain, rf	3	0	1	1
Eisenreich, rf	0	0	0	0
Stocker, ss	4	0	0	0
Schilling, p	2	0	0	0
Williams, p	0	0	0	0
Morandini, ph, 2b	1	0	0	0
Totals	**35**	**4**	**6**	**4**

Atlanta	AB	R	H	RBI
Nixon, cf	4	0	0	0
Blauser, ss	4	1	1	0
Gant, lf	5	1	1	0
McGriff, 1b	4	1	2	1
Justice, rf	2	0	0	1
Pendleton, 3b	4	0	1	0
Berryhill, c	3	0	1	0
Cabrera, ph, c	1	0	1	1
Lemke, 2b	4	0	0	0
Avery, p	2	0	0	0
Mercker, p	0	0	0	0
Sanders, ph	1	0	0	0
McMichael, p	0	0	0	0
Pecota, ph	1	0	0	0
Wohlers, p	0	0	0	0
Totals	**35**	**3**	**7**	**3**

```
PHILLIES      100  100  001   1 – 4
Atlanta       000  000  003   0 – 3
```

E—Batiste (2), Gant (1). LOB—PHILLIES 5, Atlanta 6. 2B—Kruk (2). HR—Dykstra (2), Daulton (1). S—Schilling. SF—Chamberlain, Justice.

PHILLIES	IP	H	R	ER	BB	SO
Schilling	8	4	2	1	3	9
Williams (W, 2–0)	1	3	1	1	0	1
Andersen (S, 1)	1	0	0	0	0	2

Atlanta	IP	H	R	ER	BB	SO
Avery	7	4	2	1	2	5
Mercker	1	0	0	0	0	2
McMichael	1	1	1	1	0	0
Wohlers (L, 0–1)	1	1	1	1	0	1

Schilling pitched to 2 batters in the 9th. WP—Avery.
Time—3:21. Attendance—52,032.

Game Six   October 13—Phillies 6, Braves 3

Atlanta	AB	R	H	RBI
Nixon, cf	3	1	1	0
Blauser, ss	4	1	2	3
Gant, lf	4	0	0	0
McGriff, 1b	1	0	0	0
Justice, rf	4	0	0	0
Pendleton, 3b	4	0	1	0
Berryhill, c	4	0	0	0
Lemke, 2b	3	1	1	0
Maddux, p	0	0	0	0
Mercker, p	0	0	0	0
Sanders, ph	1	0	0	0
McMichael, p	0	0	0	0
Wohlers, p	0	0	0	0
Pecota, ph	1	0	0	0
Totals	**29**	**3**	**5**	**3**

PHILLIES	AB	R	H	RBI
Dykstra, cf	4	2	1	0
Morandini, 2b	5	1	1	2
Kruk, 1b	4	0	0	0
Hollins, 3b	2	1	1	2
Batiste, 3b	0	0	0	0
Daulton, c	4	0	2	2
Eisenreich, rf	4	0	0	0
Thompson, lf	4	1	2	0
Stocker, ss	3	0	0	0
Greene, p	0	1	0	0
Jordan, ph	1	0	0	0
West, p	0	0	0	0
Williams, p	0	0	0	0
Totals	**31**	**6**	**7**	**6**

```
Atlanta      000  010  200 – 3
PHILLIES     002  022  00x – 6
```

E—Justice (1), Lemke (2), Maddux (1), Thompson (1). DP—PHILLIES 1. LOB—Atlanta 6, PHILLIES 9. 2B—Daulton (1). 3B—Morandini (1). HR—Hollins (2), Blauser (2). S—Maddux 2, Greene 2.

Atlanta	IP	H	R	ER	BB	SO
Maddux (L, 1–1)	5²/₃	6	6	5	4	3
Mercker	¹/₃	0	0	0	0	0
McMichael	²/₃	1	0	0	2	0
Wohlers	1¹/₃	0	0	0	0	1

PHILLIES	IP	H	R	ER	BB	SO
Greene (W, 1–1)	7	5	3	3	5	5
West	1	0	0	0	0	1
Williams (S, 2)	1	0	0	0	0	2

PB—Daulton. Time—3:04. Attendance—62,502.

FINAL 1993 LCS STATISTICS

Phillies Batting

	Avg.	G	AB	R	H	TB	2B	3B	HR	RBI	SH	SF	HP	BB	IBB	SO	SB	CS	GI DP	Slug Pct.
Andersen	.000	3	0	0	0	0	0	0	0	0	0	0	0	0	0	0	0	0	0	.000
Batiste	1.000	4	1	0	1	1	0	0	0	1	0	0	0	0	0	0	0	0	0	1.000
Chamberlain	.364	4	11	1	4	7	3	0	0	1	0	1	0	1	1	3	0	0	0	.636
Daulton	.263	6	19	2	5	9	1	0	1	3	0	0	0	6	1	3	0	0	0	.474
Duncan	.267	3	15	3	4	8	0	2	0	0	0	0	0	0	0	5	0	0	0	.533
Dykstra	.280	6	25	5	7	14	1	0	2	2	0	0	0	5	1	8	0	0	0	.560
Eisenreich	.133	6	15	0	2	3	1	0	0	1	0	0	0	0	0	2	0	0	0	.200
Greene	.000	2	0	1	0	0	0	0	0	0	2	0	0	1	0	0	0	0	0	.000
Hollins	.200	6	20	2	4	11	1	0	2	4	0	0	0	5	0	4	1	0	1	.550
Incaviglia	.167	3	12	2	2	5	0	0	1	1	0	0	0	0	0	3	0	0	0	.417
Jackson	.250	1	4	0	1	1	0	0	0	1	0	0	0	0	0	3	0	0	0	.250
Jordan	.000	2	1	0	0	0	0	0	0	0	0	0	0	1	0	0	0	0	0	.000
Kruk	.250	6	24	4	6	13	2	1	1	5	0	0	0	4	0	5	0	0	0	.542
Longmire	.000	1	1	0	0	0	0	0	0	0	0	0	0	0	0	1	0	0	0	.000
Mason	.000	2	0	0	0	0	0	0	0	0	0	0	0	0	0	0	0	0	0	.000
Morandini	.250	4	16	1	4	6	0	1	0	2	0	0	0	0	0	3	1	0	0	.375
Mulholland	.000	1	2	0	0	0	0	0	0	0	0	0	0	0	0	1	0	0	0	.000
Pratt	.000	1	1	0	0	0	0	0	0	0	0	0	0	0	0	1	0	0	0	.000
Rivera	.000	1	0	0	0	0	0	0	0	0	0	0	0	0	0	0	0	0	0	.000
Schilling	.000	2	5	0	0	0	0	0	0	0	1	0	0	0	0	2	0	0	0	.000
Stocker	.182	6	22	0	4	5	1	0	0	1	0	1	0	2	2	5	0	0	0	.227
Thigpen	.000	2	0	0	0	0	0	0	0	0	0	0	0	0	0	0	0	0	0	.000
Thompson	.231	6	13	2	3	4	1	0	0	0	0	0	0	1	1	2	0	0	0	.308
West	.000	3	0	0	0	0	0	0	0	0	0	0	0	0	0	0	0	0	0	.000
Williams	.000	4	0	0	0	0	0	0	0	0	0	0	0	0	0	0	0	0	0	.000
Totals	.227	6	207	23	47	87	11	4	7	22	3	2	0	26	6	51	2	0	1	.420

Braves Batting

	Avg.	G	AB	R	H	TB	2B	3B	HR	RBI	SH	SF	HP	BB	IBB	SO	SB	CS	GI DP	Slug Pct.
Avery	.500	2	4	1	2	3	1	0	0	0	0	0	0	0	0	1	0	0	0	.750
Belliard	.000	2	1	1	0	0	0	0	0	0	1	0	0	0	0	1	0	0	0	.000
Berryhill	.211	6	19	2	4	7	0	0	1	3	0	0	0	1	0	5	0	0	1	.368
Blauser	.280	6	25	5	7	14	1	0	2	4	0	0	0	4	0	7	0	0	0	.560
Bream	1.000	1	1	1	1	1	0	0	0	0	0	0	0	0	0	0	0	0	0	1.000
Cabrera	.667	3	3	0	2	2	0	0	0	1	0	0	0	0	0	1	0	0	0	.667
Gant	.185	6	27	4	5	8	3	0	0	3	0	0	0	2	0	9	0	1	1	.296
Glavine	.000	1	3	0	0	0	0	0	0	0	0	0	0	0	0	0	0	0	0	.000
Justice	.143	6	21	2	3	4	1	0	0	4	0	2	0	3	0	3	0	0	0	.190
Lemke	.208	6	24	2	5	7	2	0	0	4	0	0	0	1	0	6	0	0	0	.292
Maddux	.250	2	4	1	1	1	0	0	0	0	2	0	0	0	0	1	0	0	0	.250
McGriff	.435	6	23	6	10	15	2	0	1	4	0	0	0	4	1	7	0	0	0	.652
McMichael	.000	4	0	0	0	0	0	0	0	0	0	0	0	0	0	0	0	0	0	.000
Mercker	.000	5	0	0	0	0	0	0	0	0	0	0	0	0	0	0	0	0	0	.000
Nixon	.348	6	23	3	8	10	2	0	0	4	2	0	0	5	0	6	0	2	0	.435

	Avg.	G	AB	R	H	TB	2B	3B	HR	RBI	SH	SF	HP	BB	IBB	SO	SB	CS	GI DP	Slug Pct.
Olson	.333	2	3	0	1	2	1	0	0	0	0	0	1	0	0	1	0	0	0	.667
Pecota	.333	4	3	1	1	1	0	0	0	0	0	0	0	1	0	1	0	0	0	.333
Pendleton	.346	6	26	4	9	13	1	0	1	5	0	0	0	0	0	2	0	0	0	.500
Sanders	.000	5	3	0	0	0	0	0	0	0	0	0	0	0	0	1	0	0	0	.000
Smoltz	.000	1	1	0	0	0	0	0	0	0	0	0	0	1	0	1	0	0	0	.000
Stanton	.000	1	0	0	0	0	0	0	0	0	0	0	0	0	0	0	0	0	0	.000
Tarasco	.000	2	1	0	0	0	0	0	0	0	0	0	0	0	0	1	0	0	0	.000
Wohlers	.000	4	0	0	0	0	0	0	0	0	0	0	0	0	0	0	0	0	0	.000
Totals	.274	6	215	33	59	88	14	0	5	32	5	2	1	22	1	54	0	3	2	.409

Phillies Pitching

	W–L	ERA	G	GS	CG	GF	SV	IP	H	R	ER	HR	HB	BB	IBB	SO	WP
Andersen	0–0	15.43	3	0	0	2	1	2.1	4	4	4	0	0	1	1	3	0
Greene	1–1	9.64	2	2	0	0	0	9.1	12	10	10	3	0	7	0	7	0
Jackson	1–0	1.17	1	1	0	0	0	7.2	9	1	1	0	1	2	0	6	0
Mason	0–0	0.00	2	0	0	0	0	3.0	1	0	0	0	0	0	0	2	0
Mulholland	0–1	7.20	1	1	0	0	0	5.0	9	5	4	0	0	1	0	2	0
Rivera	0–0	4.50	1	0	0	0	0	2.0	1	1	1	1	0	1	0	2	0
Schilling	0–0	1.69	2	2	0	0	0	16.0	11	4	3	0	0	5	0	19	0
Thigpen	0–0	5.40	2	0	0	1	0	1.2	1	1	1	1	0	1	0	3	0
West	0–0	13.50	3	0	0	0	0	2.2	5	5	4	0	0	2	0	5	0
Williams	2–0	1.69	4	0	0	3	2	5.1	6	2	1	0	0	2	0	5	0
Totals	4–2	4.75	6	6	0	6	3	55.0	59	33	29	5	1	22	1	54	0

Braves Pitching

	W–L	ERA	G	GS	CG	GF	SV	IP	H	R	ER	HR	HB	BB	IBB	SO	WP
Avery	0–0	2.77	2	2	0	0	0	13.0	9	5	4	1	0	6	3	10	2
Glavine	1–0	2.57	1	1	0	0	0	7.0	6	2	2	1	0	0	0	5	0
Maddux	1–1	4.97	2	2	0	0	0	12.2	11	8	7	2	0	7	1	11	0
McMichael	0–1	6.75	4	0	0	2	0	4.0	7	3	3	1	0	2	1	1	0
Mercker	0–0	1.80	5	0	0	0	0	5.0	3	1	1	0	0	2	0	4	0
Smoltz	0–1	0.00	1	1	0	0	0	6.1	8	2	0	0	0	5	0	10	0
Stanton	0–0	0.00	1	0	0	0	0	1.0	1	0	0	0	0	1	0	0	0
Wohlers	0–1	3.38	4	0	0	4	0	5.1	2	2	2	2	0	3	1	10	1
Totals	2–4	3.15	6	6	0	6	0	54.1	47	23	19	7	0	26	6	51	3

NLCS RECORDS

NLCS Career Records Set, Tied or Extended

Terry Pendleton—Most games, total series (extends own record), 32
Terry Pendleton—Most at-bats, total series, 129
*Terry Pendleton—Most games, third base (extends own record), 32
*Terry Pendleton—Consecutive errorless games, third base (extends), 31
Terry Pendleton—Most total series, third baseman (tied), 5
John Smoltz—Most strikeouts, total series, 44
Francisco Cabrera—Most pinch-hits, total series (tied), 3
Sid Bream—Most consecutive series played, 4
*Danny Jackson—Most overall clubs started for, total series, 4
Mariano Duncan—Most clubs, total series (tied), 3

NLCS Single-Series Records Set or Tied

Darren Daulton—Most consecutive walks, series, 4
Mariano Duncan—Most triples, series (tied), 2
Steve Avery—Most wild pitches, series (tied), 2
Kim Batiste—Most errors, third baseman, series (tied), 2
Philadelphia—Most one-run victories, series (tied), 3
*Atlanta—Most runs, consecutive games, series, 23
*Both Clubs—Most strikeouts, series, 105

NLCS Single-Game Records Set or Tied

Game 1

*Curt Schilling—Most consecutive strikeouts, start of game, 5
*Curt Schilling—Most consecutive strikeouts, game, 5
Steve Avery—Most intentional walks issued, game (tied), 3
Steve Avery—Most intentional walks issued, inning (tied), 2
Steve Avery—Most hits, pitcher, game (tied), 2
Wes Chamberlain—Most doubles, game (tied), 2
Jeff Blauser—Most strikeouts, game (tied), 3
Ron Gant—Most strikeouts, game (tied), 3
Both Clubs—Most doubles, game, 8 (Phillies 5, Braves 3)

Game 2

Tommy Greene—Most consecutive hits allowed, inning (tied), 5
Ron Gant—Most doubles, game (tied), 2
*Atlanta—Most runs, game, 14
Atlanta—Most hits, game (tied), 16
Atlanta—Most consecutive hits, inning, 6 (1 walk during streak)
Atlanta—Most home runs, inning, club (tied), 2 (3d inning)
*Both Clubs—Most home runs, game, 6 (Braves 4, Phillies 2)

Game 3

*Mariano Duncan—Most triples, game, 2
*Philadelphia—Most triples, game, 3
*Philadelphia—Most consecutive triples, 2
Philadelphia—Most triples, inning, 2
Both Clubs—Most doubles, game, 8 (Braves 5, Phillies 3)

Game 4

Darren Daulton—Most walks, game, 4
John Kruk—Most strikeouts, game, 4
Otis Nixon—Most sacrifice bunts, game (tied), 2
Atlanta—Most strikeouts, 9-inning game, 15
*Philadelphia—Most left on base, game, 15
*Both Clubs—Most strikeouts, 9-inning game (tied), 21 (Braves 15, Phillies 6)
*Both Clubs—Most left on base, game, 26 (Phillies 15, Braves 11)

Game 5

Wes Chamberlain—Most outfield assists, game (tied), 2

Game 6

Tommy Greene—Most sacrifice bunts, game (tied), 2
Greg Maddux—Most sacrifice bunts, game (tied), 2
Both Clubs—Most sacrifice bunts, game (tied), 4

*Indicates overall LCS record

An Unpleasant Ending

At the very least, major league baseball's 90th World Series was going to be a study in contrasts.

On the one hand, there were the smooth, methodical Toronto Blue Jays, a coldly efficient, generally colorless crew that resembled a band of professional assassins. With an all-star cast of free agents and trade acquisitions, the Blue Jays were the best team that money could buy, an extraordinarily high-salaried collection of mercenaries who in the 17th year of Toronto's existence as an American League franchise had put together the club's 11th straight winning season.

Winning had become synonymous with Blue Jay baseball. Since 1989, the team had appeared in five League Championship Series. Although it blew a couple of the earlier ones, it had become the first team since the 1977–1978 New York Yankees to win two straight American League pennants and was the winner of the 1992 World Series, having beaten the Atlanta Braves in six games.

The Phillies, on the other hand, had no such resume. They were a team that had struggled for a decade before a group of overachievers came together and put forth some of the best years of their careers while forging a championship season that almost no one had expected.

It took only a few glances at the Toronto newspapers to tell what at least that part of the world thought of the Phillies. When the Phils arrived for the opening of the Series, headlines and articles brutally mocked the players, giving them descriptions such as "a motley crew of hairy, beer-soused brutes" and "long-haired, slack-jawed, pot-bellied and snarly lipped." One newspaper, overcome with its own hilarity, went so far as to create a comic strip character it named "Phat Phil."

The Phillies and Blue Jays did have a few things in common, though. They held spring training in adjoining communities in Florida, Toronto's Grant Field in Dunedin being just three miles down the road from the Phils' Jack Russell Stadium in Clearwater. The teams had met many times over the years in Grapefruit League games; in fact, just as their last game of the 1993 season would be against each other, the two had been opponents in their first outings of the year in an exhibition game.

Even Billy Penn, high atop City Hall, wore a Phillies cap for the post-season festivities.

The Phillies were even once called the Blue Jays. In 1944 new Phils president Bob Carpenter ran a contest to find a new name for his club. The winning entry was Blue Jays. The club altered its logo and added a blue jay to its uniforms, but hardly anyone accepted the new name and the club never officially dropped its old name. The secondary name, Blue Jays, lingered in the background until it was finally abandoned in 1949.

Toronto had once been the site of a Phillies farm team, too. From 1948 to 1950, the Phils operated their Triple-A International League team in Toronto. The Maple Leafs, as they were called then, finished fifth twice and seventh once while serving as the final step before reaching the majors for a number of future Whiz Kids, including manager Eddie Sawyer and 1950 Most Valuable Player Jim Konstanty, who was converted into a relief pitcher while toiling in Toronto.

There was one other link between the two teams. The third base coach for the Blue Jays was none other than Nick Leyva, the previous manager of the Phillies. Leyva had been dismissed by the Phillies after 13 games of the 1991 season and the following year had landed in the Toronto organization as manager of the Triple-A club at Syracuse before joining the big club during the 1993 season.

If the Braves, though, were one of the best teams in baseball, the Blue Jays were certainly the best. Whether it was pitching, hitting or fielding, they seemed to have no weakness.

Toronto had posted a 95–67 record during the regular season, the fourth best in club history, and finished seven games ahead of the second place Yankees. The Blue Jays had made their initial move into first place on June 26, had surged to a five-game lead by the All Star break, but had fallen out of the lead on July 20. From then on, they were either in first or tied for the lead the remainder of the season. Deadlocked with the Yankees on September 9, the Blue Jays went 17–4 the rest of the way to win their third straight American League East Division title. Then they downed the Chicago White Sox in six games in the American League Championship Series for the pennant.

The Blue Jays' strongest weapon was their offense. The team's league-leading .279 batting average was the highest ever recorded by the franchise and its 847 runs, which ranked second in the league, were also the most in club history.

In 1993, the Blue Jays' hitters accomplished the rare feat of placing first, second and third in the batting race. First baseman John Olerud led the league in hitting with a .363 average. He was followed by designated-hitter Paul Molitor with a .332 and second baseman Roberto Alomar with .326. It was the first time in the American League that three batters from the same team had gone one-two-three in hitting.

Vet Stadium's center field decoration marked the occasion.

The only other time such an achievement occurred was in 1893 when the Phillies' Billy Hamilton, Sam Thompson and Ed Delahanty did it.

Molitor (211) and Olerud (200) also placed first and second in the league in hits, a feat accomplished by teammates just 12 times in the American League since 1900. The Blue Jays also had three players with more than 100 RBI—Joe Carter, Molitor and Olerud.

The Toronto pitching staff, although not as overpowering as the team's offense, was led by 19-game winner Pat Hentgen, 14-game winner Juan Guzman, who ranked second in the league in strikeouts, and 12-game winner Dave Stewart, the aging warrior who was still regarded as one of the toughest hurlers in baseball. Duane Ward with a league-leading total of 45 saves was the main occupant of what was otherwise a less than overwhelming bullpen.

With all this talent, Toronto was the heavy favorite as the Series began. That had little effect, though, on the Phillies. There was a feeling on the club that if it could beat a team as strong as the Braves, it could beat anybody else, too.

"We've been underdogs all year," said Pete Incaviglia. "The Braves were supposed to kill us. But we play as gutsy a baseball as anybody."

Before much longer, the Phillies would demonstrate that trait to the rest of the world.

GAME ONE—BLUE JAYS 8, PHILLIES 5

The Phillies' first venture into a World Series in 10 years showed not only that they had every right to be on the same field as the vaunted Blue Jays, but also that there might have been a different outcome if the Phils had had a little better luck.

The Phillies outhit the Blue Jays, 11–10, but wound up leaving 11 men (to Toronto's four) on base, including five in scoring position.

Three different times the Phillies had leads, but couldn't hold them, finally folding under a three-run Toronto barrage in the seventh inning that gave the American League champs an 8–5 victory.

It didn't help the Phillies' cause that Milt Thompson and Lenny Dykstra couldn't get their signals straight on a fly ball that deflected off Thompson's glove and went for a three-base error and led to a run. Nor did it help that Kevin Stocker lost his balance and stumbled rounding third base and had to retreat instead of scoring what would have been a key run. Or that John Kruk struck out with the bases loaded in the sixth, the only time he was retired all night.

Kruk, ribbed more than any other Phil for his appearance by the Toronto media, had a big offensive night otherwise, slugging three hits, walking once, scoring twice and driving in two runs. Mariano Duncan also had three hits as the Phillies showed their willingness not to back down against the fire-balling slants of Guzman and his successors from the Toronto bullpen.

Perhaps the most surprising aspect of the game was the difficulty Curt Schilling had on the mound after two brilliant outings in the League Championship Series. Obviously not as sharp as he was in the two games against Atlanta, Schilling ran into trouble in the second when he gave up four hits and two runs. Then he yielded solo home runs to Devon White in the fifth and Olerud in the sixth before getting knocked out in the seventh after surrendering two more hits.

"I thought Schilling had good enough stuff to win," said manager Jim Fregosi. "He just didn't make enough good pitches when he needed to. If you get the ball up and out over the plate, they are going to hit it."

Curiously, Fregosi used what had to be a somewhat rusty Ricky Jordan as the Phillies' designated hitter instead of either Incaviglia or Wes Chamberlain. Jordan fanned twice and got one hit in five trips to the plate.

The Blue Jays made three errors in the game.

The Phillies jumped out to a 2–0 lead in the first inning. Dykstra walked, stole second and rode home on Kruk's single. After Dave Hollins walked, Kruk scored from second on a single by Darren Daulton.

Toronto came right back in the second to tie. Carter and Olerud singled, and both moved up on a passed ball by Daulton. Carter scored on a single by Molitor, and Olerud followed him to the plate when Tony Fernandez forced out Molitor at second.

In the third, the Phillies regained the lead as Duncan singled, stole second and rode home on a single by Kruk. Toronto answered in the bottom half when Thompson and Dykstra both went after White's routine fly to left-center. As they narrowly missed colliding, the ball bounced off Thompson's mitt with White reaching third. He scored a minute later on Carter's sacrifice fly.

Kevin Stocker grabs for his throat after a throw bounced up and hit him while Roberto Alomar was stealing second base.

The Phillies again took the lead with one run in the fifth. This time, Duncan hit a high fly off the wall in left, winding up at third with a triple. He scored on a wild pitch by Guzman.

White slammed a home run to deep right for Toronto in the fifth. Then the Phillies tried to come back in the sixth and actually got three hits by Jordan, Dykstra and Duncan and a walk to Stocker but couldn't score as Thompson hit into a doubleplay and Kruk fanned.

The Blue Jays got their first lead of the night on Olerud's home run to right in the sixth. Then they erupted with three more runs in the seventh. One out singles by Pat Borders and Rickey Henderson kayoed Schilling.

David West came in and served up back-to-back doubles to White and Alomar before Larry Andersen arrived to put out the fire.

Trailing 8–4, the Phillies had a chance in the eighth when Stocker singled and Dykstra reached first on a rare error by Alomar, who earlier had made several sparkling fielding plays. But they couldn't score again until the ninth when they got their last run. Kruk beat out an infield single and reached second when Molitor threw wildly to first. He scored with two outs on Jim Eisenreich's single.

GAME TWO—PHILLIES 6, BLUE JAYS 4

On a team full of extroverts, Jim Eisenreich is one of the quietest players on the Phillies. But as he demonstrated all season, he is the master of good timing.

Playing in his first World Series, the soft-spoken outfielder socked a boisterous three-run homer that couldn't have come at a better time. Combining with the spectacular play of Dykstra, it was just what the Phillies needed to even the Series at one game apiece with a 6–4 victory.

Eisenreich's clutch home run culminated a five-run third inning in which the Phillies roughed up the heretofore almost indestructible Stewart, the former Phils pitcher who went 10–3 in post-season games after the Phillies let him go. It was Eisenreich's first extra base hit since September 17.

"That was a hit I'll always cherish," he said. "I really felt comfortable at the plate."

Sharing honors with Eisenreich was Dykstra, who turned in two spectacular catches while crashing into the wall and whose seventh inning home run gave the Phillies a vital insurance run.

"I always think I have to do something right out there," Dykstra said. "That was a big win for us."

Indeed it was. The Toronto press and fans had spent the last two days ridiculing the Phillies for their hair styles and body sizes, and had even questioned how the Phils could possibly compete on the same level as the antiseptic Blue Jays.

The Phils had the perfect answer as they bombed 12 hits, played flawless defense and got solid pitching.

Terry Mulholland started for the Phils. Despite control problems and trouble with the Sky Dome mound, he didn't allow a hit until the third. By then, the Phillies had a 5–0 lead.

That came when the Phils battered Stewart, the scowling, former four-time 20-game winner, with a barrage in which eight men went to the plate. Dykstra opened the inning with a walk and went to second on a wild pitch.

Duncan also walked, and Kruk followed with a single that scored Dykstra. Hollins then blooped a single to center that scored Duncan.

One out later, up stepped Eisenreich, who had been in somewhat of a slump in the last month. On an 0–2 pitch, he slammed a drive into the right-center field bleachers, chasing home Kruk and Hollins before him, and giving the Phillies their biggest lead of the post-season games.

Carter hit a high fly that just cleared the short left field wall for a two-run homer in the fourth. Then a single by Alomar and an RBI double by Fernandez chased Mulholland in the sixth.

Dykstra led off the seventh with a high fly over the Phillies' bullpen in right for a vitally important run. It was his seventh home run in post-season play and tied him for first in that category among active players.

Dykstra's homer was just a topping for the splendid night he had. He also made two fine catches in which he saved extra base hits while crashing into the wall. The first time was on White's drive in the third. The second came on a blast by Alomar in the fourth.

"I'm not afraid to say I made a couple of big plays," Dykstra said in what was maybe the biggest understatement of the night.

Roger Mason replaced Mulholland and pitched one and two-thirds strong innings. His only flaw was a double to Molitor in the eighth. One out later, Mitch Williams arrived on the mound to perform his usual late-inning high-wire act.

Paying no attention to the runner, Williams let Molitor steal third. Olerud followed with a sacrifice fly, and suddenly the Phillies' lead was down to 6–4. Williams walked Alomar, who promptly stole second. He also tried to steal third, but Williams—in the middle of his windup—wheeled and threw to Hollins to nail the sliding Alomar and end the inning. It turned out that the Phillies had been tipped off to Alomar's penchant for such tricks in a report prepared by veteran Phils scout Ray Shore.

"I was a little nervous, but once I got through the eighth, I felt pretty good," Williams said.

The Phillies, who had the bases loaded with one out and couldn't score in the eighth, still had to endure a frantic ninth inning by Williams and his cardiac-inducing sidekick, Kim Batiste.

After a leadoff walk to Fernandez, Ed Sprague ripped a hot shot to Batiste, who had just entered the game as a defensive replacement at third base. The young infielder had a sure doubleplay ball, but he threw low to Duncan at second. Duncan managed to short-hop the throw and get a force-out.

All was forgotten a moment later when Pat Borders bounced a grounder to Stocker at short. Stocker flipped to Duncan at second, and the return throw to Kruk at first completed a game-ending doubleplay and sent the Phillies back to Philadelphia all even in the Series.

GAME THREE—BLUE JAYS 10, PHILLIES 3

For the Phillies, it was all downhill after the pre-game ceremony when a couple of local celebrities helped to launch the first World Series game in Philadelphia in 10 years.

Soon after Daryl Hall sang the National Anthem and Mike Schmidt threw out the first ball, the Blue Jays jumped all over Phils starter Danny Jackson for three runs in the first inning. Toronto continued its assault the rest of the game, and by the time it was over, the Phillies had been blown out, 10–3.

Because of a rain storm, the game began 72 minutes late. It didn't end until well after midnight, and by that time, most of the huge crowd of 62,689 had long before headed for the exits.

Pre-game controversy swirled around the Blue Jays as manager Cito Gaston elected to bench Olerud, the American League batting champion, and insert Molitor into the lineup at first base (the designated hitter is not used in National League cities during the Series), instead of using Molitor at third in place of the light-hitting but good fielding Sprague.

The fuzzy logic of that move, which was based on the notion that the lefthanded Olerud shouldn't have to bat against southpaw Jackson, was soon forgotten as Molitor slammed a triple and home run in the first three innings and wound up with three hits and three RBI. Alomar added four hits to pace a 13-hit Toronto attack.

"Our team has been playing like that all year," said Gaston. "They go out and play hard. Tonight we managed to come up with a well-pitched game, and the guys put some runs on the board."

The Blue Jays got six strong innings from Hentgen, who gave up just five hits and one run before retiring for the night.

"We had a lot of opportunities, but we just didn't get the big hit when we needed it," said Fregosi.

The Phillies had nine hits altogether, but left six runners in scoring position, including five of them with less than two outs.

"I don't think you have to make any more of this (the loss) than what it is," said Daulton. "We can't panic now. We've had a lot of games likes this before, and we've come back and got the job done."

The Phillies did come up with several fine defensive plays, particularly a diving catch in left by Incaviglia on a fifth inning drive by Carter, and a diving grab in center by Dykstra on Borders' smash in the eighth.

But the Phils needed more than good defense in this game. Although the rain delay may have taken some of the excitement out of the fans, nobody admitted it affected the players. Some people looked for that as an excuse for Jackson's slow start.

"The rain delay (the first at the start of a World Series game since 1968) had nothing to do with it [his ineffectiveness]," said Jackson. "It was my pitching. I was just too strong. When I'm too strong, I don't get the pitches where I want them."

That was particularly true in the first inning when the first three batters got on base, two of them scoring on Molitor's triple. Carter's sacrifice fly brought in Molitor.

The Blue Jays added four hits in the third but managed only one run on Molitor's two-out homer, which was followed by three straight singles before Jackson escaped the inning.

After Jackson departed, Toronto lit up Ben Rivera for four more runs. The Blue Jays scored once in the sixth when Alomar singled, stole second and third and scored on a sacrifice fly by Fernandez. Three more runs crossed in the seventh with Henderson's double and White's triple preceding a walk, a single by Alomar that kayoed Rivera, another walk and a sacrifice fly by Sprague.

All along, the Phillies were having trouble with Hentgen. They had men on second and third with one out in the first but couldn't cash in. Kruk's double in the fourth was also wasted. One run finally came home in the sixth on walks to Kruk and Daulton and an RBI single by Eisenreich.

"Hentgen pitched a great game," said Eisenreich. "I can't give him enough credit. He pitched six strong innings."

After Hentgen left, the Phillies rattled for-mer teammate Danny Cox for three hits and a walk in the seventh but could get just one run. Singles by Thompson, Dykstra and Duncan pushed the run across before a walk to Kruk loaded the bases. Hollins' doubleplay grounder ended the threat.

Darren Daulton is met at the plate by Dave Hollins and Jim Eisenreich after his two-run homer in Game Four.

After Toronto scored two more times against Andersen in the ninth, the Phillies managed one more run on a home run to right by Thompson.

Blue Jays Todd Stottlemyre smacks his chin on the ground as he slides into third.

GAME FOUR—BLUE JAYS 15, PHILLIES 14

In a contest filled with bizarre twists and an unbelievable outcome, the Phillies incurred what was certifiably the most devastating loss in club history.

With a chance to even the Series and set themselves in good shape for a final push for the World Championship, the Phillies blew a five-run lead in the eighth inning when once again atrocious relief pitching failed to do the job.

Coming in the kind of situation in which it did, it was a thoroughly crushing defeat and left a teary Phillies clubhouse deflated and bewildered. Never before had a Phillies team suffered such a difficult defeat.

It was a game in which records fell by the bushel en route to the final 15–14 outcome, which made it the highest scoring game in World Series history, far surpassing the old record of 22 set in 1936 by the New York Yankees and Giants.

"This will go down in the annals as one of the all-time World Series games," said Fregosi. "It was unbelievable."

The two teams combined for 31 hits, 12 of them for extra bases. Dykstra hit two home runs and Daulton one, while Dykstra, Duncan, Thompson, White, Alomar and Fernandez all had three hits apiece.

"It's a terrible loss," sighed Thompson, who in the final innings of the third game and early innings of the fourth had hit for the cycle. "But it was for real. We all saw what happened."

What happened on this foggy, drizzling night was that neither starting pitcher Tommy Greene nor Todd Stottleyre lasted three innings, that some strange managerial moves took place, that both bullpens with a few exceptions were horrible, that the Phillies wasted four-run and five-run innings and finally that the Blue Jays rocked Andersen and Williams for six runs in the eighth to overcome a five-run Phillies lead and win.

Williams was torched for three hits and three runs while walking one after he entered with one out, one run in and two men on base in the eighth. By the time the inning was over, the Blue Jays had sent 11 men to the plate and had the lead.

"It was the toughest loss of my career," Williams said. "I don't have any excuses. They hit everything I threw. I just didn't get the job done."

Neither did a lot of others on the mound. Toronto pounded Greene for three runs in the first inning, getting a leadoff double by Henderson, two walks and two singles. In the bottom half of the inning, Stottlemyre put his name in the record book with four walks, three of them in a row. Thompson's bases-loaded triple gave the Phils a 4–3 lead.

Dykstra began a huge night in which he scored four runs and drove in four with a two-run homer in the second following a single by Greene. But the Phils' 6–3 lead was short-lived as the Blue Jays routed Greene with four runs in the third.

Dykstra doubled and scored on Duncan's single to tie the score at 7–7 in the fourth. In the fifth, the Phils took a 12–7 lead, batting around and scoring on two-run homers by Daulton and Dykstra and an RBI double by Thompson.

With West pitching in the sixth, the Blue Jays picked up two runs. West had not retired a batter in two previous World Series outings with the Minnesota Twins.

Lenny Dykstra is greeted by Milt Thompson after a Game Four home run.

The Phillies came back with single runs in the sixth and seventh innings. In the sixth, Hollins doubled and scored on a single by Thompson. In the seventh, after a single by Duncan and walks to Kruk and Hollins loaded the bases, Daulton was hit by a pitch to force in a run with one out. But the Phils left the bases loaded without further damage.

That led to the eighth with the Phillies seemingly holding a comfortable 14–9 lead. Before the inning was over, the Blue Jays had knocked out

Andersen, pummelled Williams and, combining four hits with two walks and an error, had pushed over six runs and left the Phillies in a state of shock.

The Toronto explosion all came after Andersen had retired the first batter. Carter singled and Olerud walked before Hollins was handcuffed by a hard grounder by Molitor that let in a run. Williams entered and gave up a single to Fernandez and a walk to Borders before striking out Sprague in what would have been an inning-ending out. Instead, Henderson's RBI single and a two-run triple by White followed before the side was finally retired.

The deflated Phillies went meekly in the eighth and ninth, getting retired in order in each frame with four of the six batters striking out.

It was an ugly ending to a weird game, which saw a little bit of everything, including a breakdown in the Blue Jays' telephone to the bullpen, resulting in the wrong pitcher warming up and the right one (Tony Castillo) getting extra time to warm up when summoned to the mound.

The four-hour, 14-minute skirmish was the longest nine-inning game in World Series history.

GAME FIVE—PHILLIES 2, BLUE JAYS 0

With their backs against the wall in a game they had to win, the Phillies showed once again what they're made of.

A lot of teams would have folded after the crushing defeat of the previous night. But that is not in the Phillies' make-up. The fiercely determined bunch played their final home game of the season with perhaps more intensity than imaginable.

And they came away with a pulsating victory behind the stout pitching of Curt Schilling, who hurled the Phillies' first complete game in a World Series since Robin Roberts did it in the second game of 1950 and the first shutout ever tossed in a Fall Classic by a Phillies pitcher.

Contrasted to the previous night's slugfest, the Phillies' 2–0 victory was a stunning reversal of form. Instead of 29 runs and 31 hits, there were only 10 hits in the game, five by each team.

But what was more stunning was the way the Phils came back. They refused to let the season end on a sour note, overcoming the embarrassment of their 15–14 loss in Game Four with a masterfully played game.

"We had no choice," said Kruk. "We had to win, and we had to get nine innings from our starter. After all the running everybody did last night, we needed a pitchers' game."

The Phillies low-keyed their resiliency, but there was no question that they were planning on sending the Series back to Toronto. Fregosi even informed them before the game that there would be a work-out on their day off back at Sky Dome.

"I think the beautiful thing about winning that game," said Andersen, "was just the act of coming back from that 15–14 embarrassment. It was our way of saying we didn't quit. That just epitomized what this team's been able to do all year."

"It would have been very easy to have been down," added Hollins. "But we weren't going to do that, and the fans weren't going to let us do that. They kept us up. They were just great."

Schilling needed no prodding from anybody. The big righthander stood up in the clubhouse before the game and told his teammates that he was going to give it everything he had.

"I was upset (the previous night) just because of the fact that we'd given a game away," he said. "So, I wanted the ball. I wanted the responsibility. If you don't want the ball in these situations, why show up?"

Schilling didn't allow a Blue Jay to get as far as second base until the sixth inning, and then the third Phillies doubleplay of the night erased the threat. In the eighth, the first two Blue Jays hit safely, but with men on first and third, Henderson hit a hard smash that Schilling knocked down near the mound. Pinch-runner Will Canate started to go home, but Schilling's throw to Daulton trapped him in a rundown. After that out, Schilling retired the next five Blue Jays in a row.

Caught in a rundown, Will Canate is tagged out by Dave Hollins near third base in a key play in Game Five.

"I started to run out of gas in the seventh," Schilling said. "I know when Daulton tells me we'll be using mirrors to get these guys out, I'm starting to lose it.

"In the eighth, I looked in the bullpen, and there was nobody up. It pumped me up. I knew this team would go to Toronto based on what I did. If I had to point to one inning in my career where I gave everything I had for one inning, that was the inning."

Helpfully, Schilling's teammates made his job a little more comfortable by giving him some early runs. Although the Phillies didn't exactly jump all over Blue Jays starter Guzman, they made good use of what they had.

In the first inning, Dykstra manufactured a run. He led off with a walk, stole second and scampered to third when catcher Borders' throw skipped into center field. Dykstra then romped home from third on Kruk's ground-out to second.

"The one thing I wanted to do for Curt was somehow get on in the first and put up a number for him," said Dykstra. "That way, he'd relax and not have to worry.

"I told him before the game," Dykstra added. "Let's just play baseball like we did when we were eight years old. It's the same game, so let's have some fun."

After scoring without a hit, the Phillies used two hits to get another run in the second. This time, Daulton led off with a double to right-center. He moved to third on Eisenreich's ground-out to first. Then with two outs and Schilling due up next, the Blue Jays elected to pitch to Stocker, and the rookie responded by grounding a double down the right field line to score Daulton.

"I've had big hits in my career, but never in a game like this," Stocker said. "That was the most satisfying hit I ever had. I was just glad to hit the ball someplace and drive in a run."

The Phillies had only three hits the rest of the game, including two in the third inning. In the fourth, Guzman walked the bases loaded with two outs, but the Phils failed to score. Kruk and Hollins were walked by Cox leading off the eighth, but then Cox struck out the side.

Curt Schilling pitched brilliantly in Game Five, sending the Series back to Toronto.

Game Six—Blue Jays 8, Phillies 6

For the second time in three games, Mitch Williams couldn't hold a lead. And that cost the Phillies the World Series.

Joe Carter rocked Williams for a three-run home run in the bottom of the ninth inning to give the Blue Jays a come-from-behind, 8–6 victory and the World Championship, four games to two.

Largely through the heroics of Dykstra, the Phillies had entered the last inning clinging to a 6–5 lead. Dykstra's three-run homer in the seventh had anchored a rousing Phillies comeback in which they scored five runs in the inning to overcome a 4–1 deficit.

But Williams, just as he had done in the fourth game, couldn't protect the Phils' lead, and his team lost the second game in the last three that it should have won. Thus, a storybook season came to an abrupt and bittersweet ending.

"We never quit," said Dykstra. "We tried and tried and tried again. But it just wasn't enough."

To his credit, Williams, who had become the whipping boy of Phillies fans and who received death threats after the fourth game, did not run and hide after the game was over. He neither alibied nor apologized for his misfortune.

"There are no excuses," he said. "I just didn't get the job done. I threw a fastball down and in. It was a bad pitch. I'll have to deal with it. But don't expect me to curl up and hide because I gave up a home run in the World Series."

At least publicly, Williams's teammates stood behind him, Mulholland even going to the trouble of dragging the beleaguered reliever away from the hordes of media hounds besieging him in the somber Phils locker room.

"We wouldn't have been here if it wasn't for him," Kruk said in a statement repeated over and over by Phillies players.

To the end, the Phillies never gave up. They could easily have done just that after the Blue Jays rocked Mulholland for three runs in the first inning. But they battled back, eventually knocking out Stewart, the Toronto starter, and were ultimately a scant two outs away from sending the World Series to the seventh game.

"I couldn't be prouder of these guys," said Fregosi. "They tried as hard as they could. They just came up a little short."

The game began as a definite downer for the Phillies when Toronto strung together a walk to White, a triple by Molitor, a sacrifice fly by Carter, a double by Olerud and a single by Alomar to produce three runs between the first and second outs of the first inning.

The Phillies came back with one run in the fourth when with two outs Daulton doubled and scored on a single by Eisenreich. Toronto, however, offset that with a run in the bottom of the fourth. Alomar doubled, went to third on a ground-out and scored on a sacrifice fly by Sprague.

After Molitor slugged a home run in the fifth, Mulholland departed at the end of the inning. Mason came on and pitched superbly for the next two and one-third innings.

The Phillies launched their comeback in the seventh by sending 10 men to the plate in a wild inning that kayoed Stewart. Stocker opened with a walk and Mickey Morandini followed with a single. Then Dykstra hit a towering drive into the right field seats for his fourth home run of the Series. Only one other player—Reggie Jackson with five in 1977—has hit more home runs in a Series.

The Phils weren't through, yet. Duncan singled, stole second and scored on a single by Hollins. Then Daulton walked and Eisenreich singled to load the bases. Pinch-hitting, Incaviglia slapped a fly ball to right-center that scored Hollins with the final run of the inning.

Despite his strong performance, Mason was lifted after getting one out in the eighth in a move that was debated long after the Series had ended. Near disaster followed. West came on to walk one batter before being re-

Mariano Duncan had a big Series, hitting .345 and leading the Phils with 10 hits.

placed by Andersen, who hit one batter and walked another before escaping a bases-loaded jam without damage.

Andersen's pitch that had hit Fernandez came after the batter had hit a grounder to Kruk at first. It was ruled that the ball hit Fernandez's foot and was a dead ball, although replays clearly showed otherwise. Had that been the third out, maybe the Blue Jays wouldn't have had a chance to go so deep in their order in the next inning.

Fregosi brought in Williams in the ninth in another move that would be second-guessed through most of the winter. And for the umpteenth time this year, Williams walked the leadoff batter (Henderson). He got White to fly out to left but then served up a single to Molitor. That led to Carter. After missing badly on a second strike, Carter took Williams's 2–2 offering and hammered it deep into the left field stands for a three-run homer.

It was only the third time a home run had decided a World Series, the first being Harry Hooper's homer that gave the Boston Red Sox the decision over the Phillies in 1915. The second was Bill Mazeroski's blow that gave the Pittsburgh Pirates victory over the Yankees in the 1960 Fall Classic. And it made the Blue Jays the first team since the Yankees in 1977–1978 to win back-to-back World Series.

"It was a weird feeling, watching that ball go out," Dykstra said. "Helpless. I can't really describe it. I didn't want to watch it.

"I really thought this was meant to be," he added. "We battled and battled and battled. But we had two heartbreaking losses. We were the second best team in baseball this year, and that's nothing to be ashamed of. Now, it's over. Toronto's the better ball team. That's it. Uncle."

* * *

In the aftermath of their stunning loss to the Blue Jays, the Phillies could find solace in the fact that they waged a furious fight before succumbing in only the team's fifth visit to a World Series.

Characteristic of the team throughout the season, the Phillies refused to back down, even in the face of the enormously talented Blue Jays. And relentlessly and with unbending determination, the Phils kept picking themselves up off the mat each time they got knocked down.

The Phillies were outhit as a team, .311 to .274, and outscored, 45–36. They lost two games they should have won but came within one swing of Joe Carter's bat of becoming the first team in Phils history ever to go to the seventh game of a World Series.

The Phillies got a marvelous Series from center fielder Lenny Dykstra. Although Paul Molitor was chosen Most Valuable Player of the Series, Dykstra was surely the Phils' Most Valuable Player, hitting .348 with four home runs and eight RBI and attracting worldwide attention with his hustling style of play.

First baseman John Kruk also hit .348, while second baseman Mariano Duncan hit .345 and left fielder Milt Thompson hit .313. They were the only consistent hitters in the Phils' lineup, however, the rest of the team batting a combined .223.

Except for Curt Schilling's fifth game masterpiece, the Phillies had no outstanding pitching performances from its starters, although it was given a workmanlike job from Terry Mulholland in the second game.

The Blue Jays did not have particularly good pitching, either, but their hitting was outstanding. Except for the bottom of the order, there was not a weak hitter in the lineup. Molitor, Roberto Alomar and Tony Fernandez carried especially hot bats throughout the tournament.

In the end, it was the Phillies' bullpen that let it down. Roger Mason led the team with a 1.17 ERA in four strong outings, but the rest of the relief corp was a bust. By the time the Series arrived, David West, whose 76 games during the regular season were well over twice as many games as he'd ever thrown in a single year, and 40-year-old Larry Andersen were out of gas. And Mitch Williams's once-crackling fastball had been reduced to an

82–mph balloon that was so ineffective that he had to resort much of the time to a highly mediocre slider.

Despite that, manager Jim Fregosi persisted in using Williams in critical situations and was burned because of his refusal to try another approach, a tactic that was the subject of heated debate among fans long after the Series was over. Many questioned Fregosi's bullpen moves, although few would acknowledge that the Phils' pilot really had no other viable options.

"Mitch Williams did the job for us all year," Fregosi said. "I told him that we wouldn't have gotten this far without him."

But Williams had lost so much of his zip by the time the fatal ninth inning of the sixth game arrived that the Blue Jays and especially Carter were happy to see him beckoned from the bullpen.

Mitch Williams lost the final game when he served up a three-run homer to Joe Carter in the bottom of the ninth.

"With Mitch out there, you knew something good would happen," said Carter after his three-run homer had ended the Series. "I knew his velocity was not good. The only pitch he was throwing for strikes was the slider."

To his credit, Williams stood up to the parade of inquisitors who descended upon his locker, patiently answering wave after wave of questions.

"The one thing that bothers me is I let my teammates down," he said. "They busted their butts all year, and I let them down. I threw the pitch that cost us the World Series. But I'm going to deal with it. I'm not going to go home and commit suicide. The bottom line is, I let us down in big situations. But I can carry that burden. It's my job to do that. And going home and sulking about it does not bring that ball back over the fence. It does not give us the win."

Many of Williams's teammates tried to defend him, some claiming that threats to his life and vandalism at his New Jersey home after Game Four had placed undue pressure on the hurler.

"We would not be here without Mitch Williams," said Daulton. "He has nothing to hang his head about. That guy [Carter] gets paid to hit, and he came out on top this time. You have to tip your hat to him."

The day after the game, all the Phillies returned quietly to Philadelphia except Williams, who flew directly to his winter home in Texas. Because they chose not to announce their arrival time in advance, the Phils were greeted by only about 600 fans at Philadelphia Airport.

The team also declined offers of a victory parade to celebrate its National League pennant. Instead, the players began scattering for the winter. It figured that some of them would not be back.

"We'll never have a team like this again," said Fregosi, noting how it was a team that cared deeply about each other and that fought so gallantly in one of the most glorious seasons any Philadelphia team ever put together.

WORLD SERIES BOX SCORES

Game One   October 16—Blue Jays 8, Phillies 5

PHILLIES	AB	R	H	RBI
Dykstra, cf	4	1	1	0
Duncan, 2b	5	2	3	0
Kruk, 1b	4	2	3	2
Hollins, 3b	4	0	0	0
Daulton, c	4	0	1	1
Eisenreich, rf	5	0	1	1
Jordan, dh	5	0	1	0
Thompson, lf	3	0	0	0
Incaviglia, lf	1	0	0	0
Stocker, ss	3	0	1	0
Totals	**38**	**5**	**11**	**4**

Toronto	AB	R	H	RBI
Henderson, lf	3	1	1	0
White, cf	4	3	2	2
Alomar, 2b	4	0	1	2
Carter, rf	3	1	1	1
Olerud, 1b	3	2	2	1
Molitor, dh	4	0	1	1
Fernandez, ss	3	0	0	1
Sprague, 3b	4	0	1	0
Borders, c	4	1	1	0
Totals	**32**	**8**	**10**	**8**

```
PHILLIES     201  010  001 – 5
Toronto      021  011  30x – 8
```

E—Thompson (1), Alomar (1), Carter (1), Sprague (1). DP—PHILLIES 1, Toronto 1. LOB—PHILLIES 11, Toronto 4. 2B—White (1), Alomar (1). 3B—Duncan (1). HR—White (1), Olerud (1). SB—Dykstra (1), Duncan (1), Alomar (1). CS—Fernandez (1). SF—Carter.

PHILLIES	IP	H	R	ER	BB	SO
Schilling (L, 0–1)	6⅓	8	7	6	2	3
West	0	2	1	1	0	0
Andersen	⅔	0	0	0	1	1
Mason	1	0	0	0	0	1

Toronto	IP	H	R	ER	BB	SO
Guzman	5	5	4	4	4	6
Leiter (W, 1–0)	2⅔	4	0	0	1	2
Ward (S, 1)	1⅓	2	1	0	0	3

West pitched to 2 batters in the 7th. WP—Guzman. PB—Daulton.
Time—3:27. Attendance—52,011.

Game Two   October 17—Phillies 6, Blue Jays 4

PHILLIES	AB	R	H	RBI
Dykstra, cf	4	2	2	1
Duncan, 2b	4	1	1	0
Kruk, 1b	5	1	2	1
Hollins, 3b	4	1	2	1
Batiste, 3b	0	0	0	0
Daulton, c	5	0	1	0
Eisenreich, rf	4	1	1	3
Incaviglia, lf	4	0	1	0
Thompson, pr, lf	0	0	0	0
Jordan, dh	4	0	1	0
Stocker, ss	3	0	1	0
Totals	**37**	**6**	**12**	**6**

Toronto	AB	R	H	RBI
Henderson, lf	3	0	0	0
White, cf	4	0	1	0
Molitor, dh	3	2	2	0
Carter, rf	4	1	1	2
Olerud, 1b	3	0	0	1
Alomar, 2b	3	1	1	0
Fernandez, ss	3	0	2	1
Sprague, 3b	4	0	0	0
Griffin, pr	0	0	0	0
Borders, c	4	0	1	0
Totals	**31**	**4**	**8**	**4**

```
PHILLIES      005  000  100 – 6
Toronto       000  201  010 – 4
```

DP—PHILLIES 1, Toronto 1. LOB—PHILLIES 9, Toronto 5. 2B—White (2), Molitor (1), Fernandez (1). HR—Carter (1), Dykstra (1), Eisenreich (1). SB—Molitor (1), Alomar (2). CS—Stocker (1), Henderson (1), Alomar (1). SF—Olerud.

PHILLIES	IP	H	R	ER	BB	SO
Mulholland (W, 1–0)	5²/₃	7	3	3	2	4
Mason	1²/₃	1	1	1	0	2
Williams (S, 1)	1²/₃	0	0	0	2	0

Toronto	IP	H	R	ER	BB	SO
Stewart (L, 0–1)	6	6	5	5	4	6
Castillo	1	3	1	1	0	0
Eichhorn	¹/₃	1	0	0	1	0
Timlin	1²/₃	2	0	0	0	2

WP—Stewart. BK—Stewart. Time—3:35. Attendance—52,062.

Game Three   October 19—Blue Jays 10, Phillies 3

Toronto	AB	R	H	RBI
Henderson, lf	4	2	2	0
White, cf	4	2	1	1
Molitor, 1b	4	3	3	3
Carter, rf	4	1	1	1
Alomar, 2b	5	2	4	2
Fernandez, ss	3	0	2	2
Sprague, 3b	4	0	0	1
Borders, c	4	0	0	0
Hentgen, p	3	0	0	0
Cox, p	1	0	0	0
Ward, p	0	0	0	0
Totals	**36**	**10**	**13**	**10**

PHILLIES	AB	R	H	RBI
Dykstra, cf	5	0	1	0
Duncan, 2b	5	0	2	1
Kruk, 1b	3	1	2	0
Hollins, 3b	3	0	0	0
Daulton, c	3	0	0	0
Eisenreich, rf	4	0	1	1
Incaviglia, lf	3	0	0	0
Thigpen, p	0	0	0	0
Morandini, ph	0	0	0	0
Andersen, p	0	0	0	0
Stocker, ss	4	0	1	0
Jackson, p	1	0	0	0
Chamberlain, ph	1	0	0	0
Rivera, p	0	0	0	0
Thompson, lf	2	2	2	1
Totals	**34**	**3**	**9**	**3**

```
Toronto     301  001  302 – 10
PHILLIES    000  001  101 –  3
```

DP—Toronto 2. LOB—Toronto 7, PHILLIES 9. 2B—Henderson (1), Kruk (1). 3B—White (1), Molitor (1), Alomar (1). HR—Thompson (1), Molitor (1). SB—Alomar 2 (4). SF—Carter, Fernandez, Sprague.

Toronto	IP	H	R	ER	BB	SO
Hentgen (W, 1–0)	6	5	1	1	3	6
Cox	2	3	1	1	2	2
Ward	1	1	1	1	0	2

PHILLIES	IP	H	R	ER	BB	SO
Jackson (L, 0–1)	5	6	4	4	1	1
Rivera	1 1/3	4	4	4	2	3
Thigpen	1 2/3	0	0	0	1	0
Andersen	1	3	2	2	0	0

HBP—Henderson by Thigpen. Time—3:16. Attendance—62,689.

Game Four   October 20—Blue Jays 15, Phillies 14

Toronto	AB	R	H	RBI
Henderson, lf	5	2	2	2
White, cf	5	2	3	4
Alomar, 2b	6	1	2	1
Carter, rf	6	2	3	0
Olerud, 1b	4	2	1	0
Molitor, 3b	4	2	1	1
Griffin, 3b	0	0	0	0
Fernandez, ss	6	2	3	5
Borders, c	4	1	1	1
Stottlemyre, p	0	0	0	0
Butler, ph	1	1	0	0
Leiter, p	1	0	1	0
Castillo, p	1	0	0	0
Sprague, ph	1	0	0	0
Timlin, p	0	0	0	0
Ward, p	0	0	0	0
Totals	**44**	**15**	**17**	**14**

PHILLIES	AB	R	H	RBI
Dykstra, cf	5	4	3	4
Duncan, 2b	6	1	3	1
Kruk, 1b	5	0	0	0
Hollins, 3b	4	3	2	0
Daulton, c	3	2	1	3
Eisenreich, rf	4	2	1	1
Thompson, lf	5	1	3	5
Stocker, ss	4	0	0	0
Greene, p	1	1	1	0
Mason, p	1	0	0	0
Jordan, ph	1	0	0	0
West, p	0	0	0	0
Chamberlain, ph	1	0	0	0
Andersen, p	0	0	0	0
Williams, p	0	0	0	0
Morandini, ph	1	0	0	0
Thigpen, p	0	0	0	0
Totals	**41**	**14**	**14**	**14**

Toronto	304	002	060 – 15	
PHILLIES	420	151	100 – 14	

E—Hollins (1). LOB—Toronto 10, PHILLIES 8. 2B—Henderson (2), White (3), Carter (1), Leiter (1), Dykstra (1), Hollins (1), Thompson (1). 3B—White (2), Thompson (1). HR—Dykstra 2 (3), Daulton (1). SB—Henderson (1), White (1), Dykstra (2), Duncan (2).

Toronto	IP	H	R	ER	BB	SO
Stottlemyre	2	3	6	6	4	1
Leiter	2²/₃	8	6	6	0	1
Castillo (W, 1–0)	2¹/₃	3	2	2	3	1
Timlin	²/₃	0	0	0	0	2
Ward (S, 2)	1¹/₃	0	0	0	0	2

PHILLIES	IP	H	R	ER	BB	SO
Greene	2¹/₃	7	7	7	4	1
Mason	2²/₃	2	0	0	1	2
West	1	3	2	2	0	0
Andersen	1¹/₃	1	3	1	1	2
Williams (L, 0–1)	²/₃	3	3	3	1	1
Thigpen	1	1	0	0	0	0

HBP—Daulton by Castillo, Molitor by West.
Time—4:14. Attendance—62,731.

Game Five   October 21—Phillies 2, Blue Jays 0

Toronto	AB	R	H	RBI
Henderson, lf	3	0	0	0
White, cf	3	0	0	0
Alomar, 2b	3	0	1	0
Carter, rf	4	0	0	0
Olerud, 1b	4	0	0	0
Molitor, 3b	4	0	1	0
Fernandez, ss	3	0	0	0
Borders, c	3	0	2	0
Canate, pr	0	0	0	0
Knorr, c	0	0	0	0
Guzman, p	2	0	0	0
Butler, ph	1	0	1	0
Cox, p	0	0	0	0
Totals	**30**	**0**	**5**	**0**

PHILLIES	AB	R	H	RBI
Dykstra, cf	2	1	0	0
Duncan, 2b	4	0	0	0
Kruk, 1b	3	0	1	1
Hollins, 3b	3	0	1	0
Batiste, 3b	0	0	0	0
Daulton, c	4	1	1	0
Eisenreich, rf	4	0	0	0
Thompson, lf	3	0	0	0
Stocker, ss	2	0	1	1
Schilling, p	2	0	1	0
Totals	**27**	**2**	**5**	**2**

Toronto	000	000	000 – 0
PHILLIES	110	000	00x – 2

E—Borders (1), Duncan (1). DP—Toronto 1, PHILLIES 3. LOB—Toronto 6, PHILLIES 8.
2B—Daulton (1), Stocker (1). CS—Alomar (2). S—Schilling.

Toronto	IP	H	R	ER	BB	SO
Guzman (L, 0–1)	7	5	2	1	4	6
Cox	1	0	0	0	2	3

PHILLIES	IP	H	R	ER	BB	SO
Schilling (W, 1–1)	9	5	0	0	3	6

Time—2:53. Attendance—62,706.

Game Six   October 23—Blue Jays 8, Phillies 6

PHILLIES	AB	R	H	RBI
Dykstra, cf	3	1	1	3
Duncan, dh	5	1	1	0
Kruk, 1b	3	0	0	0
Hollins, 3b	5	1	1	1
Batiste, 3b	0	0	0	0
Daulton, c	4	1	1	0
Eisenreich, rf	5	0	2	1
Thompson, lf	3	0	0	0
Incaviglia, ph, lf	0	0	0	1
Stocker, ss	3	1	0	0
Morandini, 2b	4	1	1	0
Totals	**35**	**6**	**7**	**6**

Toronto	AB	R	H	RBI
Henderson, lf	4	1	0	0
White, cf	4	1	0	0
Molitor, dh	5	3	3	2
Carter, rf	4	1	1	4
Olerud, 1b	3	1	1	0
Griffin, pr, 3b	0	0	0	0
Alomar, 2b	4	1	3	1
Fernandez, ss	3	0	0	0
Sprague, 3b, 1b	2	0	0	1
Borders, c	4	0	2	0
Totals	**33**	**8**	**10**	**8**

```
PHILLIES      000  100  500 – 6
Toronto       300  110  003 – 8
```

E—Alomar (2), Sprague (2). LOB—PHILLIES 9, Toronto 7. 2B—Daulton (2), Olerud (1), Alomar (2). 3B—Molitor (2). HR—Molitor (2), Carter (2), Dykstra (4). SB—Dykstra (4), Duncan (3). SF—Incaviglia, Carter, Sprague.

PHILLIES	IP	H	R	ER	BB	SO
Mulholland	5	7	5	1	1	1
Mason	2⅓	1	0	0	0	2
West	0	0	0	0	1	0
Andersen	⅔	0	0	0	1	0
Williams (L, 0–2)	⅓	2	3	3	1	0

Toronto	IP	H	R	ER	BB	SO
Stewart	6	4	4	4	4	2
Cox	⅓	3	2	2	1	1
Leiter	1⅔	0	0	0	1	2
Ward (W, 1–0)	1	0	0	0	0	0

Stewart pitched to 3 batters in the 7th. West pitched to 1 batter in the 8th. HBP—Fernandez by Andersen. Time—3:26. Attendance—52,195.

FINAL WORLD SERIES STATISTICS

Phillies Batting

	G	AB	R	H	2B	3B	HR	RBI	SO	BB	Avg.	PO	A	E	Pct.
Greene, p	1	1	1	1	0	0	0	0	0	0	1.000	0	0	0	—
Schilling, p	2	2	0	1	0	0	0	0	1	0	.500	0	3	0	1.000
Dykstra, cf	6	23	9	8	1	0	4	8	4	7	.348	19	1	0	1.000
Kruk, 1b	6	23	4	8	1	0	0	4	7	7	.348	42	3	0	1.000
Duncan, 2b-dh	6	29	5	10	0	1	0	2	7	1	.345	10	17	1	.964
Thompson, lf-pr	5	16	3	5	1	1	1	6	2	1	.313	10	0	1	.909
Hollins, 3b	6	23	5	6	1	0	0	2	5	6	.261	9	9	0	1.000
Eisenreich, rf	6	26	3	6	0	0	1	7	4	2	.231	18	0	0	1.000
Daulton, c	6	23	4	5	2	0	1	4	5	4	.217	31	4	0	1.000
Stocker, ss	6	19	1	4	1	0	0	1	5	5	.211	8	13	0	1.000
Jordan, dh-ph	3	10	0	2	0	0	0	0	2	0	.200	0	0	0	—
Morandini, ph-2b	3	5	1	1	0	0	0	0	2	1	.200	2	0	0	1.000
Incaviglia, ph-lf	4	8	0	1	0	0	0	1	4	0	.125	7	0	0	1.000
Chamberlain, ph	2	2	0	0	0	0	0	0	1	0	.000	0	0	0	—
Jackson, p	1	1	0	0	0	0	0	0	1	0	.000	0	0	0	—
Mason, p	4	1	0	0	0	0	0	0	0	0	.000	0	0	0	—
Andersen, p	4	0	0	0	0	0	0	0	0	0	.000	0	0	0	—
Batiste, 3b	2	0	0	0	0	0	0	0	0	0	.000	0	1	0	1.000
Mulholland, p	2	0	0	0	0	0	0	0	0	0	.000	1	1	0	1.000
Rivera, p	1	0	0	0	0	0	0	0	0	0	.000	0	0	0	—
Thigpen, p	2	0	0	0	0	0	0	0	0	0	.000	0	1	0	1.000
West, p	3	0	0	0	0	0	0	0	0	0	.000	0	0	0	—
Williams, p	3	0	0	0	0	0	0	0	0	0	.000	0	1	0	1.000
Totals	6	212	36	58	7	2	7	35	50	34	.274	157	54	2	.991

Blue Jays Batting

	G	AB	R	H	2B	3B	HR	RBI	SO	BB	Avg.	PO	A	E	Pct.
Leiter, p	3	1	0	1	1	0	0	0	0	0	1.000	0	0	0	—
Molitor, dh-1b-3b	6	24	10	12	2	2	2	8	0	3	.500	7	3	0	1.000
Butler, ph	2	2	1	1	0	0	0	0	0	0	.500	0	0	0	—
Alomar, 2b	6	25	5	12	2	1	0	6	3	2	.480	10	21	2	.939
Fernandez, ss	6	21	2	7	1	0	0	9	3	3	.333	11	8	0	1.000
Borders, c	6	23	2	7	0	0	0	1	1	2	.304	50	2	1	.981
White, cf	6	24	8	7	3	2	1	7	7	4	.292	16	0	0	1.000
Carter, rf	6	25	6	7	1	0	2	8	4	0	.280	12	0	2	.857
Olerud, 1b	5	17	5	4	1	0	1	2	1	4	.235	36	0	0	1.000
Henderson, lf	6	22	6	5	2	0	0	2	2	5	.227	8	0	0	1.000
Sprague, 3b-ph-1b	5	15	0	1	0	0	0	2	6	1	.067	4	9	2	.867
Hentgen, p	1	3	0	0	0	0	0	0	1	0	.000	0	0	0	—
Guzman, p	2	2	0	0	0	0	0	0	1	0	.000	0	1	0	1.000
Castillo, p	2	1	0	0	0	0	0	0	1	0	.000	0	0	0	—
Cox, p	3	1	0	0	0	0	0	0	0	0	.000	1	0	0	1.000
Griffin, pr-3b	3	0	0	0	0	0	0	0	0	0	.000	0	0	0	—
Canate, pr	1	0	0	0	0	0	0	0	0	0	.000	0	0	0	—
Eichhorn, p	1	0	0	0	0	0	0	0	0	0	.000	0	0	0	—
Knorr, c	1	0	0	0	0	0	0	0	0	0	.000	3	0	0	1.000

	G	AB	R	H	2B	3B	HR	RBI	SO	BB	Avg.	PO	A	E	Pct.
Stewart, p	2	0	0	0	0	0	0	0	0	0	.000	1	1	0	1.000
Stottlemyre, p	1	0	0	0	0	0	0	0	0	1	.000	0	0	0	—
Timlin, p	2	0	0	0	0	0	0	0	0	0	.000	0	0	0	—
D. Ward, p	4	0	0	0	0	0	0	0	0	0	.000	0	0	0	—
Totals	**6**	**206**	**45**	**64**	**13**	**5**	**6**	**45**	**30**	**25**	**.311**	**159**	**45**	**7**	**.967**

Phillies Pitching

	G	CG	IP	H	R	BB	SO	HB	WP	W	L	Sv	Pct.	ER	ERA
Thigpen	2	0	$2^2/_3$	1	0	1	0	1	0	0	0	0	—	0	0.00
Mason	4	0	$7^2/_3$	4	1	1	7	0	0	0	0	0	—	1	1.17
Schilling	2	1	$15^1/_3$	13	7	5	9	0	0	1	1	0	.500	6	3.52
Mulholland	2	0	$10^2/_3$	14	8	3	5	0	0	1	0	0	1.000	8	6.75
Jackson	1	0	5	6	4	1	1	0	0	0	1	0	.000	4	7.20
Andersen	4	0	$3^2/_3$	5	5	3	3	1	0	0	0	0	—	5	12.27
Williams	3	0	$2^2/_3$	5	6	4	1	0	0	0	2	1	.000	6	20.25
Greene	1	0	$2^1/_3$	7	7	4	1	0	0	0	0	0	—	7	27.00
Rivera	1	0	$1^1/_3$	4	4	2	3	0	0	0	0	0	—	4	27.00
West	3	0	1	5	3	1	0	1	0	0	0	0	—	3	27.00
Totals	**6**	**1**	**$52^1/_3$**	**64**	**45**	**25**	**30**	**3**	**0**	**2**	**4**	**1**	**.333**	**44**	**7.57**

Blue Jays Pitching

	G	CG	IP	H	R	BB	SO	HB	WP	W	L	Sv	Pct.	ER	ERA
Timlin	2	0	$2^1/_3$	2	0	0	4	0	0	0	0	0	—	0	0.00
Eichhorn	1	0	$^1/_3$	1	0	1	0	0	0	0	0	0	—	0	0.00
Hentgen	1	0	6	5	1	3	6	0	0	1	0	0	1.000	1	1.50
Ward	4	0	$4^2/_3$	3	2	0	7	0	0	1	0	2	1.000	1	1.93
Guzman	2	0	12	10	6	8	12	0	1	0	1	0	.000	5	3.75
Stewart	2	0	12	10	9	8	8	0	1	0	1	0	.000	9	6.75
Leiter	3	0	7	12	6	2	5	0	0	1	0	0	1.000	6	7.71
Castillo	2	0	$3^1/_3$	6	3	3	1	1	0	1	0	0	1.000	3	8.10
Cox	3	0	$3^1/_3$	6	3	5	6	0	0	0	0	0	—	3	8.10
Stottlemyre	1	0	2	3	6	4	1	0	0	0	0	0	—	6	27.00
Totals	**6**	**0**	**53**	**58**	**36**	**34**	**50**	**1**	**2**	**4**	**2**	**2**	**.667**	**34**	**5.77**

WORLD SERIES RECORDS

Individual and team records set or tied during the 1993 World Series between the Toronto Blue Jays and Philadelphia Phillies:

Individual Records Set

Batting
Most sacrifice flies, series—3, Joe Carter, Toronto; old record, 2, held by many.

Most sacrifice flies, career—4, Joe Carter, Toronto; old record, 3, Brooks Robinson, Baltimore, and Dave Concepcion, Cincinnati.

Most RBI by a shortstop, series—9, Tony Fernandez, Toronto; old record, 7, Bucky Dent, New York Yankees, 1978.

Individual Records Tied

Batting
Most hits, six-game series—12, Roberto Alomar and Paul Molitor, Toronto; also accomplished by Billy Martin, New York Yankees, 1953.

Most extra-base hits, six-game series—6, Paul Molitor and Devon White, Toronto; also accomplished by Willie Stargell, Pittsburgh, 1979.

Most at-bats, inning—2, Roberto Alomar, Toronto, Game 4, eighth inning, accomplished many times.

Most runs, game—4, Lenny Dykstra, Game 4, Philadelphia; accomplished seven times, most recently by Carney Lansford, Oakland, Game 3, 1989.

Pitching
Most walks, inning—4, Todd Stottlemyre, Game 4, first inning; accomplished five times, most recently by Tom Glavine, Atlanta, Game 5, 1991, sixth inning.

Most consecutive walks—3, Stottlemyre, Game 4; accomplished five times, most recently by Tom Glavine, Atlanta, Game 5, 1991.

Team Records Set

Batting
Most total runs, game—29, Toronto (15), Philadelphia (14), Game 4; old record, 22, New York Yankees (18), New York Giants (4), Game 2, 1936.

Most runs by losing team—14, Philadelphia, Game 4; old record, 9, New York Yankees, Game 7, 1960.

Most runs, six-game series—45, Toronto; old record, 43, New York Yankees, 1936.

Most runs by losing team, six-game series—36, Philadelphia; old record, 28, Los Angeles, 1977.

Most total runs, first four games—65, Toronto (37), Philadelphia (28); old record, 56, New York Yankees (37), Chicago Cubs (19), 1932.

Most total players with run scored, game—16, Toronto (9), Philadelphia (7), Game 4; old record, 15, Pittsburgh (9), New York Yankees (6), Game 7, 1960.

Most total hits, six-game series—122, Toronto (64), Philadelphia (58); old record, 120, Brooklyn (64), New York Yankees (56), 1953, and New York Yankees (68), Los Angeles (52), 1978.

Most extra-base hits, six-game series—26, Toronto; old record, 22, Brooklyn, 1953.

Most triples, series—5, Toronto; old record, 4, New York Giants, 1917, and New York Yankees, 1922 and 1953.

Most total bases, six-game series—105, Toronto; old record, 103, Brooklyn, 1953.

Most RBI, six-game series—45, Toronto; old record, 41, New York Yankees, 1936.

Most total RBI, six-game series—80, Toronto (45), Philadelphia (35); old record, 61, New York Yankees (41), New York Giants (20), 1936.

Most sacrifice flies, game—3, Toronto, Game 3; old record, 2; accomplished many times.

Most total sacrifice flies, game—3, Toronto (3), Philadelphia (0), Game 3; old record, 2; accomplished many times.

Most sacrifice flies, series—7, Toronto; old record, 5, Pittsburgh, 1979.

Most total sacrifice flies, series—8, Toronto (7), Philadelphia (1); old record, 7, Philadelphia (4), Kansas City (3), 1980.

Most walks, six-game series—34, Philadelphia; old record, 33, New York Yankees, 1981.

Most total walks, six-game series—59, Philadelphia (34), Toronto (25); old record, 53, New York Yankees (33), Los Angeles (20), 1981.

Most strikeouts, six-game series—50, Philadelphia; old record, 49, St. Louis Browns, 1944, and Kansas City, 1980.

Pitching

Most total appearances, six-game series—44, Philadelphia (23), Toronto (21); old record, 41, Toronto (25), Atlanta (16), 1992.

Miscellaneous

Longest game—4:14, Game 4; old record, 4:13, New York Mets at Oakland, Game 2, 1973.

Longest nine-inning game—4:14, Game 4; old record, 3:48, Baltimore at Pittsburgh, Game 4, 1979. Team records tied.

Batting

Fewest sacrifices, six-game series—0, Toronto; accomplished three times.

Most extra bases on long hits, six-game series—41, Toronto; also accomplished by New York Yankees, 1953.

Most players with run scored, game—9, Toronto, Game 4; accomplished five times.

Most innings with runs, game—6, Philadelphia, Game 4; accomplished three times.

Most runs, eighth inning—6, Toronto, Game 4; also accomplished by Baltimore, Game 4, 1979, and Chicago Cubs, Game 2, 1908.

Most total hits, game—32, Toronto (18), Philadelphia (14), Game 4; also accomplished by New York Yankees (19) vs. Pittsburgh Pirates (13), Game 2, 1960.

Most total triples, six-game series—7, Toronto (5), Philadelphia (2); also accomplished by New York Yankees (4), New York Giants (3), 1923.

Most Home Runs in a World Series

5—Reggie Jackson, New York Yankees, 1977 vs. Los Angeles (6 games).

4—Lenny Dykstra, Philadelphia, 1993 vs. Toronto (6 games).

4—Willie Aikens, Kansas City, 1980 vs. Philadelphia (6 games).

4—Gene Tenace, Oakland, 1972 vs. Cincinnati (7 games).

4—Hank Bauer, New York Yankees, 1958 vs. Milwaukee Braves (7 games).

4—Duke Snider, Brooklyn, 1955 vs. New York Yankees (7 games).

4—Duke Snider, Brooklyn, 1952 vs. New York Yankees (7 games).

4—Lou Gehrig, New York Yankees, 1928 vs. St. Louis Cardinals (4 games).

4—Babe Ruth, New York Yankees, 1926 vs. St. Louis Cardinals (7 games).

The
Aftermath

Just because the long season had ended, it didn't mean the Phillies would go into hibernation for the winter. In the aftermath of the club's World Series appearance, there was every indication that the club would remain very much in the news during the off-season.

There was no parade down Broad Street for the Phillies following their return from Toronto. The club decided that it didn't want one. What it got instead was a 25-minute ceremony at City Hall that took place at lunch time in early November.

A wildly enthusiastic crowd, much of it below voting age and variously estimated to number between five and 10,000, showed up to brush up on its hero-worshipping and to cheer the 30-second sound bites offered by the speakers.

"They can call us misfits. They can call us castoffs. Vagabonds. But they have to call us National League champions," intoned general manager Lee Thomas in a statement that summarized the Phillies' season.

To this, manager Jim Fregosi added: "It [the 1993 season] has been the best experience of my baseball career."

Five players—Kevin Stocker, Curt Schilling, Lenny Dykstra, John Kruk and Darren Daulton—spoke, several of them promising a World Series victory in 1994.

The longest and perhaps the most descriptive commentary was provided by Dykstra. "We worked hard. We believed in ourselves," he said at one point. "We stuck together, and that's what makes this so special."

Sticking together, however, may have had useful applications during the season, but it was not a staple of the Phillies' approach in the weeks that followed the City Hall celebration. At that point, a chink in the club's one-for-all, all-for-one facade appeared.

It all revolved around reliever Mitch Williams, the enigmatic lefthander who had punctuated an atrocious post-season by delivering a home run pitch to Joe Carter that won the World Series for the Blue Jays.

In the midst of the Series, Williams had received threats on his life and his New Jersey home had been vandalized. And his ineffective performance was the subject of conversation throughout the area among fans and media who had conveniently forgotten the hurler's many contributions to the team, including his sparkling save in the deciding game of the League Championship Series against the Braves.

A forthright fellow with a seemingly thick skin, Williams, who set an all-time club record with 43 saves in 1993, never tried to find excuses for his mistakes. He always accepted the blame, and in post-season interviews from his ranch in Texas, including several on national television, he was quick to admit that he deserved the goat horns for the Series. He also said that he was looking forward to returning to the Phillies in 1994.

There were many doubters, though, who believed that Williams should not return to the Phillies, that he had lost his effectiveness, especially his fastball, and that he would be the target of too much fan abuse if he came back the next season. Although Williams's teammates had loyally supported him during the post-season games, some of the most vocal doubters were teammates who suddenly turned on him, particularly Dykstra and Schilling. Both went public with comments that strongly proclaimed that the reliever should go elsewhere.

Williams, of course, took issue with the remarks, defending himself and expressing bewilderment at his teammates' views. It also came out that many people, including Williams, did not find much humor in Schilling's placing a towel over his head to hide his eyes while he sat on the bench when Williams was pitching, a scene that was shown repeatedly on television during post-season play.

Just as the level of dissent heightened, the situation took an unexpected twist when Thomas suddenly traded Williams to the Houston Astros for two pitchers, Doug Jones, an aging reliever seven years Williams's senior who had a terrible 1993 season, and Jeff Juden, a 22-year-old minor leaguer who is viewed as a possible big league starter.

While more Phillies came out saying they thought the trade was "the best thing" for Williams, Thomas insisted he was not pressured to make the swap, either by his own players or by the view that the Phillies' second highest all-time save leader could not pitch again in Philadelphia. He was prepared, he said, to see Williams working again the next year with the Phils and made the deal only because the Astros suggested it.

Nonetheless, the trade was part of what was probably Thomas's most important off-season task—that of restructuring the Phillies' bullpen.

Before the Williams deal, the Phillies had already made another attempt to bolster a bullpen that had stumbled badly during the latter stages of the 1993 season. Thomas had sent reserve outfielder Ruben Amaro to the Cleveland Indians in exchange for relief pitcher Heathcliff Slocumb, a 27-year-old righthander who had previously toiled with the Chicago Cubs and whom the Phils expected to use as a set-up man.

Amaro, a Philadelphia native and the younger half of the only father-son combination ever to play with the Phillies, had not played much with the Phils in 1993 after filling in for the injured Dykstra for much of the previous year. He didn't figure to see much action in 1994, either, and was hoping to hook on with another team.

Also leaving the Phillies was pitcher Kyle Abbott, who had come to the club with Amaro in the trade with the California Angels for Von Hayes. Abbott, who spent the entire 1993 season with Scranton/Wilkes-Barre after posting an unbecoming 1–14 record with the Phils in 1992, was released so he could play in Japan for the 1994 season.

In other post-season player activity before the end of the year, the Phillies gave Dykstra a four-year extension on his contract that would produce $27.5 million, picked up the third year option on Mariano Duncan's contract and re-

In a controversial departure, Mitch Williams was traded to Houston.

signed Jim Eisenreich to a one-year contract after the outfielder had become a free agent following the end of the season.

Phillies players also came in for a different kind of windfall after the season when they were awarded a World Series losers' share of $91,222.27 each, a new record. Twenty-nine individuals, including 22 players, the manager and six coaches, received full shares. Eighteen other players and 24 nonuniformed personnel were awarded fractional shares.

The winning Blue Jays received full shares valued at $127,920.77 per man, also a new World Series record.

In post-season honors, Thomas was chosen National League executive of the year by *The Sporting News,* Fregosi was named National League manager of the year by *Associated Press* and Dykstra won a Silver Slugger award for being the top hitter at his position in the league.

Dykstra came in second in the balloting for Most Valuable Player, finishing well behind the winner, Barry Bonds of the San Francisco Giants. Bonds polled 372 points with 24 first and four second place votes in the balloting by the Baseball Writers' Association of America. Dykstra had 267 points with four firsts, 20 seconds, three thirds and one fourth.

Lenny Dykstra was runner-up in the MVP voting and won a Silver Slugger award.

Darren Daulton was seventh in the voting with 79 points, placing behind the Atlanta Braves' Dave Justice (183), Fred McGriff (177) and Ron Gant (176) and the Giants' Matt Williams (103).

Although they weren't overwhelmed with awards, the Phillies went into the off-season knowing that they had earned a special place in the club's long and occasionally glorious history. On any list of top Phillies teams, the 1993 club certainly ranked among the best, perhaps exceeded only by the 1980 team, the Phils' only World Series winner.

It was truly a remarkable year, one in which a band of gritty, determined, hard-working, sometimes zany players came together to produce an unexpected but memorable and completely satisfying result.

One More Look

PHILLIES POST-SEASON ROSTER

MANAGER: Jim Fregosi (11)

COACHES: John Vukovich (18)
Larry Bowa (2)
Denis Menke (14)
Mel Roberts (26)
Johnny Podres (46)
Mike Ryan (9)

TRAINER: Jeff Cooper

ASST. TRAINER: Mark Andersen

TEAM PHYSICIAN: Dr. Phillip Marone

No.		B-T	Ht.	Wt.	Born	Birthplace	Residence
	Pitchers						
47	Andersen, Larry	R-R	6-3	205	5/6/53	Portland, OR	San Diego, CA
49	Greene, Tommy	R-R	6-5	227	4/6/67	Lumberton, NC	Richmond, VA
27	Jackson, Danny	L-L	6-0	205	1/5/62	San Antonio, TX	Overland Park, KS
48	Mason, Roger	R-R	6-6	220	9/19/58	Bellaire, MI	Bellaire, MI
45	Mulholland, Terry	R-L	6-3	215	3/9/63	Uniontown, PA	Glendale, AZ
34	Rivera, Ben	R-R	6-8	240	1/11/68	San Pedro de Macoris, DR	San Pedro de Macoris, DR
38	Schilling, Curt	R-R	6-4	220	11/16/66	Anchorage, AK	Kennett Square, PA
37	Thigpen, Bobby	R-R	6-3	222	7/17/63	Tallahassee, FL	St. Petersburg, FL
40	West, David	L-L	6-6	240	9/1/64	Memphis, TN	Eden Prairie, MN
99	Williams, Mitch	L-L	6-4	205	11/17/64	Santa Ana, CA	Arlington, TX

No.		B-T	Ht.	Wt.	Born	Birthplace	Residence
	Catchers						
10	Daulton, Darren	L-R	6-2	205	1/3/62	Arkansas City, KS	Safety Harbor, FL
23	Pratt, Todd	R-R	6-3	227	2/9/67	Bellevue, NE	Sunrise, FL
	Infielders						
5	Batiste, Kim	R-R	6-0	193	3/15/68	New Orleans, LA	Prairieville, LA
7	Duncan, Mariano	R-R	6-0	191	3/13/63	San Pedro de Macoris, DR	Cherry Hill, NJ
15	Hollins, Dave	S-R	6-1	207	5/25/66	Buffalo, NY	Orchard Park, NY
17	Jordan, Ricky	R-R	6-3	210	5/26/65	Richmond, CA	Gold River, CA
29	Kruk, John	L-L	5-10	210	2/9/61	Charleston, WV	Burlington, WV
12	Morandini, Mickey	L-R	5-11	183	4/22/66	Kittanning, PA	Valparaiso, IN
19	Stocker, Kevin	S-R	6-1	178	2/13/70	Spokane, WA	Spokane, WA
	Outfielders						
44	Chamberlain, Wes	R-R	6-2	219	4/13/66	Chicago, IL	Chicago, IL
4	Dykstra, Lenny	L-L	5-10	190	2/10/63	Santa Ana, CA	Devon, PA
8	Eisenreich, Jim	L-L	5-11	195	4/18/59	St. Cloud, MN	Blue Springs, MO
22	Incaviglia, Pete	R-R	6-1	230	4/2/64	Pebble Beach, CA	Colleyville, TX
16	Longmire, Tony	L-R	6-1	197	8/12/68	Vallejo, CA	Vallejo, CA
25	Thompson, Milt	L-R	5-11	200	1/5/59	Washington, DC	Ballwin, MO

HIGHS, LOWS OF THE
1993 SEASON

Team Batting

Most runs, inning, Phillies: 7—9/3 at CIN (5th); 9/17 at MTL (65th)

Most runs, inning, Opp: 7—5/5 at SF (5th); 7/1 at STL (3rd); 7/9 vs SF (2nd); 9/8 vs CHI (8th)

Most runs, game, Phillies: 18—5/30 at COL

Most runs, game, Opposition: 15—7/9 vs SF

Most hits, inning, Phillies: 7—5/28 at COL (4th)

Most hits, inning, Opposition: 7—7/9 vs SF (2nd)

Most hits, game, Phillies: 20—5/28 at COL

Most hits, game, Opposition: 23—7/9 vs SF

Most homers, game, Phillies: 6—5/30 at COL (ties club record)

Most homers, game, Opposition: 4—4/9 vs CHI; 9/6 vs CHI; 9/29 at PIT

Most stolen bases, game, Phillies: 5—4/10 vs CHI

Most stolen bases, game, Opposition: 4—5/21 vs MTL

Most doubles, game, Phillies: 6—5/23 vs MTL; 5/28 at COL

Most doubles, game, Opposition: 5—7/3 vs SD; 7/9 vs SF; 8/12 vs MTL; 8/28 vs CIN

Most triples, game, Phillies: 3—8/29 vs CIN

Most triples, game, Opposition: 3—6/17 vs FLA

Most extra-base hits, game, Phillies: 10—4/18 at CHI

Most extra-base hits, game, Opposition: 8—7/9 vs SF

Most walks, game, Phillies: 12—8/7 at FLA (10 inn)

Most strikeouts, game, Phillies: 14—4/20 vs SD

Most left on base, game, Phillies: 17—7/7 vs LA (20 innings)

Individual Batting

Most hits, game: 5—Kruk, 5/17 at FLA & 7/27 vs STL

Most runs, game: 4—Daulton, 5/30 at COL

Most doubles, game: 3—Dykstra, 5/23 vs MTL; Hollins, 5/28 at COL

Most triples, game: 2—Duncan, 6/7 vs HOU; Morandini, 8/29 vs CIN

Most HR, game: 2—Daulton, 4/9 vs CHI, 5/30 at COL, 7/16 at SD & 8/7 at FLA; Kruk, 4/18 at CHI & 8/18 at COL; Chamberlain, 4/18 at CHI; lncaviglia, 5/24 vs NY, 7/31 vs PIT & 8/28 vs CIN; Pratt, 8/1 vs PIT; Dykstra, 9/9 vs CHI

Most extra-base hits, game: 3—Chamberlain, 4/18 at CHI; Dykstra, 5/23 vs MTL; Hollins, 5/28 at COL; Eisenreich, 6/9 vs HOU; Pratt, 8/1 vs PIT; lncaviglia, 8/28 vs CIN

Most RBI, game: 6—Daulton, 7/28 vs STL; 5–Daulton, 4/9 vs CHI and 8/7 at FLA; Incaviglia, 5/20 vs MTL; Morandini, 7/10 vs SF; Dykstra, 9/9 vs CHI

Most walks, game: 3—Daulton, 4/7 at HOU, 4/29 at SD & 8/7 at FLA; Hollins, 4/17 at CHI & 6/4 vs COL; Dykstra, 4/24 vs LA, 6/20 vs FLA, 6/23 vs ATL, 7/10 vs SF & 7/21 at LA; Kruk, 5/7 vs STL, 5/22 vs MTL, 5/31 at CIN, 6/1 at CIN, 6/18 vs FLA & 7/23 at SF; Eisenreich, 9/22 vs FLA

Most stolen bases, game: 3—Dykstra, 4/10 vs CHI

Longest hitting streak: 18 games—Duncan, 8/28–9/19

Longest RBI streak: 6 games—Incaviglia, 6/22–28

Longest run scored streak: 15—Dykstra, 6/6–20

Longest stolen base streak: 18—Dykstra, 5/17–7/24

Pinch home runs: Morandini, 7/30 vs PIT; Duncan, 9/7 vs CHI

Grand slams: Duncan, 5/9 vs STL & 9/28 at PIT; Daulton, 5/10 vs PIT & 7/28 vs STL; Incaviglia, 5/20 vs MTL; Eisenreich, 6/14 at MTL; Morandini, 7/10 vs SF; Batiste, 8/13 vs NY

Individual Pitching

Most strikeouts, game, Phillies: 14—Mulholland, 6/4 vs COL

Most walks, game, Phillies: 8—Greene, 9/24 vs ATL

Longest walkless streak, Phillies: 26 innings—Mulholland, 5/29–6/9

Fewest hits, game, Phillies (CG): 3—Greene, 9/3 at CIN; 4—Mulholland, 4/5 at HOU; Schilling, 4/11 vs CHI; Rivera, 8/31 at CHI

Longest winning streak: 8 games—Greene (4/13–6/5)

Longest losing streak: 5 games—Schilling (6/21–7/11)

Longest consec. scoreless IP streak (starter): 17.0—Greene, 5/12–24 & Mulholland, 5/29–6/4

Longest consec. scoreless IP streak (reliever): 13.1—West, 4/14–5/15 & Andersen, 6/1–7/3

Longest consec. scoreless IP streak (pitcher): 17.0—Greene & Mulholland

Most innings, game, starter: 10.0 innings—Mulholland, 5/8 vs STL

Most innings, game, relief: 6.0 innings—Mk Williams, 7/7 vs LA (20 inn)

Miscellaneous Team

Longest winning streak: 6 games (6/9–14)

Longest losing streak: 4 games (7/11–17)

Longest game, innings: 20 innings, 7/7 vs LA

Longest game, time: 6:10—7/7 vs LA (20 inn); 3:43—9/25 vs ATL (9 inn)

Shortest game, time: 2:02—5/12 vs PIT

Largest crowd, home: 60,985—4/9 vs CHI

Largest crowd, road: 63,193—8/17 at COL

Most games above .500: 35 games (9/24, 94–59; 9/28, 96–61)

Most errors, game: 5—5/28 at COL

Largest margin of victory: 17 runs—5/30 at COL (18–1 win)

Largest margin of defeat: 11 runs—7/8 vs SF (13–2 loss)

Biggest come-from-behind win: 8 runs—4/26 vs SF (won 9–8, trailed 8–0)

PHILLIES TEAM
TOTALS

	Home W/L	Road W/L	Totals W/L
Vs. East			
vs. Chicago	3–4	3–3	6–7
vs. Florida	6–1	3–3	9–4
vs. Montreal	5–2	2–4	7–6
vs. New York	4–2	6–1	10–3
vs. Pittsburgh	4–2	3–4	7–6
vs. St. Louis	6–0	2–5	8–5
Totals	**28–11**	**19–20**	**47–31**
Vs. West			
vs. Atlanta	3–3	3–3	6–6
vs. Cincinnati	4–2	4–2	8–4
vs. Colorado	4–2	5–1	9–3
vs. Houston	3–3	4–2	7–5
vs. Los Angeles	5–1	5–1	10–2
vs. San Diego	3–3	3–3	6–6
vs. San Francisco	2–4	2–4	4–8
Totals	**24–18**	**26–16**	**50–34**
Overall Totals	**52–29**	**45–36**	**97–65**

	Phi.	Opp.
Double Plays	123	142
Triple Plays	0	0
Left on Base	1281	1202
Grand Slam HR	8	3
Home Runs—Home	80	57
Home Runs—Road	76	72

	Home W/L	Road W/L	Totals W/L
Shutouts	5–0	6–2	11–2
SHO—Individual	3–0	5–1	8–1
Extra Innings	6–1	5–6	11–7
One-Run Decisions	14–7	9–13	23–20
Two-Run Decisions	8–4	12–9	20–13
Vs. LH Starters	19–7	12–11	31–18
vs. RH Starters	33–22	33–25	66–47
Grass Fields	0–0	30–19	30–19
Artificial Fields	52–29	15–17	67–46
Day Games	15–6	11–14	26–20
Night Games	37–23	34–22	71–45

Larry Bowa

PHILLIES COACHES

Denis Menke

Johnny Podres

Mike Ryan

Mel Roberts

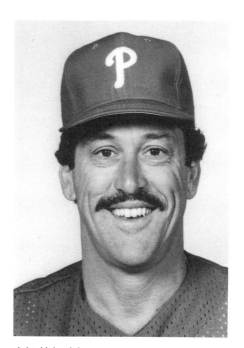

John Vukovich

MAJOR LEAGUE STANDINGS

National League

East

East	W	L	Pct.	GB
PHILLIES	**97**	**65**	**.599**	—
Montreal	94	68	.580	3
St. Louis	87	75	.537	10
Chicago	84	78	.519	14
Pittsburgh	75	87	.463	23
Florida	64	98	.395	34
New York	59	103	.364	39

West	W	L	Pct.	GB
Atlanta	104	58	.642	—
San Francisco	103	59	.636	1
Houston	85	77	.525	19
Los Angeles	81	81	.500	23
Cincinnati	73	89	.451	31
Colorado	67	95	.414	37
San Diego	61	101	.377	43

American League

East	W	L	Pct.	GB
Toronto	95	67	.586	—
New York	88	74	.543	7
Baltimore	85	77	.525	10
Detroit	85	77	.525	10
Boston	80	82	.494	15
Cleveland	76	86	.469	19
Milwaukee	69	93	.426	26

West	W	L	Pct.	GB
Chicago	94	68	.580	—
Texas	86	76	.531	8
Kansas City	84	78	.519	10
Seattle	82	80	.506	12
California	71	91	.438	23
Minnesota	71	91	.438	23
Oakland	68	94	.420	26

PHILLIES 1993 ROSTER TRANSACTIONS

Date	Name	Description
1-08-93	Incaviglia, Pete	Signs Phillies contract 1993-94 (opt '95)
1-10-93	Parris, Steve	Signs Phillies contract
1-20-93	Schilling, Curt	Signs Phillies contract
1-21-93	Lockett, Ron	Signs Phillies contract
1-24-93	Borland, Toby	Signs Phillies contract
1-30-93	Eisenreich, Jim	Signs Phillies contract
2-09-93	Jordan, Ricky	Signs Phillies contract
2-20-93	Ayrault, Bob	Signs Phillies contract
2-20-93	Mulholland, Terry	Signs Phillies contract
2-20-93	Pratt, Todd	Signs Phillies contract
2-20-93	Rivera, Ben	Signs Phillies contract
2-20-93	Williams, Mike	Signs Phillies contract
2-26-93	Williams, Cary	Signs Phillies contract
2-27-93	Combs, Pat	Signs Phillies contract
2-27-93	Greene, Tommy	Signs Phillies contract
2-28-93	Brantley, Cliff	Signs Phillies contract
2-28-93	Brink, Brad	Signs Phillies contract
2-28-93	Chamberlain, Wes	Signs Phillies contract
2-28-93	Lindsey, Doug	Signs Phillies contract
3-01-93	Fletcher, Paul	Signs Phillies contract
3-02-93	Abbott, Kyle	Signs Phillies contract
3-02-93	Jackson, Jeff	Signs Phillies contract
3-03-93	Bell, Juan	Signs Phillies contract
3-03-93	Hollins, Dave	Signs Phillies contract
3-03-93	Morandini, Mickey	Signs Phillies contract
3-04-93	Amaro, Ruben	Signs Phillies contract 1993–94
3-04-93	Batiste, Kim	Signs Phillies contract
3-04-93	Nuneviller, Tom	Signs Phillies contract
3-13-93	Borland, Toby	Optioned from the Phillies to Scranton
3-13-93	Brantley, Cliff	Optioned from the Phillies to Scranton
3-13-93	Longmire, Tony	Optioned from the Phillies to Scranton
3-13-93	Williams, Cary	Outrighted from the Phillies to Scranton
3-13-93	Williams, Mike	Optioned from the Phillies to Scranton
3-16-93	Farmer, Mike	Optioned from the Phillies to Reading
3-16-93	Jackson, Jeff	Optioned from the Phillies to Reading
3-16-93	Lockett, Ron	Optioned from the Phillies to Scranton
3-16-93	Nuneviller, Tom	Optioned from the Phillies to Reading
3-22-93	Brink, Brad	Optioned from the Phillies to Scranton
3-22-93	Parris, Steve	Optioned from the Phillies to Scranton
3-26-93	DeJesus, Jose	Placed on Sdl-15 day disabled list
3-29-93	Abbott, Kyle	Optioned from the Phillies to Scranton
4-01-93	Amaro, Ruben	Optioned from the Phillies to Scranton
4-01-93	Combs, Pat	Optioned from the Phillies to Scranton
4-01-93	Fletcher, Paul	Optioned from the Phillies to Scranton
4-01-93	Lindsey, Doug	Optioned from the Phillies to Scranton
4-04-93	Andersen, Larry	Outrighted from Scranton to the Phillies
4-04-93	Andersen, Larry	Signs Phillies contract

Date	Name	Description
4-04-93	DeJesus, Jose	Transferred to Edl-60 day disabled list
4-04-93	Green, Tyler	Outrighted from Reading to the Phillies
4-04-93	Green, Tyler	Signs Phillies contract
4-13-93	Davis, Mark	Acquired from Atlanta to the Phillies in exchange for Brad Hassinger
4-13-93	Green, Tyler	Optioned from the Phillies to Scranton
4-14-93	Parris, Steve	Recalled from Scranton (ntr)
4-14-93	Parris, Steve	Designated for assignment
4-19-93	Parris, Steve	Outrighted from the Phillies to the Dodgers
4-19-93	Parris, Steve	Claimed on waivers
4-28-93	Lindsey, Doug	Recalled from Scranton to the Phillies
4-28-93	Pratt, Todd	Placed on Sdl-15 day disabled list
5-08-93	Andersen, Larry	Placed on Sdl-15 day disabled list
5-14-93	Williams, Mike	Recalled from Scranton to the Phillies
5-23-93	Pratt, Todd	Sent to Scranton for rehab.
5-23-93	Williams, Mike	Optioned from the Phillies to Scranton
5-24-93	Brantley, Cliff	Designated for assignment
5-24-93	Mauser, Tim	Outrighted from Scranton to the Phillies
5-24-93	Mauser, Tim	Signs Phillies contract
5-26-93	Andersen, Larry	Reinstated from disabled list
5-26-93	Ayrault, Bob	Optioned from the Phillies to Scranton
5-26-93	Lindsey, Doug	Optioned from the Phillies to Scranton
5-26-93	Pratt, Todd	Recalled from rehab. list
5-27-93	Brantley, Cliff	Outrighted from the Phillies to Montreal
5-27-93	Brantley, Cliff	Waiver claim
5-27-93	Pratt, Todd	Reinstated from disabled list
6-01-93	Bell, Juan	Outrighted from the Phillies to Milwaukee
6-06-93	Millette, Joe	Outrighted from Scranton to the Phillies
6-06-93	Millette, Joe	Signs Phillies contract
6-11-93	Hollins, Dave	Placed on Sdl-15 day disabled list
6-12-93	Ayrault, Bob	Recalled (ntr) from Scranton to the Phillies
6-12-93	Ayrault, Bob	Outrighted from the Phillies to Seattle
6-13-93	Manto, Jeff	Outrighted from Scranton to the Phillies
6-13-93	Manto, Jeff	Signs Phillies contract
6-16-93	Chamberlain, Wes	Placed on Sdl-15 day disabled list
6-17-93	Amaro, Ruben	Recalled from Scranton to the Phillies
6-28-93	Hollins, Dave	Reinstated from disabled list
6-28-93	Millette, Joe	Optioned from the Phillies to Scranton
6-29-93	DeJesus, Jose	Sent to Clearwater for rehab.
7-02-93	Davis, Mark	Released
7-02-93	Williams, Mike	Recalled from Scranton to the Phillies
7-03-93	Duncan, Mariano	Placed on Sdl-15 day disabled list
7-03-93	Mason, Roger	Acquired from San Diego to the Phillies in exchange for Tim Mauser
7-03-93	Mauser, Tim	Outrighted from the Phillies to San Diego
7-03-93	Millette, Joe	Recalled from Scranton to the Phillies
7-04-93	Chamberlain, Wes	Reinstated from disabled list
7-04-93	Manto, Jeff	Designated for assignment
7-07-93	Millette, Joe	Optioned from the Phillies to Scranton
7-07-93	Stocker, Kevin	Outrighted from Scranton to the Phillies
7-07-93	Stocker, Kevin	Signs Phillies contract

Date	Name	Description
7-09-93	Amaro, Ruben	Optioned from the Phillies to Scranton
7-09-93	Manto, Jeff	Outrighted from the Phillies to Scraton
7-10-93	Fletcher, Paul	Recalled from Scranton to the Phillies
7-18-93	Duncan, Mariano	Reinstated from disabled list
7-18-93	Fletcher, Paul	Optioned from the Phillies to Scranton
7-28-93	DeJesus, Jose	Recalled from rehab. list
7-28-93	Greene, Tommy	Placed on Sdl-15 day disabled list
7-31-93	Green, Tyler	Recalled from Scranton to the Phillies
8-03-93	DeJesus, Jose	Reinstated from disabled list
8-03-93	DeJesus, Jose	Outrighted from the Phillies to Clearwater
8-11-93	DeLeon, Jose	Outrighted from the Phillies to Chicago White Sox
8-11-93	Green, Tyler	Optioned from the Phillies to Scranton
8-11-93	Thigpen, Bobby	Acquired from Chicago White Sox to the Phillies in exchange for Jose DeLeon
8-12-93	Greene, Tommy	Reinstated from disabled list
8-30-93	Farmer, Mike	Recalled (ntr) from Reading to the Phillies (ntr)
8-30-93	Farmer, Mike	Outrighted from the Phillies to Reading
8-30-93	Lockett, Ron	Recalled from Reading to the Phillies (ntr)
8-30-93	Lockett, Ron	Outrighted from the Phillies to Reading
8-30-93	Williams, Mike	Optioned from the Phillies to Scranton
8-31-93	Longmire, Tony	Recalled from Scranton to the Phillies
9-01-93	Amaro, Ruben	Recalled from Scranton to the Phillies
9-01-93	Foster, Kevin	Outrighted from Scranton to the Phillies
9-01-93	Manto, Jeff	Outrighted from Scranton to the Phillies
9-01-93	Pall, Donn	Acquired from Chicago White Sox to the Phillies
9-05-93	Williams, Mike	Recalled from Scranton to the Phillies
9-08-93	Lindsey, Doug	Recalled from Scranton to the Phillies (ntr)
9-08-93	Lindsey, Doug	Outrighted from the Phillies to Chicago White Sox
9-09-93	Abbott, Kyle	Recalled from Scranton to the Phillies (ntr)
9-09-93	Borland, Toby	Recalled from Reading to the Phillies (ntr)
9-09-93	Brink, Brad	Recalled from Scranton to the Phillies
9-09-93	Combs, Pat	Recalled from Scranton to the Phillies (ntr)
9-09-93	Fletcher, Paul	Recalled from Scranton to the Phillies (ntr)
9-09-93	Green, Tyler	Recalled from Scranton to the Phillies (ntr)
9-09-93	Jackson, Jeff	Recalled from Reading to the Phillies (ntr)
9-09-93	Millette, Joe	Recalled from Scranton to the Phillies (ntr)
9-09-93	Nuneviller, Tom	Recalled from Reading to the Phillies (ntr)

Club Batting

Club	AVG	G	AB	R	OR	H	TB	2B	3B	HR	GS
San Francisco	.276	162	5557	808	636	1534	2373	269	33	168	1
Philadelphia	**.274**	**162**	**5685**	**877**	**740**	**1555**	**2422**	**297**	**51**	**156**	**8**
Colorado	.273	162	5517	758	967	1507	2329	278	59	142	3
St. Louis	.272	162	5551	758	744	1508	2192	262	34	118	5
Chicago	.270	163	5627	738	739	1521	2327	259	32	161	2
Pittsburgh	.267	162	5549	707	806	1482	2179	267	50	110	0
Houston	.267	162	5464	716	630	1459	2235	288	37	138	0
Cincinnati	.264	162	5417	722	785	1457	2185	261	28	137	5
Atlanta	.262	162	5515	767	559	1444	2248	239	29	169	4
Los Angeles	.261	162	5588	675	662	1458	2138	234	28	130	2
Montreal	.257	163	5493	732	682	1410	2118	270	36	122	1
San Diego	.252	162	5503	679	772	1386	2140	239	28	153	2
New York	.248	162	5448	672	744	1350	2126	228	37	158	4
Florida	.248	162	5475	581	724	1356	1897	197	31	94	4
Totals	.264	1135	77489	10190	10190	20427	30909	3588	513	1956	41

Club Pitching

Club	W–L	ERA	G	CG	SHO	REL	SV	IP
Atlanta	104–58	3.14	162	18	16	353	46	1455.0
Houston	85–77	3.49	162	18	14	324	42	1441.1
Los Angeles	81–81	3.50	162	17	9	346	36	1472.2
Montreal	94–68	3.55	163	8	7	385	61	1456.2
San Francisco	103–59	3.61	162	4	9	414	50	1456.2
Philadelphia	**97–65**	**3.95**	**162**	**24**	**11**	**350**	**46**	**1472.2**
New York	59–103	4.05	162	16	8	297	22	1438.0
St. Louis	87–75	4.09	162	5	7	423	54	1453.0
Florida	64–98	4.13	162	4	5	409	48	1440.1
Chicago	84–78	4.18	163	8	5	422	56	1449.2
San Diego	61–101	4.23	162	8	6	397	32	1437.2
Cincinnati	73–89	4.51	162	11	8	375	37	1434.0
Pittsburgh	75–87	4.77	162	12	5	384	34	1445.2
Colorado	67–95	5.41	162	9	0	453	35	1431.1
Totals	1134–1134	4.04	1135	162	110	5332	599	20284.2

Club Fielding

Club	PCT	G	PO	A	E	TC	DP	TP	PB
San Francisco	.984	162	4370	1733	101	6204	169	0	15
Pittsburgh	.983	162	4337	1816	105	6258	161	1	19
Atlanta	.983	162	4365	1769	108	6242	146	0	13
Chicago	.982	163	4349	1889	115	6353	162	0	14
Cincinnati	.980	162	4302	1633	121	6056	133	0	12
Florida	.980	162	4321	1703	125	6149	130	0	29
Houston	.979	162	4324	1652	126	6102	141	0	7
Los Angeles	.979	162	4418	1838	133	6389	141	0	15
Philadelphia	**.977**	**162**	**4418**	**1536**	**141**	**6095**	**123**	**0**	**12**
St. Louis	.975	162	4359	1890	159	6408	157	1	14
New York	.975	162	4314	1781	156	6251	143	0	4
Montreal	.975	163	4370	1827	159	6356	144	2	14
San Diego	.974	162	4313	1616	160	6089	129	0	20
Colorado	.973	162	4294	1760	167	6221	149	0	11
Totals	.978	1135	60854	24443	1876	87173	2028	4	199

Team Records

RBI	SH	SF	HP	BB	IBB	SO	SB	CS	GIDP	LOB	SHO	SLG	OBP
759	102	50	46	516	88	930	120	65	121	1155	5	.427	.340
811	**84**	**51**	**42**	**665**	**70**	**1049**	**91**	**32**	**107**	**1281**	**2**	**.426**	**.351**
704	70	52	46	388	40	944	146	90	125	978	13	.422	.323
724	59	54	27	588	50	882	153	72	128	1177	8	.395	.341
706	67	42	34	446	61	923	100	43	131	1133	10	.414	.325
664	76	52	55	536	50	972	92	55	129	1199	6	.393	.335
656	82	47	40	497	58	911	103	60	125	116	8	.409	.330
669	63	66	32	485	42	1025	142	59	104	1125	10	.396	.324
712	73	50	36	560	46	946	125	48	127	1165	9	.408	.331
639	107	47	27	492	48	937	126	61	105	1162	8	.383	.321
682	100	50	48	542	65	860	228	56	95	1166	5	.386	.326
633	80	50	59	443	43	1046	92	41	111	1090	8	.389	.312
632	89	47	24	448	43	879	79	50	108	1011	4	.390	.305
542	58	43	51	498	39	1054	1117	56	122	1183	14	.346	.314
9533	110	701	567	7104	743	13358	1714	788	1638	15941	110	.399	.327

H	R	ER	HR	HB	BB	IBB	SO	WP	BK	OPPAVG
1297	559	507	101	22	480	59	1036	46	9	.240
1363	630	559	117	41	476	52	1056	60	12	.251
1406	662	573	103	37	567	68	1043	47	20	.254
1369	682	574	119	47	521	38	934	46	12	.249
1385	636	585	168	50	442	46	982	33	18	.253
1419	**740**	**647**	**129**	**37**	**573**	**33**	**1117**	**74**	**7**	**.252**
1483	744	647	139	50	434	61	867	32	14	.269
1553	744	660	152	43	383	50	775	40	7	.276
1437	724	661	135	32	598	58	945	85	20	.261
1514	739	673	153	43	470	61	905	43	21	.273
1470	772	675	148	34	558	72	947	57	14	.266
1510	785	718	158	44	508	36	996	47	8	.272
1557	806	766	153	46	485	43	832	55	11	.280
1664	967	860	181	41	609	66	913	82	22	.294
20427	10190	9105	1956	567	7104	743	13358	747	195	.264

PHILLIES AMONG LEAGUE LEADERS

Hitting

Batting Average		
8	Kruk	.316

Runs		
1	Dykstra	143
T7	Hollins	104
10	Kruk	100

Doubles		
2	Dykstra	44

Stolen Bases		
10	Dykstra	37

On-Base Percentage		
2	Kruk	.430
3	Dykstra	.420
10	Daulton	.392

Grand Slams		
T2	Duncan	2
T2	Daulton	2

At-Bats		
1	Dykstra	637

Sacrifice Bunts		
T6	Rivera	13
T6	Schilling	13

Runs Batting In		
6	Daulton	105

Hits		
1	Dykstra	194

Total Bases		
T4	Dykstra	307

Triples		
T3	Morandini	9

Walks		
1	Dykstra	129
3	Daulton	117
4	Kruk	111

Extra Base Hits		
T4	Dykstra	69
10	Daulton	63

Hitting Streaks		
4	Duncan	18

Games Played		
T2	Dykstra	161

Pitching

Earned Run Average		
10	Mulholland	3.25

Saves		
T4	Williams	43

Games		
T2	West	76

Strikeouts		
4	Schilling	186
7	Greene	167

Winning Percentage		
2	Greene	.800
8	Schilling	.696

Wild Pitches		
1	Greene	15
T3	Rivera	13

Earned Runs		
3	Schilling	105

Wins		
T8	Schilling	16
T8	Greene	16

Complete Games		
T2	Schilling	7
T2	Greene	7
T2	Mulholland	7

Innings Pitched		
6	Schilling	235.1

Walks		
6	Rivera	85
7	Jackson	80

Games Finished		
5	Williams	57

Hits		
5	Schilling	234

Runs		
3	Schilling	114

*T designates a tie.

PHILLIES INDIVIDUAL HIGHLIGHTS

Larry Andersen

Phillies righthanded set-up man . . . Had staff's best strikeout-per-inning pitched ratio (67–61.2) . . . Was only scored upon in 22 of his 65 appearances . . . Had a 13.1 scoreless inning streak, 5/31–7/3 and a streak of 18.1 IP without allowing an earned run, 5/13–7/7 . . . Finished the season with a 12.2 walkless streak over 15 games . . . On DL, 5/8–26 with an inflammation in his right shoulder . . . Was 1–0, 1.14 ERA in 32 games at the Vet . . . Righthanders hit .199 against him.

Kim Batiste

Began season sharing shortstop duties with Juan Bell, ended up as back-up third baseman . . . Made 35 starts (20 at SS; 15 at 3B) and appeared in a total of 56 games at 3d and 24 at short . . . Had a career-high 4 hits, 6/2 at CIN (HR, 2B, 2 1B) . . . Hit his 1st career grand slam, 8/13 vs NY, the 4 RBI were also a career-high . . . Hit .349 (15–43) against lefthanders; .300 (24–80) at the Vet; .311, 21 RBI with runners in scoring position.

Wes Chamberlain

Platooned in right field with Eisenreich . . . Started 74 games (Phils were 47–27 in his starts) . . . Led club with 10 assists . . . Made just one error in his last 107 games . . . 34 of 80 hits went for extra-bases . . . Hit .328 against lefthanders; .310 at the Vet.

Darren Daulton

Led the team in RBI for the 2d straight season . . . Is 1st lefthanded Phillie to have consecutive 100 RBI seasons since Johnny Callison had 104 and 101 in 1964 and 1965 . . . Was the hardest player in the NL to double up (twice in 510 AB) and finished tied for 2d grand slams, 3d in walks, tied for 4th RBI/AB ratio (4.9), 6th in RBI, tied for 8th in intentional walks (12), tied for 9th in extra-base

Larry Andersen, in a 1933 uniform, was scored on in only 22 of his 65 appearances.

Wes Chamberlain led Phils outfielders with 10 assists.

hits, 10th in on-base percentage, and 10th in HR/AB ratio (21.3) . . . Is 1st Phillie catcher to reach 100 walks in a season . . . Had 4 two-HR games; most since Mike Schmidt had 5 in 1983 . . . Had 26 multiple RBI games, Phils were 18–8 in those games . . . Had a career-high 6 RBI, 7/28 vs STL, most by a Phil since Chamberlain had 6, 7/31/91 vs SD . . . Elected starting catcher for the 1st time, it was his 2d All-Star appearance . . . Threw out 33% (43 of 129) of runners attempting to steal . . . Started 143 of the 162 games.

Mariano Duncan

Made 110 starts, 48 at shortstop, 62 at second . . . Phillies were 70–40 in his starts . . . Hit 2 grand slams (2d and 3d of career), 5/9 vs STL and 9/28 at PIT . . . Tied his career-high 5 RBI, 9/28 at PIT . . . Had 73 RBI, surpassing previous career-high of 55, set in 1990 . . . On DL, 7/3–18 with a strained right hamstring . . . Had a career-best 18-game hit streak, 8/28–9/19, .355 (27–76); it was best on club and 4th best in NL . . . Also had a 13-game hitting streak, 5/21–6/8, .368 (21–57) . . . Hit .316, 60 RBI with runners in scoring position . . . Was suspended for 3 games, 9/20–22, for charging Frank Castillo, 9/9 vs CHI after nearly being hit by pitch, following a Dykstra HR.

Lenny Dykstra

Had a season worthy of MVP honors, scoring a ML-leading, career-high 143 runs, most in NL since 1932 when Chuck Klein led the NL with 152 . . . Phils

Jim Eisenreich had the highest batting average (.318) among regulars.

were 34–2 when he scored at least 2 runs . . . Also led the NL in hits, walks and at-bats; finished 2d in doubles, tied for 2d in games, 3d in on-base % (.420), tied for 4th in total bases (307), tied for 4th in extra-base hits (69), tied for 6th in multiple hit games (54), 9th hardest to fan (once every 12.1 AB), 9th hardest to double up (79.6) and 10th in stolen bases . . . Walked 129 times to break Mike Schmidt club record (128) set in 1963 . . . His 154 career stolen bases as a Phillie ranks him 8th all-time . . . Is the 1st NL player to reach base 300 times (via hit, walk, & HBP) in a season since Tony Gwynn in 1987 and just the 3d NL player since 1958 (Pete Rose did it 5 times) . . . Led team with 17 HR vs righthanders . . . Missed only one game all season, 9/29 at PIT.

Jim Eisenreich

Pinch-hitting role changed to platooning position, making 77 starts (Phils were 45–32 in those starts) . . . Had just 35 strikeouts in 392 plate appearances (once every 11.2) . . . 2d on club with career-high 152 games . . . Played 114 straight games without an error; has just one error in his last 228 games . . . Tied his career-best 13-game hit streak, .365 (19–52) . . . Set new career-highs in average, games and hits . . . Hit .322 vs righthanders; .327 at the Vet; .303, 47 RBI with runners in scoring position.

Tommy Greene

Went 1–1, 1.96 ERA, 3 BB, 17 SO in 7 spring training games, but still began season as Phils 5th starter . . . Made sole relief appearance, 4/9 vs CHI . . . Named NL Pitcher of the Week, 5/24–30, 2–0, 2 CG, 1.50 ERA, 3 BB, 13 SO . . . NL and Phillies Pitcher of the Month for May (led NL with 5–0 mark, 1.45 ERA), becoming 1st Phillie pitcher to win the award since Mitch Williams in August, 1991 and 1st starter since Shane Rawley, August, 1985 . . . Began the season 8–0, best start since Steve Carlton went 8–0 in 1981 . . . Had a streak of 5 straight CG, 5/12–6/5, most since Carlton had 6 straight in 1982 . . . Those 5 straight CG were all victories, Carlton was also last to do that in 1972 . . . Had a 21.0 walkless inning streak, 5/24–6/5 . . . Became 1st Phillie righty to win 11 games before the All-Star break since Jim Lonborg in 1976 . . . On the DL with a strained right groin, 7/28–8/12 . . . Pitched a staff-best 3-hitter and struck out a career-high 11, 9/3 at CIN . . . Hit in 5 straight games, .500, one HR, 6 RBI, 9/3–24 . . . Finished

Tommy Greene had the team's best winning percentage (.800).

2d among NL leaders in winning % (.800), tied for 2d in CG, tied for 3d in win streak (8 games), 5th in strikeouts per 9 IP (7.5), 7th in opponents average vs him (.233) and in strikeouts and tied for 8th in wins . . . Was one of 3 Phillies to pitch 200 innings; it was 2d time in career he reached the 200 mark . . . Phillies went 23–7 in his 30 starts; he went 10–0 in 16 games at the Vet and 9–1 in 15 starts vs the West.

Dave Hollins

Scored 104 runs, 2d to Dykstra on the team and 7th in the NL . . . He is the 1st Phillie with back-to-back 100-run seasons since Juan Samuel in 1984–85 . . . Also ranked 4th on the team in walks, tied for 6th in the NL . . . Tied his career-high with 93 RBI . . . Had 23 multiple RBI games . . . Collected a career-high 4 hits, 9/27 at PIT . . . 7 of his 18 HR went to the opposite field and 5 were game-winners . . . Phils went 14–4 when he homered . . . Selected to his 1st All-Star game, doubled in his only at-bat . . . On DL 6/11–28; had surgery to remove a fractured hook of the hamate bone in his right wrist . . . Returned to action an amazing 2 weeks later.

Pete Incaviglia

Platooned with Thompson in left field . . . Had 86 starts (80 in LF, 6 in RF) . . . Missed 6 games with a strained left calf, sustained when running the bases, 9/14 at NY . . . Had career-high 11-game hit streak, 8/17–9/3, .474 (18–38), 3 HR, 11 RBI . . . Knocked in a career-high 89 runs; had 88 RBI in 1986 with Texas . . . Has club's best AB-per-RBI ratio (4.1), AB-per-HR ratio (4.1), AB-per-HR ratio (15.3) and leads club in slugging % . . . Hit 304, 66 RBI with runners in scoring position.

Danny Jackson

Pitched over 200 innings for the 5th time in his career and 2d straight . . . Threw a 3–0 CG on 6/12 at NY, his 1st CG since 7/18/89 vs PHI and 1st shutout since 9/4/88 at CHI . . . Threw his 2d CG, 7/31 vs PIT . . . Missed one start in August with a sore rib cage . . . Allowed 12 home runs, but only one in his last 11 starts (72.2 IP) . . . Struck out a season-high 8, 8/29 vs CIN . . . Donated $18,000 ($500 per win, $100 per SO) to the People's Emergency Center for homeless women and children in Philadelphia.

Ricky Jordan had the most Phillies pinch-hits (16) since 1982.

Ricky Jordan

Led the team with 16 pinch-hits; most for a Phillie since Greg Gross had 18 in 1982 and most by a righthander since Tony Taylor had 17 in 1974 . . . Has a .307 (39–127) career pinch-hitting average . . . Made 24 starts, all at 1st base, 5 HR, 13 RBI . . . Had made just 2 errors in his last 79 games in the field . . . Hit .300 (27–90) vs righthanders; .317 (26–82) at the Vet.

John Kruk

NL's 1st Player of the Week, 4/5–11, .476, 2 HR, 5 RBI . . . Finished 2d in the NL with a .430 on-base percentage, 4th in walks, 8th in average and 10th in runs . . . His average has not dipped below .309 at any point since ending the 1991 season at .294 . . . Had 2 career-high 5-hit games, 5/17 at FLA and 7/27 vs STL; also had 16 3-hit games and 1 4-hit game . . . Has the Phillies best all-time on-base percentage, .397; Richie Ashburn is 2d, .394 . . . His .310 (710–2292) career average as a Phillie is 9th on club's all-time list . . . Elected starting 1st baseman for the All-Star Game; it was his 1st start, 3d appearance . . . Missed the final 2 games of the season with lower back stiffness.

Tony Longmire

Hit .304, 136 H, 6 HR, 67 RBI in 120 games for AAA Scranton . . . Set a Scranton record with 36 doubles . . . Selected as an in-season and post-season International League All-Star . . . Recalled 8/31 . . . Pinch-hit single off Jose Rijo was the 1st hit of his career, 9/4 at CIN . . . His 1st ML run was a game-winner in 12th inning, 9/22 vs FLA . . . Started 1st ML game 9/29 at PIT . . . Got 1st ML RBI with pinch-single, 10/1 at STL.

Roger Mason

Was 0–7, 3.24 ERA in 34 games with the Padres . . . 5–5 in 34 games as a Phillies . . . Struck out a season-high 4 batters, twice, 4/20 vs PHI and 6/4 vs FLA . . . Traded to Phillies, 7/3 for Tim Mauser . . . Earned 1st win of the season as a Phillie, 7/19 at LA . . . He combined on 2 shutouts with the Phils: with Greene, 7/21 at LA and with Jackson, 8/29 vs CIN . . . Pitched a season-high 4.0 innings with Phils, 7/9 vs SF.

Mickey Morandini

Finished 2d among NL second basemen with a .990 fielding % . . . Had a 66-game errorless streak snapped, 9/25 vs ATL (1st error since 5/31 at CIN) . . . Had 100 starts at second base . . . Led club and finished tied for 3d with 9 triples . . . Hit 1st career grand slam and had career-high 5 RBI, 7/10 vs SF; it was 1st slam by Phillie 2d baseman since Juan Samuel hit one 8/12/87 vs CHI . . . Had a career-high 12-game streak, 8/27–9/29 . . . Had 13 stolen bases in 15 attempts; 37–44 lifetime.

Terry Mulholland, who was traded early in 1994 to the New York Yankees, tied for the team lead in shutouts and complete games.

Terry Mulholland

Phillies Opening Day starter for the 3d straight season and won for the 1st time, 3–1, 4/5 at HOU . . . Threw back-to-back CG victories, 5/2 at LA and 5/8 vs STL . . . Pitched a career-high 10.0 innings in his 3d CG of the season, 5/8 vs STL; Steve Carlton was the last Phillie to go that distance, 8/12/82 at HOU . . . Missed a start in May with an inflamed left foot which limited his play on 5/14 at ATL . . . Threw the 1st SHO ever at Mile High Stadium, 5/29 at COL . . . Struck out a career-high 14, 6/4 vs COL; it was 4th time in his career he has had a 10+ strikeout game and the most by a Phillie since Carlton, 9/21/82 at STL . . . 14 SO was also the most by a NL pitcher in a 9.0 inning game . . . Named NL starter for the All-Star game; it was also his 1st All-Star appearance . . . Allowed 3 HR in a game for the 1st time in his career 8/8 at FLA . . . Pitched to just 3 batters 9/6 vs CHI, had to leave the game with a left hip flexer strain . . . Did not pitch again until 9/30 at PIT when he threw 1 inning in relief . . . Finished tied for 2d in the NL in CG, tied for 3d in shutouts, tied for 6th with fewest walks per 9.0 innings (1.9) and 10th in ERA . . . Donated $24,000 ($2,000 per win) to the Philadelphia Department of Recreation to expand baseball programs in the city.

Todd Pratt

This was his 1st full season as Daulton's back-up . . . Phils were 12–7 in his 19 starts . . . Had 5 HR and 11 RBI when started . . . On DL, 4/28–5/26 with a sprained right ankle . . . 4 of his 5 HR were hit to the opposite field . . . Went .353 (18–51), 4 HR and 10 RBI in the 2d half . . . Had 1st career 2-HR game, 8/1 vs PIT; also had career-high 3 hits . . . Hit .318, 8 RBI with runners in scoring position . . . Hit in 8 of last 10 games, .419 (13–31) with 7 extra-base hits.

Ben Rivera

Because of rain and off days early in the season, made a start in extended spring training, 5/6 . . . Was 1st Phillie pitcher to face the expansion teams and won both, 10–3, 5/17 at FLA and 15–9, 5/28 at COL . . . Struck out a career-high 9, 6/2 at CIN and 8/31 at CHI . . . Won 5 straight games, 6/13–7/4 . . . Scratched from start, 7/19 at LA, after suffering a contusion of the rt. index finger during B.P. . . . Threw 1st CG SHO of season, 8/31 at CHI, winning 7–0 . . . His 13 wins are the most he has had in any professional season . . . Had 13 successful sacrifice bunts, tied for 6th best in the NL.

Ben Rivera set a career high with 13 wins.

Curt Schilling

Phillies Player of the Month for April, 4–1, 2.54 ERA, 2 CG SHO and September, 4–1, 3.47, 35 SO . . . Tied for NL lead with 1.000 fielding % . . . Also finished tied for 2d in the NL in CG, tied for 3d in shutouts, 4th in strikeouts, 5th in innings, 7th in strikeouts per 9.0 IP (7.1), 8th in winning % (.696), tied for 8th in wins and tied for 9th with fewest walks per 9–0 IP (2.2) . . . Set a new career-high with 235.1 IP; 2d straight season he reached the 200 IP mark . . . Had 11 games with at least 7 SO; 15 with at least 6 and 20 with a min. of 5 . . . Had a career-best 7-game win streak, 7/18–9/20 . . . Also had 6-game win streak, 4/23–6/11 and 5-game losing streak, 6/21–7/11 . . . Initiated "Curt's Pitch for ALS" and donated $15,060 to the cause.

Kevin Stocker

Hit .233, 54 R, 73 H, 17 RBI in 83 games at AAA Scranton . . . Made his ML debut 7/7 vs LA (played all 20 innings) . . . Earned his 1st ML hit, 7/8 vs SF off Bill Swift and hit his 1st HR in the same game, off Rod Beck . . . Had 2 10-game hit streaks in his first 33 games, 7/18–8/5 and 8/12–22 . . . Had 5 three-hit games . . . Joined the team in early July, but managed to lead the team and finish tied for 9th in the NL with 8 hit by pitches.

Bobby Thigpen

Opened season ranking 14th on all-time save list . . . His 193 saves over last 6 seasons were 2d only to Eckersley over that stretch . . . Began season in bullpen with CHI Sox, but not as closer . . . Earned only save of season 5/16 at TEX . . . Finished 11 games for Sox . . . Was 0–0, 5.71, 1 SV with Sox before traded to Phillies, 8/10 for Jose DeLeon . . . Made his Phillies & NL debut, 8/13 vs NY, winning his 1st NL game, 1.0 IP, 1 SO . . . Finished 5 games for Phillies.

Milt Thompson

Platooned with Incaviglia in left field . . . Finished tied for 2d on club with 6 outfield assists . . . Made just one error in his last 125 games . . . Threw out 2 runners at the plate, 5/16 at ATL . . . Was on base (via hit, walk or HBP) in 68 of 79 starts (Phils were 49–30 in his starts) . . . Had 3 hits and made an excellent catch of a potential grand slam, 4/29 at SD . . . Hit .320 (8–25) as a pinch-hitter; .293, 36 RBI with runners in scoring position.

David West

First full season in the bullpen . . . Finished tied for 2d in the NL with 76 appearances, a new Phillies record for a lefthander . . . Don Carman held the previous record of 71, set in 1985 . . . His 76 appearances this year matched his career total . . . Earned 1st ML save, 4/18 at CHI . . . Had a total of 3 saves . . . Led Phillies bullpen in wins, appearances, IP, and strikeouts . . . Phillies Player of the Month for July, 2–0, 0.87 ERA in 15 appearances . . . Had a 13.1 scoreless inning streak, 4/14–5/14 . . . Opponents hit just .194 against him.

Mitch Williams

Set a new Phillies record with 43 saves . . . Steve Bedrosian held the old record, 40 saves in 1987 . . . His 102 career saves as a Phillies puts him in 2d place on the all-time list behind Bedrosian (103) . . . Finished 4th among NL leaders with 43 saves and 5th with 57 finished games . . . 51 of his 65 appearances were save situations . . . Converted 13 straight save opportunities, 7/18–8/24 . . . Earned a save in 4 of his last 5 appearances.

PHILLIES WINNINGEST SEASONS

Year	W	L	Pct.	Finish	GA/B
1976	101	61	.623	1	9
1977	101	61	.623	1	5
1993	97	65	.599	1	3
1899	94	58	.617	3	9
1964	92	70	.568	2T	1
1916	91	62	.594	2	2½
1950	91	63	.589	1	2
1980	91	71	.562	1	1
1915	90	62	.592	1	7
1983	90	72	.556	1	6
1978	90	72	.556	1	1½
1982	89	73	.549	2	3
1913	88	63	.579	2	12½
1917	87	65	.571	2	10
1892	87	66	.568	4	16½
1952	87	67	.565	4	9½
1963	87	75	.537	4	12
1966	87	75	.537	4	8

PHILLIES' PAST WINNERS

1915: 90–62–1   7 GA

Regular Season—Clinched pennant on September 29 with 5–0 win over the Boston Braves in Boston.

World Series—Lost to Boston Red Sox, four games to one after winning the first game at Baker Bowl.

1950: 91–63   2 GA

Regular Season—Won pennant October 1 with 4–1 victory over the Brooklyn Dodgers in 10 innings at Ebbets Field.

World Series—Lost in four straight games to the New York Yankees, losing the first three by one run each.

1976: 101–61   9 GA

Regular Season—Clinched NL East division title September 26 with 4–1 victory over the Montreal Expos at Montreal.

LCS—Lost all three games to Cincinnati Reds in best-of-three series.

1977: 101–61   5 GA

Regular Season—Captured NL East title with 15–9 victory over the Chicago Cubs on September 27 at Wrigley Field.

LCS—After winning the first game, lost three straight to the Los Angeles Dodgers.

1978: 90–72   1¹/₂ GA

Regular Season—Claimed division flag on September 20 with 10–8 victory over the Pittsburgh Pirates at Three Rivers Stadium.

LCS—Lost three out of four games to the Los Angeles Dodgers.

1980: 91–71   1 GA

Regular Season—Clinched flag on October 4 at Montreal with 6–4 victory over the Expos in 11 innings.

LCS—Won three out of five from the Houston Astros, coming from behind, 5–2, in the eighth to win the final game, 8–7, in 10 innings.

World Series—Captured the Phillies' first World Championship by defeating the Kansas City Royals four games to two, winning the final game, 4–1, at Veterans Stadium.

1983: 90–72   6 GA

Regular Season—Gained division title September 28 with 13–6 win over the Chicago Cubs at Wrigley Field.

LCS—Won three out of four with the Los Angeles Dodgers to take club's fourth NL pennant, winning the last game, 7–2, at the Vet.

World Series—A first-game victory was followed by four straight losses to the Baltimore Orioles.

PHILLIES KEY GAMES

PHILLIES GET THEIR FIRST OPENING DAY WIN SINCE 1984

April 5—Phillies 3, Astros 1

PHILLIES	AB	R	H	RBI
Dykstra, cf	4	0	0	0
Morandini, 2b	4	0	1	0
Kruk, 1b	2	2	1	0
Hollins, 3b	4	0	1	0
Daulton, c	3	1	1	1
Thompson, lf	3	0	0	0
Incaviglia, lf	1	0	1	1
Eisenreich, rf	4	0	1	1
J. Bell, ss	4	0	0	0
Mulholland, p	3	0	0	0
Totals	**32**	**3**	**6**	**3**

Houston	AB	R	H	RBI
Biggio, 2b	4	1	1	0
Finley, cf	4	0	0	0
Bagwell, 1b	3	0	0	0
Anthony, rf	4	0	1	0
Caminiti, 3b	4	0	1	0
Gonzalez, lf	4	0	0	0
Cedeno, ss	3	0	0	0
Taubensee, c	3	0	0	0
Drabek, p	2	0	0	0
James, ph	1	0	1	0
Parker, pr	0	0	0	0
Hernandez, p	0	0	0	0
E. Bell, p	0	0	0	0
Totals	**32**	**1**	**4**	**0**

PHILLIES	000	200	001 – 3
Houston	100	000	000 – 1

E—J. Bell 2 (2), Taubensee (1). DP—PHILLIES 1, Houston 1. LOB—PHILLIES 5, Houston 5. 2B—Kruk (1), Daulton (1), James (1). SB—Morandini (1). CS—Kruk (1).

PHILLIES	IP	H	R	ER	BB	SO
Mulholland (W, 1–0)	9	4	1	0	1	3

Houston	IP	H	R	ER	BB	SO
Drabek (L, 0–1)	8	4	2	2	2	7
Hernandez	1/3	1	1	1	1	0
E. Bell	2/3	1	0	0	0	0

Time—2:19. Attendance—44,560.

EIGHT HOME RUNS, TWO BY DAULTON, HIT IN HOME OPENER LOSS TO CUBS

April 9—Cubs 11, Phillies 7

Chicago	AB	R	H	RBI
Wilson, cf	5	1	1	0
Sanchez, ss	4	1	0	0
Grace, 1b	4	3	2	2
May, lf	4	3	3	5
Sosa, rf	4	1	2	0
Buechele, 3b	5	0	2	1
Wilkins, c	4	1	0	0
Vizcaino, 2b	5	1	1	3
Castillo, p	2	0	1	0
McElroy, p	1	0	0	0
Assenmacher, p	1	0	1	0
Myers, p	0	0	0	0
Totals	**39**	**11**	**11**	**14**

PHILLIES	AB	R	H	RBI
Dykstra, cf	4	1	1	1
Morandini, 2b	5	0	2	0
Kruk, 1b	4	2	2	1
Hollins, 3b	4	2	1	0
Daulton, c	4	2	2	5
Thompson, lf	3	0	0	0
Incaviglia, rf	4	0	1	0
Bell, ss	3	0	0	0
West, p	0	0	0	0
Jordan, ph	1	0	1	0
Green, p	0	0	0	0
Rivera, p	1	0	0	0
Greene, p	0	0	0	0
Chamberlain, ph	1	0	0	0
DeLeon, p	0	0	0	0
Duncan, ss	2	0	0	0
Totals	**36**	**7**	**10**	**7**

```
Chicago    033  000  302 – 11
PHILLIES   301  010  020 – 7
```

E—Wilkins (1). DP—Chicago 1, PHILLIES 1. LOB—Chicago 6, PHILLIES 6. 2B—Wilson (4), Kruk (5). 3B—Sosa (1). HR—Dykstra (1), Kruk (1), Daulton 2 (3), Grace (1), May 2 (2), Vizcaino (1). SB—Thompson (1).

Chicago	IP	H	R	ER	BB	SO
Castillo	4^1/$_3$	5	5	5	2	2
McElroy (W, 1–0)	1^2/$_3$	1	0	0	1	4
Assenmacher	1^2/$_3$	4	2	2	0	2
Myers (S, 1)	1^1/$_3$	0	0	0	1	2

PHILLIES	IP	H	R	ER	BB	SO
Rivera (L, 0–1)	2^1/$_3$	7	6	6	2	1
Greene	2^2/$_3$	1	0	0	0	1
DeLeon	1^1/$_3$	1	1	1	0	2
West	1^2/$_3$	2	2	2	1	4
Green	1	2	2	2	2	1

WP—West. Time—3:06. Attendance—60,985.

PHILS SWEEP REDS FOR FIRST TIME AT HOME SINCE 1968

April 14—Phillies 9, Reds 2

Cincinnati	AB	R	H	RBI
Samuel, 2b	5	1	0	0
Kelly, cf	4	0	1	0
Larkin, ss	3	0	1	0
Sabo, 3b	4	0	0	0
Milligan, 1b	2	0	1	0
Varsho, lf	2	0	0	0
Kaiser, p	0	0	0	0
Cadaret, p	0	0	0	0
Roberts, ph	1	0	0	0
Reardon, p	0	0	0	0
Sanders, rf	3	0	0	0
Oliver, c	4	1	2	0
Browning, p	2	0	0	0
Landrum, p	0	0	0	0
Espy, lf	2	0	1	0
Totals	**32**	**2**	**6**	**0**

PHILLIES	AB	R	H	RBI
Dykstra, cf	5	2	2	0
Duncan, 2b	5	2	3	0
Kruk, 1b	5	0	1	1
Hollins, 3b	5	1	2	2
Daulton, c	4	2	1	0
Incaviglia, lf	5	1	2	3
Chamberlain, rf	4	1	3	1
Eisenreich, rf	1	0	0	0
Bell, ss	4	0	2	2
Rivera, p	2	0	0	0
DeLeon, p	0	0	0	0
Jordan, ph	0	0	0	0
West, p	0	0	0	0
Totals	**40**	**9**	**16**	**9**

```
Cincinnati    000  000  200 – 2
PHILLIES      002  041  02x – 9
```

E—Milligan (2), Daulton (1). DP—PHILLIES 1. LOB—Cincinnati 9, PHILLIES 10. 2B—Dykstra (3), Duncan (1), Daulton (2), Bell (3). SB—Dykstra (5), Duncan (1). S—Rivera.

Cincinnati	IP	H	R	ER	BB	SO
Browning (L, 0–2)	$4^2/_3$	9	5	5	1	5
Landrum	$^1/_3$	2	1	1	0	0
Kaiser	1	2	1	1	0	1
Cadaret	1	1	0	0	1	1
Reardon	1	2	2	0	0	1

PHILLIES	IP	H	R	ER	BB	SO
Rivera (W, 1–1)	6	4	0	0	4	7
DeLeon	1	2	2	2	1	1
West	2	0	0	0	0	2

WP—DeLeon 2. Time—2:43. Attendance—21,111.

Hollins' three-run homer wins in 11th inning

April 18—Phillies 11, Cubs 10 (11)

PHILLIES	AB	R	H	RBI
Dykstra, cf	6	1	1	0
Duncan, 2b	5	3	3	1
Kruk, 1b	5	3	2	4
Hollins, 3b	6	1	3	3
Daulton, c	4	1	1	0
Chamberlain, rf	4	2	3	3
Eisenreich, rf	1	0	0	0
Incaviglia, lf	6	0	0	0
DeLeon, p	0	0	0	0
West, p	0	0	0	0
Batiste, ss	5	0	1	0
Jackson, p	3	0	0	0
Andersen, p	1	0	1	0
MDavis, p	0	0	0	0
Williams, p	0	0	0	0
Thompson, lf	1	0	0	0
Totals	**47**	**11**	**15**	**11**

Chicago	AB	R	H	RBI
Wilson, cf	5	1	1	1
McElroy, p	1	0	0	0
Scanlan, p	0	0	0	0
Myers, ph	1	0	0	0
Sanchez, ss	5	1	3	0
Grace, 1b	4	0	1	1
May, lf	5	1	2	1
Sosa, rf	5	0	0	0
Buechele, 3b	4	3	1	1
Vizcaino, 2b	2	0	1	0
Plesac, p	0	0	0	0
Smith, ph	0	1	0	0
Shields, 2b	2	1	1	0
Lake, c	3	0	0	0
Walbeck, c	3	1	2	3
Hibbard, p	2	0	0	0
Bautista, p	0	0	0	0
Yelding, 2b	1	0	0	0
Wilkins, ph	0	0	0	0
Maldonado, lf	3	1	2	3
Totals	**46**	**10**	**14**	**10**

PHILLIES	201	002	120	03 – 11
Chicago	000	000	224	02 – 10

E—Batiste (1). DP—PHILLIES 1, Chicago 1. LOB—PHILLIES 8, Chicago 12. 2B—Dykstra (4), Duncan (2), Hollins (4), Daulton (3), Chamberlain (2), May (1). HR—Kruk 2 (4), Hollins (1), Chamberlain 2 (2), Buechele (1), Walbeck (1), Maldonado (1). SB—Wilson (2), May (2), Buechele (1). S—Grace. WP – Williams.

PHILLIES	IP	H	R	ER	BB	SO
Jackson	6²/₃	5	2	2	4	0
Andersen	¹/₃	2	2	2	1	1
Davis	1¹/₃	2	2	2	1	0
Williams (W, 1–0)	1²/₃	3	2	2	0	2
DeLeon	¹/₃	2	2	2	1	0
West (S, 1)	²/₃	0	0	0	0	0

Chicago	IP	H	R	ER	BB	SO
Hibbard	5²/₃	6	5	5	2	2
Bautista	1	2	1	1	0	1
Plesac	1¹/₃	3	2	2	1	1
McElroy	2	1	0	0	0	2
Scanlan (L, 0–2)	1	3	3	3	2	1

Andersen pitched to 3 batters in the 8th.
Time—3:36. Attendance—28,758.

KRUK HOMERS IN 14TH TO BEAT PADRES

April 20—Phillies 4, Padres 3 (14)

San Diego	AB	R	H	RBI	PHILLIES	AB	R	H	RBI
Gardner, 2b	4	0	2	1	Dykstra, cf	6	1	2	0
Sherman, pr	0	0	0	0	Morandini, 2b	4	0	1	0
Scott, p	0	0	0	0	Incaviglia, rf	3	0	0	0
Rodriguez, p	0	0	0	0	Kruk, 1b	6	2	2	1
Gutierrez, ss	1	0	0	0	Hollins, 3b	5	0	0	0
Gwynn, rf	6	0	0	0	Daulton, c	6	1	2	1
Sheffield, 3b	6	1	1	0	Chamberlain, rf	4	0	1	0
McGriff, 1b	3	0	1	1	Williams, p	0	0	0	0
Plantier, lf	6	1	1	0	Andersen, p	0	0	0	0
D. Bell, cf	5	0	0	0	Jordan, ph	1	0	0	0
Shipley, ss	5	1	2	1	West, p	0	0	0	0
Walters, c	4	0	0	0	Pratt, ph	1	0	0	0
Eiland, p	2	0	0	0	Ayrault, p	0	0	0	0
Gomez, p	0	0	0	0	Thompson, lf	5	0	1	0
Valesquez, ph	1	0	0	0	Batiste, ss	6	0	1	1
Teufel, 2b	1	0	0	0	Greene, p	3	0	0	0
Mason, p	0	0	0	0	Davis, p	0	0	0	0
Clark, ph	1	0	0	0	Eisenreich, rf	0	0	0	0
Hernandez, p	0	0	0	0	Duncan, 2b	3	0	0	0
Totals	**45**	**3**	**7**	**3**	**Totals**	**53**	**4**	**10**	**3**

```
San Diego   010  000  011  000  00 – 3
PHILLIES    000  120  000  000  01 – 4
```

Two outs when winning run scored. E—Sheffield 2 (6), D. Bell (1), Williams (1). DP—PHILLIES 3. LOB—San Diego 5, PHILLIES 12. 2B—Gardner (3), Plantier (1), Shipley (5), Chamberlain (3). HR—Kruk (5). SB—Gwynn 2 (7), McGriff (2), Dykstra (6). CS—McGriff (1).

San Diego	IP	H	R	ER	BB	SO
Eiland	5²/₃	8	3	3	3	2
Gomez	1¹/₃	0	0	0	0	1
Scott	1	0	0	0	0	2
Rodriguez	1²/₃	0	0	0	0	2
Mason	2¹/₃	0	0	0	1	4
Hernandez (L, 0–2)	1²/₃	2	1	1	0	3

PHILLIES	IP	H	R	ER	BB	SO
Greene	7²/₃	5	2	2	2	9
Davis	¹/₃	0	0	0	0	0
Williams	1	2	1	0	0	1
Andersen	1	0	0	0	0	1
West	3	0	0	0	1	4
Ayrault (W, 1–0)	1	0	0	0	2	1

PB—Walters. Time—4:27. Attendance—21,074.

Phils overcome 8–0 deficit to beat Giants in 10 innings

April 26—Phillies 9, Giants 8 (10)

San Francisco	AB	R	H	RBI
McGee, rf	6	1	2	0
Martinez, cf	5	0	2	2
Lewis, cf	2	0	0	0
Clark, 1b	4	0	0	0
Williams, 3b	4	1	0	0
Bonds, lf	2	2	0	0
R. Thompson, 2b	2	2	0	0
Reed, c	1	0	0	0
Clayton, ss	6	1	2	2
Manwaring, c	1	0	0	1
Benjamin, 2b	2	0	0	0
Brantley, p	4	1	2	2
Hickerson, p	0	0	0	0
Rogers, p	0	0	0	0
Jackson, p	0	0	0	0
Carreon, ph	0	0	0	0
Righetti, p	0	0	0	0
Beck, p	0	0	0	0
Benzinger, ph	1	0	1	0
Minutelli, p	0	0	0	0
Totals	**40**	**8**	**9**	**7**

PHILLIES	AB	R	H	RBI
Dykstra, cf	5	1	0	0
Morandini, 2b	5	2	2	0
Kruk, 1b	2	0	1	0
Eisenreich, 1b	3	2	3	2
Hollins, 3b	3	1	0	1
Daulton, c	3	2	0	0
Incaviglia, rf	4	0	1	2
M. Thompson, lf	5	0	2	2
Duncan, ss	3	0	2	1
Batiste, ss	2	0	0	0
Andersen, p	0	0	0	0
Rivera, p	1	0	0	0
DeLeon, p	0	0	0	0
Jordan, ph	1	0	0	0
Ayrault, p	0	0	0	0
Chamberlain, ph	1	0	0	0
Davis, p	0	0	0	0
Pratt, ph	1	0	0	0
West, p	0	0	0	0
Bell, ss	0	1	0	0
Totals	**39**	**9**	**11**	**8**

```
San Francisco   022  202  000   0 – 8
PHILLIES        000  003  410   1 – 9
```

Two outs when winning run scored. E—Clayton (7), Benjamin (1). Hollins 3 (3). DP—San Francisco 1. LOB—San Francisco 18, PHILLIES 10. 2B—McGee (3), Martinez (2), Morandini (4), Duncan (3). 3B—Clayton (1), Morandini (1). CS—Martinez (1). SF—Manwaring, Hollins.

San Francisco	IP	H	R	ER	BB	SO
Brantley	5 1/3	4	3	3	3	1
Hickerson	2/3	2	0	0	0	0
Rogers	1/3	1	4	3	3	0
Jackson	2/3	1	0	0	0	0
Righetti	1/3	2	1	1	0	0
Beck	1 2/3	0	0	0	0	4
Minutelli (L, 0–1)	2/3	1	1	0	1	0

PHILLIES	IP	H	R	ER	BB	SO
Rivera	2 2/3	3	4	2	6	4
DeLeon	2 1/3	2	2	1	3	2
Ayrault	1	2	2	2	1	2
Davis	1	1	0	0	1	0
West	2	0	0	0	3	3
Andersen (W, 1–0)	1	1	0	0	0	2

HBP—Incaviglia by Brantley, Manwaring by Ayrault. WP—Brantley 2, Hickerson, Minutelli. Time—4:33. Attendance—17,170.

Thompson's three hits, game-saving catch downs Padres

April 29—Phillies 5, Padres 3

PHILLIES	AB	R	H	RBI
Dykstra, cf	5	1	1	1
Duncan, 2b	3	0	0	0
Jordan, 1b	4	1	0	0
Hollins, 3b	5	0	2	0
Daulton, c	2	1	0	0
Chamberlain, rf	4	1	1	0
Eisenreich, rf	1	0	0	0
Thompson, lf	4	1	3	2
J. Bell, ss	4	0	1	2
Jackson, p	3	0	1	0
Andersen, p	0	0	0	0
West, p	0	0	0	0
Williams, p	0	0	0	0
Totals	**35**	**5**	**9**	**5**

San Diego	AB	R	H	RBI
Shipley, ss	5	0	0	0
Gwynn, rf	5	1	1	0
Sheffield, 3b	4	1	1	0
McGriff, 1b	2	0	1	0
D. Bell, cf	3	0	0	0
Velasquez, lf	1	0	1	2
Teufel, 2b	3	1	1	0
Gardner, ph	0	0	0	0
Gutierrez, 2b	0	0	0	0
Clark, lf	4	0	2	1
Geren, c	4	0	1	0
Seminara, p	1	0	0	0
Stillwell, ph	1	0	0	0
Scott, p	0	0	0	0
Walters, ph	1	0	0	0
Hernandez, p	0	0	0	0
Sherman, ph	1	0	0	0
Totals	**35**	**3**	**8**	**3**

```
PHILLIES      104  000  000 – 5
San Diego     000  000  120 – 3
```

E—Hollins (4), Shipley (2). DP—PHILLIES 1. LOB—PHILLIES 10, San Diego 8. 2B—Hollins (6), J. Bell (4), Clark (1). 3B—Teufel (1). HR—Dykstra (3). SB—Sheffield (4). CS—Duncan (1), McGriff (2). S—Jackson.

PHILLIES	IP	H	R	ER	BB	SO
Jackson (W, 2–0)	7 1/3	7	3	2	2	4
Andersen	0	1	0	0	0	0
West	2/3	0	0	0	1	0
Williams (S, 9)	1	0	0	0	0	1

San Diego	IP	H	R	ER	BB	SO
Seminara (L, 1–2)	5	8	5	1	3	3
Scott	2	1	0	0	1	3
Hernandez	2	0	0	0	0	0

Andersen pitched to 1 batter in the 8th. HBP—Duncan by Seminara, Jordan by Seminara. Time—2:43. Attendance—14,399.

Mulholland goes 10 innings to defeat Cardinals

May 8—Phillies 2, Cardinals 1 (10)

St. Louis	AB	R	H	RBI		PHILLIES	AB	R	H	RBI
Pena, 2b	4	0	1	0		Dykstra, cf	4	0	0	0
O. Smith, ss	5	0	1	0		Duncan, ss	4	0	0	0
Jefferies, 1b	4	0	1	0		Kruk, 1b	3	0	0	0
Zeile, 3b	4	0	0	0		Hollins, 3b	4	0	1	0
Whiten, rf	4	1	3	0		Daulton, c	4	0	0	0
Lankford, cf	4	0	2	0		Incaviglia, lf	4	1	1	0
Canseco, lf	4	0	2	0		Thompson, pr	0	1	0	0
Villanueva, c	4	0	0	1		Chamberlain, rf	4	0	2	1
Cormier, p	2	0	0	0		Morandini, 2b	3	0	1	0
Woodson, ph	1	0	0	0		Mulholland, p	3	0	0	0
Perez, p	0	0	0	0		Eisenreich, ph	0	0	0	0
Murphy, p	0	0	0	0		Jordan, ph	1	0	1	1
Totals	**36**	**1**	**10**	**1**		**Totals**	**34**	**2**	**6**	**2**

```
St. Louis     010  000  000   0 – 1
PHILLIES      000  010  000   1 – 2
```

One out when winning run scored. E—Zeile (7). DP—St. Louis 1, PHILLIES 3. LOB—St. Louis 7, PHILLIES 6. 2B—Pena (5), Incaviglia (1), Chamberlain (6). SB—Thompson (3). CS—Jefferies (2), Whiten (4). S—Cormier.

St. Louis	IP	H	R	ER	BB	SO
Cormier	9	5	1	1	1	5
Perez (L, 2–2)	1/3	0	1	0	1	1
Murphy	0	1	0	0	0	0

PHILLIES	IP	H	R	ER	BB	SO
Mulholland (W, 4–3)	10	10	1	1	1	6

Time—2:38. Attendance—40,524.

DUNCAN RIPS EIGHTH INNING GRAND SLAM AGAINST LEE SMITH AS PHILS SWEEP CARDS

May 9—Phillies 6, Cardinals 5

St. Louis	AB	R	H	RBI
Lankford, cf	4	1	1	0
O. Smith, ss	5	0	0	0
Jefferies, 1b	4	1	2	3
Whiten, rf	4	0	0	0
Zeile, 3b	4	2	1	0
L. Smith, p	0	0	0	0
Alicea, 2b	4	0	3	2
Canseco, lf	3	0	0	0
Brewer, lf	1	0	0	0
Villanueva, c	4	0	0	0
Tewksbury, p	3	1	1	0
Woodson, 3b	1	0	0	0
Totals	**37**	**5**	**8**	**5**

PHILLIES	AB	R	H	RBI
Dykstra, cf	4	1	2	0
Morandini, 2b	3	0	0	0
Kruk, 1b	4	0	1	1
Hollins, 3b	4	0	0	0
Daulton, c	4	2	3	0
Chamberlain, rf	4	1	1	0
Eisenreich, rf	0	0	0	0
Thompson, lf	3	1	1	1
Duncan, ss	4	1	1	4
Schilling, p	2	0	0	0
Incaviglia, ph	1	0	1	0
Davis, p	0	0	0	0
Bell, ph	1	0	0	0
Williams, p	0	0	0	0
Totals	**34**	**6**	**10**	**6**

St. Louis	003	101	000 – 5
PHILLIES	100	100	04x – 6

E—Zeile (8), Hollins (6), Duncan (2). LOB—St. Louis 6, PHILLIES 6. 2B—Zeile (8), Alicea (1), Dykstra (6), Daulton (4), Chamberlain (7). HR—Jefferies (6), Duncan (2). SB—O. Smith (5), Kruk (2), Thompson 2 (5). S—Morandini.

St. Louis	IP	H	R	ER	BB	SO
Tewksbury	7²/₃	9	4	4	0	5
L. Smith (L, 0–1)	¹/₃	1	2	2	1	1

PHILLIES	IP	H	R	ER	BB	SO
Schilling	7	6	5	4	1	6
Davis (W, 1–0)	1	1	0	0	0	2
Williams (S, 13)	1	1	0	0	0	1

Time—2:33. Attendance—43,648.

Phils' first meeting with Marlins features 17 hits, five by Kruk

May 17—Phillies 10, Marlins 3

PHILLIES	AB	R	H	RBI
Dykstra, cf	5	1	1	0
Morandini, 2b	6	1	1	0
Kruk 1b	6	3	5	2
Hollins, 3b	6	3	3	1
Daulton, c	5	1	1	1
Eisenreich, rf	3	1	3	2
Thompson, lf	4	0	2	2
Duncan, ss	4	0	0	2
Rivera, p	2	0	0	0
Ayrault, p	1	0	0	0
West, p	1	0	1	0
Totals	**43**	**10**	**17**	**10**

Florida	AB	R	H	RBI
Carr, cf	5	0	1	1
Felix, rf	4	0	0	0
Magadan, 3b	2	0	1	0
Destrade, 1b	5	1	0	0
Santiago, c	3	0	0	1
Conine, lf	4	0	0	0
Arias, 2b	4	1	4	1
Weiss, ss	4	0	1	0
Hough, p	1	0	0	0
Natal, ph	1	0	0	0
Carpenter, p	0	0	0	0
Fariss, ph	1	1	1	0
McClure, p	0	0	0	0
Briley, ph	1	0	1	0
Corsi, p	0	0	0	0
Harvey, p	0	0	0	0
Renteria, ph	0	0	0	0
Totals	**35**	**3**	**9**	**3**

```
PHILLIES    023  021  020 – 10
Florida     000  011  100 – 3
```

E—Duncan (4), Felix (3). DP—PHILLIES 1. LOB—PHILLIES 12, Florida 17. 2B—Morandini (8), Kruk (10), Daulton (7), Eisenreich 2 (6). 3B—Hollins (1). SB—Dykstra 2 (10). CS—Dykstra (5). S—Rivera.

PHILLIES	IP	H	R	ER	BB	SO
Rivera (W, 2–2)	5	5	1	1	7	1
Ayrault	1⅓	4	2	2	3	1
West	2⅔	0	0	0	1	2

Florida	IP	H	R	ER	BB	SO
Hough (L, 2–4)	4	6	5	5	1	1
Carpenter	2	5	3	3	2	3
McClure	1	1	0	0	1	1
Corsi	1	3	2	2	1	2
Harvey	1	2	0	0	0	2

HBP—Arias by West. WP—Rivera, Carpenter.
Time—3:24. Attendance—38,519.

OTHER '93 PHILLIES

Brad Brink

Mark Davis

Jose DeLeon

Kevin Foster

INCAVIGLIA'S GRAND SLAM, FIVE RBI LEAD PHILS OVER EXPOS

May 20—Phillies 9, Expos 3

Montreal	AB	R	H	RBI
DeShields, 2b	3	0	1	0
Alou, lf	4	0	0	0
Grissom, cf	4	1	2	0
Walker, rf	3	1	1	0
Bolick, 1b	4	1	1	3
Fletcher, c	4	0	0	0
Cordero, ss	4	0	2	0
Lansing, 3b	3	0	0	0
Nabholz, p	0	0	0	0
Bottenfield, p	2	0	0	0
Fassero, p	0	0	0	0
Frazier, ph	1	0	0	0
Jones, p	0	0	0	0
VandarWal, ph	1	0	0	0
Totals	**33**	**3**	**7**	**3**

PHILLIES	AB	R	H	RBI
Dykstra, cf	5	2	2	0
Duncan, 2b	3	2	0	0
Kruk, 1b	3	1	1	0
Hollins, 3b	3	1	0	1
Daulton, c	4	1	1	2
Incaviglia, lf	4	1	2	5
Chamberlain, rf	4	0	1	0
Eisenreich, rf	0	0	0	0
Bell, ss	4	0	0	0
Schilling, p	3	1	1	0
Totals	**33**	**9**	**8**	**8**

```
Montreal      000  300  000 – 3
PHILLIES      400  200  12x – 9
```

E—Bolick (6). DP—PHILLIES 1. LOB—Montreal 6, PHILLIES 8. 2B—Walker (8), Dykstra (9), Chamberlain (9). HR—Bolick (3), Daulton (11), Incaviglia (5).

Montreal	IP	H	R	ER	BB	SO
Nabholz (L, 3–4)	1²/₃	3	4	4	3	3
Bottenfield	1²/₃	1	2	2	2	1
Fassero	1²/₃	1	0	0	2	2
Jones	3	3	3	1	0	1

PHILLIES	IP	H	R	ER	BB	SO
Schilling (W, 5–1)	9	7	3	3	2	5

HBP—Hollins by Nabholz, Lansing by Schilling. WP—Nabholz.
Time—2:51. Attendance—28,123.

Three doubles by Hollins pace 20-hit attack in first game with Rockies

May 28—Phillies 15, Rockies 9

PHILLIES	AB	R	H	RBI
Dykstra, cf	5	2	2	0
Duncan, 2b	5	0	2	0
Morandini, 2b	1	1	1	1
Kruk, 1b	6	3	2	3
Hollins, 3b	5	3	3	3
Daulton, c	6	2	2	4
Incaviglia, lf	4	1	1	1
Chamberlain, rf	5	1	2	3
West, p	0	0	0	0
Batiste, ss	5	0	3	0
Rivera, p	2	1	1	0
Mauser, p	0	0	0	0
Andersen, p	0	0	0	0
Eisenreich, rf	1	1	1	0
Totals	**45**	**15**	**20**	**15**

Colorado	AB	R	H	RBI
Young, 2b	5	1	1	0
Cole, cf	5	3	2	0
Bichette, rf	4	2	3	2
Galarraga, 1b	5	1	2	2
Jones, lf	4	1	1	0
Hayes, 3b	4	1	1	1
Girardi, c	5	0	2	1
Liriano, ss	5	0	2	1
Henry, p	1	0	0	0
Ashby, p	0	0	0	0
Tatum, ph	1	0	0	0
Ruffin, p	0	0	0	0
Benevedes, ph	1	0	0	0
Parrett, p	0	0	0	0
Clark, ph	1	0	1	0
Totals	**41**	**9**	**15**	**7**

```
PHILLIES      401  600  004 – 15
Colorado      021  010  221 – 9
```

E—Dykstra (1), Duncan 2 (9), Incaviglia (2), Batiste (2), Bichette (5). DP—PHILLIES 2, Colorado 1. LOB—PHILLIES 8, Colorado 11. 2B—Kruk (13), Hollins 3 (14), Daulton (9), Incaviglia (6), Bichette (8), Galarraga (12), Hayes (13). 3B—Bichette (1). HR—Daulton (12), Chamberlain (6). SB—Young (18), Cole 2 (16). S—Rivera 2.

PHILLIES	IP	H	R	ER	BB	SO
Rivera (W, 3–2)	6	9	6	5	4	2
Mauser	1²/₃	3	2	2	2	3
Andersen	¹/₃	0	0	0	0	0
West	1	3	1	1	0	1

Colorado	IP	H	R	ER	BB	SO
Henry (L, 2–6)	3²/₃	10	9	8	1	2
Ashby	¹/₃	3	2	2	0	1
Ruffin	4	2	0	0	1	2
Parrett	1	5	4	4	0	1

Rivera pitched to 2 batters in the 7th. HBP—Incaviglia by Henry. WP—Rivera. Time—3:17. Attendance—58,312.

Three homers in one inning help Phillies score their most runs since 1986

May 30—Phillies 18, Rockies 1

PHILLIES	AB	R	H	RBI
Dykstra, cf	5	1	2	3
Eisenreich, cf	1	0	0	0
Duncan, 2b	6	1	1	2
Kruk, 1b	5	2	2	0
Jordan, 1b	1	0	1	0
Hollins, 3b	5	2	2	2
Morandini, 2b	1	0	0	0
Daulton, c	4	4	2	2
Incaviglia, lf	6	3	4	3
Chamberlain, rf	4	0	0	0
Batiste, ss	3	3	2	3
Greene, p	4	2	3	2
Totals	**45**	**18**	**19**	**17**

Colorado	AB	R	H	RBI
Young, 2b	4	0	1	0
Cole, cf	3	0	0	0
Henry, p	0	0	0	0
Castellano, 1b	1	0	0	0
Bichette, rf	4	0	1	0
Galarraga, 1b	3	1	1	1
Wayne, p	0	0	0	0
Clark, ph	1	0	0	0
Boston, lf	4	0	0	0
Hayes, 3b	3	0	1	0
Sheaffer, c	2	0	0	0
Parrett, p	0	0	0	0
Jones, cf	1	0	0	0
Liriano, ss	3	0	0	0
Painter, p	1	0	0	0
Girardi, c	2	0	2	0
Totals	**32**	**1**	**6**	**1**

```
PHILLIES      000   054   450 – 18
Colorado      000   000   100 – 1
```

E—Henry (1), Liriano 2 (4), DP—Colorado 1. LOB—PHILLIES 6, Colorado 4. 2B—Dykstra (14), Kruk (14), Bichette (9). 3B—Incaviglia (2). HR—Duncan (4), Hollins (8), Daulton 2 (14), Batiste (1), Greene (1), Galarraga (5). CS—Young (7). S—Greene. SF—Batiste.

PHILLIES	IP	H	R	ER	BB	SO
Greene (W, 7–0)	9	6	1	1	0	6

Colorado	IP	H	R	ER	BB	SO
Painter (L, 0–2)	5⅓	7	7	7	1	4
Parrett	⅔	2	2	2	1	0
Henry	1	3	4	4	2	1
Wayne	2	7	5	5	0	2

Time—2:38. Attendance—56,710.

MULHOLLAND STRIKES OUT 14 BUT LOSES TO ROCKIES

June 4—Rockies 2, Phillies 1

Colorado	AB	R	H	RBI
Liriano, 2b	3	0	0	0
Young, ph, 2b	1	0	0	0
Jones, cf	4	1	3	0
Bichette, rf	4	0	1	0
Galarraga, 1b	4	1	2	1
Hayes, 3b	4	0	1	1
Girardi, c	4	0	0	0
Sheaffer, ph, c	0	0	0	0
Clark, lf	3	0	0	0
Castilla, ss	2	0	0	0
Castellano, ss	1	0	0	0
Blair, p	3	0	0	0
Wayne, p	0	0	0	0
Totals	**33**	**2**	**7**	**2**

PHILLIES	AB	R	H	RBI
Dykstra, cf	5	0	0	0
Morandini, 2b	5	0	2	1
Kruk, 1b	5	0	2	0
Hollins, 3b	2	0	1	0
Daulton, c	5	0	1	0
Chamberlain, rf	4	0	2	0
Thompson, lf	2	0	0	0
Batiste, ss	3	0	0	0
Eisenreich, ph	1	0	0	0
Duncan, ss	0	0	0	0
Mulholland, p	3	0	1	0
Jordan, ph	1	1	1	0
Totals	**36**	**1**	**10**	**1**

Colorado	000	000	002 – 2	
PHILLIES	000	000	001 – 1	

DP—Colorado 1. LOB—Colorado 4, PHILLIES 13. 2B—Jones (1), Bichette (12), Galarraga (13), Hayes (14), Morandini (10), Chamberlain (12), Jordan (2). CS—Hayes (2).

Colorado	IP	H	R	ER	BB	SO
Blair (W, 2–2)	8^1/$_3$	10	1	1	4	6
Wayne (S, 1)	^{2}/$_3$	0	0	0	1	1

PHILLIES	IP	H	R	ER	BB	SO
Mulholland (L, 6–5)	9	7	2	2	0	14

PB—Daulton. Time—2:32. Attendance—43,333.

With complete game, six-hitter Jackson hurls first shutout since 1988

June 12—Phillies 3, Mets 0

PHILLIES	AB	R	H	RBI
Dykstra, cf	4	1	1	0
Duncan, ss	4	0	1	1
Kruk, 1b	3	0	0	0
Daulton, c	4	0	1	0
Eisenreich, rf	4	0	1	0
Thompson, lf	3	1	0	0
Batiste, 3b	4	1	2	1
Morandini, 2b	4	0	1	1
Dn. Jackson, p	4	0	0	0
Totals	34	3	7	3

New York	AB	R	H	RBI
Coleman, lf	4	0	1	0
O'Brien, c	3	0	1	0
Murray, 1b	3	0	0	0
Bonilla, rf	4	0	1	0
Dr. Jackson, cf	4	0	0	0
Kent, 3b	3	0	2	0
McKnight, 2b	3	0	0	0
Bogar, ss	3	0	0	0
Gooden, p	2	0	0	0
Walker, ph	1	0	1	0
Telgheder, p	0	0	0	0
Totals	30	0	6	0

```
PHILLIES      001  200  000 – 3
New York      000  000  000 – 0
```

DP—PHILLIES 2. LOB—PHILLIES 7, New York 5. 2B—Daulton (13), Batiste (3), Coleman (10). 3B—Morandini (4). SB—Dykstra 2 (16). S—O'Brien.

PHILLIES	IP	H	R	ER	BB	SO
Dn. Jackson (W, 6–2)	9	6	0	0	1	5

New York	IP	H	R	ER	BB	SO
Gooden (L, 7–5)	8	7	3	3	2	7
Telgheder	1	0	0	0	0	2

HBP—Thompson by Gooden. Time—2:18. Attendance—31,814.

PHILLIES WIN SIXTH STRAIGHT WITH HELP OF EISENREICH'S GRAND SLAM

June 14—Phillies 10, Expos 3

PHILLIES	AB	R	H	RBI		Montreal	AB	R	H	RBI
Dykstra, cf	3	1	1	1		DeShields, 2b	5	0	0	0
Duncan, ss	4	2	1	0		Lansing, 3b, ss	4	0	1	0
Kruk, 1b	3	2	1	1		VanderWal, ph	1	0	0	0
Daulton, c	3	2	1	0		Grissom, cf	2	1	1	1
Incaviglia, lf	3	0	1	2		Walker, rf	4	0	1	0
Thompson, lf	0	1	0	1		Bolick, 1b	3	0	0	0
Eisenreich, rf	4	1	1	4		Alou, lf	4	1	1	2
Batiste, 3b	5	0	0	0		Cordero, ss	2	0	0	0
Morandini, 2b	4	1	2	1		Fassero, p	0	0	0	0
Mulholland, p	5	0	0	0		Colbrunn, ph	1	0	0	0
Andersen, p	0	0	0	0		Nabholz, p	0	0	0	0
						Rojas, p	0	0	0	0
						Frazier, ph	1	0	1	0
						Laker, c	4	0	1	0
						Shaw, p	1	0	0	0
						Berry, 3b	2	1	2	0
Totals	34	10	8	10		Totals	34	3	8	3

```
PHILLIES     210  020  005 – 10
Montreal     000  100  011 – 3
```

DP—Montreal 1. LOB—PHILLIES 8, Montreal 8. 2B—Dykstra (18), Duncan (8), Morandini (12). 3B—Morandini (5). HR—Kruk (6), Eisenreich (2), Alou (5). SB—Duncan (4). SF—Grissom.

PHILLIES	IP	H	R	ER	BB	SO
Mulholland (W, 8–5)	8$\frac{1}{3}$	8	3	3	3	4
Andersen	$\frac{2}{3}$	0	0	0	0	0

Montreal	IP	H	R	ER	BB	SO
Shaw (L, 1–3)	4$\frac{1}{3}$	6	5	5	3	2
Fassero	2$\frac{2}{3}$	0	0	0	3	4
Nabholz	1	1	3	3	2	0
Rojas	1	1	2	2	1	0

Nabholz pitched to 3 batters in the 9th. HBP—Daulton by Nabholz, Incaviglia by Shaw. WP—Nabholz.
Time—2:46. Attendance—13,235.

Pirates' Cooke fires first complete game of season against Phils

June 26—Pirates 4, Phillies 2

PHILLIES	AB	R	H	RBI
Dykstra, cf	4	0	1	1
Amaro, rf	4	1	2	0
Kruk, 1b	4	0	0	0
Daulton, c	4	0	0	0
Incaviglia, lf	4	0	1	1
Batiste, ss	3	0	0	0
Manto, 3b	3	0	1	0
Morandini, 2b	2	1	1	0
Schilling, p	1	0	0	0
Jordan, ph	1	0	0	0
West, p	0	0	0	0
Totals	**30**	**2**	**6**	**2**

Pittsburgh	AB	R	H	RBI
Garcia, 2b	4	1	1	1
Bell, ss	2	1	1	0
Martin, cf	4	0	1	0
Merced, rf	3	1	1	0
King, 3b	3	0	2	1
Clark, lf	3	0	1	0
Pennyfeather, cf	1	0	0	0
Slaught, c	4	0	0	0
Young, 1b	3	1	1	0
Cooke, p	3	0	1	1
Totals	**30**	**4**	**9**	**3**

```
PHILLIES      001  000  001 – 2
Pittsburgh    000  011  11x – 4
```

E—Dykstra (6). DP—PHILLIES 3, Pittsburgh 1. LOB—PHILLIES 4, Pittsburgh 6. 2B—Amaro (1), Bell (19), Young (7). HR—Garcia (3). S—Schilling. SF—King.

PHILLIES	IP	H	R	ER	BB	SO
Schilling (L, 8–3)	7	7	3	3	2	2
West	1	2	1	1	0	0

Pittsburgh	IP	H	R	ER	BB	SO
Cooke (W, 5–3)	9	6	2	2	2	10

HBP—Merced by Schilling. WP—Cooke.
Time—2:15. Attendance—39,439.

FIRST GAME ENDS AT 1 A.M. IN HISTORY-MAKING DOUBLEHEADER WITH PADRES

July 2—Padres 5, Phillies 2 (1st game)

San Diego	AB	R	H	RBI
Gutierrez, ss	3	0	1	1
Gwynn, rf	4	0	1	0
Bean, rf	0	0	0	0
Bell, cf	4	2	2	0
McGriff, 1b	3	2	1	2
Clark, lf	4	0	1	1
Teufel, 2b	3	0	0	0
Gardner, 2b	1	0	0	0
Cianfrocco, 3b	3	0	0	1
Ge. Harris, p	0	0	0	0
Geren, c	4	1	2	0
Brocail, p	1	0	0	0
Ettles, p	1	0	0	0
Martinez, p	1	0	0	0
Mason, p	0	0	0	0
Shipley, 3b	1	0	0	0
Totals	**33**	**5**	**8**	**5**

PHILLIES	AB	R	H	RBI
Dykstra, cf	4	0	0	0
Thompson, lf	4	0	1	0
Kruk, 1b	4	0	0	0
Hollins, 3b	4	0	0	0
Daulton, c	4	1	2	0
Eisenreich, rf	3	0	0	0
Duncan, ss	3	1	2	1
Morandini, 2b	3	0	1	1
Mulholland, p	1	0	0	0
Williams, p	0	0	0	0
Incaviglia, ph	1	0	0	0
West, p	0	0	0	0
Totals	**31**	**2**	**6**	**2**

```
San Diego    001  200  020 – 5
PHILLIES     001  000  100 – 2
```

DP—San Diego 1, PHILLIES 1. LOB—San Diego 4, PHILLIES 3. 2B—Clark (7), Geren 2 (5), Daulton (17), Duncan (10). HR—McGriff (17). CS—Thompson (3). S—Mulholland. SF—Cianfrocco.

San Diego	IP	H	R	ER	BB	SO
Brocail	3	2	1	1	0	0
Ettles (W, 1–0)	2	1	0	0	0	1
Martinez	1⅔	2	1	1	0	2
Mason	1⅓	1	0	0	0	2
Ge. Harris (S, 13)	1	0	0	0	0	1

PHILLIES	IP	H	R	ER	BB	SO
Mulholland (L, 9–6)	5	5	3	3	2	3
Williams	3	2	2	2	0	0
West	1	1	0	0	0	1

BK—Mason. Time—2:34.

WILLIAMS'S 10TH INNING SINGLE ENDS SECOND GAME AT 4:40 A.M.

July 2—Phillies 6, Padres 5 (10) (2d game)

San Diego	AB	R	H	RBI
Gardner, 2b	4	1	0	0
Gutierrez, ss	1	0	0	0
Shipley, 3b	5	1	1	3
Bean, rf	4	0	0	0
McGriff, 1b	3	1	2	0
Teufel, 1b	2	0	0	0
Plantier, lf	3	1	2	1
Ge. Harris, p	0	0	0	0
Cianfrocco, 3b	0	0	0	0
Bell, cf	4	0	0	0
Higgins, c	4	0	1	0
Stillwell, ss	3	0	0	0
Hoffman, p	0	0	0	0
Benes, p	2	1	0	0
Mason, p	0	0	0	0
Clark, lf	1	0	0	0
Totals	**36**	**5**	**6**	**4**

PHILLIES	AB	R	H	RBI
Amaro, cf	3	0	0	0
West, p	0	0	0	0
Dykstra, ph	1	0	0	0
Andersen, p	0	0	0	0
Duncan, ss	1	0	1	0
Greene, pr	0	0	0	0
Manto, ss	0	0	0	0
Morandini, 2b	4	1	1	0
Jordan, 1b	5	2	2	3
Hollins, 3b	4	1	0	0
Incaviglia, lf	3	1	2	0
Eisenreich, rf	5	0	2	1
Pratt, c	3	0	0	0
Daulton, c	2	0	1	1
Batiste, ss	3	0	0	0
Kruk, ph	0	0	0	0
Williams, p	1	0	1	1
DeLeon, p	1	0	0	0
Thompson, cf	2	1	0	0
Totals	**38**	**6**	**10**	**6**

```
San Diego    003  200  000  0 – 5
PHILLIES     000  130  010  1 – 6
```

One out when winning run scored. E—Shipley (6), McGriff (12), Jordan (1), Batiste (6). DP—San Diego 1. LOB—San Diego 5, PHILLIES 10. 2B—McGriff (9), Plantier (12), Duncan (11), Morandini (14). HR—Shipley (2), Jordan (3).

San Diego	IP	H	R	ER	BB	SO
Benes	7	6	4	4	1	3
Mason	1/3	0	1	1	2	1
Ge. Harris	2/3	1	0	0	1	0
Hoffman (L, 2–3)	1 1/3	3	1	1	2	2

PHILLIES	IP	H	R	ER	BB	SO
DeLeon	5	4	5	1	0	3
West	2	1	0	0	1	2
Andersen	1	1	0	0	1	2
Williams (W, 2–3)	2	0	0	0	1	2

HBP—Benes by DeLeon. WP—Hoffman, DeLeon, Williams.
Time—3:12. Attendance—54,617.

PHILLIES EDGE DODGERS IN 20-INNING MARATHON

July 7—Phillies 7, Dodgers 6 (20)

Los Angeles	AB	R	H	RBI
Butler, cf	9	1	2	0
Offerman, ss	8	2	4	0
Snyder, rf	9	0	2	2
Karros, 1b	6	0	1	1
Martinez, p	0	0	0	0
Goodwin, ph	1	0	1	0
McDowell, p	0	0	0	0
Hernandez, c	3	0	0	1
Piazza, c	8	2	2	0
Trlicek, p	2	0	0	0
Nichols, p	0	0	0	0
Davis, lf	8	0	3	0
Wallach, 3b	3	0	0	1
Daal, p	0	0	0	0
Hansen, ph	1	0	0	0
Gott, p	0	0	0	0
Rodriguez, 1b	4	0	0	0
Sharperson, 2b	3	0	0	0
Harris, 2b	5	0	0	0
Martinez, p	3	0	1	0
Webster, rf	5	1	1	0
Totals	**78**	**6**	**17**	**5**

PHILLIES	AB	R	H	RBI
Dykstra, cf	9	2	3	3
Thompson, lf	8	0	1	2
Kruk, 1b	7	1	2	2
Hollins, 3b	4	0	0	0
West, p	0	0	0	0
Chamberlain, ph	1	0	0	0
DeLeon, p	0	0	0	0
Incaviglia, ph	1	0	0	0
Mk. Williams, p	2	0	0	0
Daulton, c	7	0	1	0
Eisenreich, rf	8	1	3	0
Morandini, 2b	8	2	2	0
Stocker, ss	6	1	0	0
Mulholland, p	2	0	0	0
Mason, p	0	0	0	0
Jordan, ph	1	0	0	0
Mt. Williams, p	0	0	0	0
Andersen, p	0	0	0	0
Batiste, 3b	5	0	0	0
Totals	**69**	**7**	**12**	**7**

```
Los Angeles   000 111 002 000 000 000 01 – 6
PHILLIES      020 201 000 000 000 000 02 – 7
```

One out when winning run scored. E—Piazza (3), Hollins 2 (11), Stocker (1), Batiste (9). DP—PHILLIES 1. LOB—Los Angeles 20, PHILLIES 17. 2B—Offerman (11), Snyder (16), Piazza (12), Davis (9), Dykstra (26), Thompson (7), Daulton (18). HR—Dykstra (10), Kruk (8). SB—Butler (19), Morandini (10). CS—Goodwin (1). S—Stocker, Mulholland.

Los Angeles	IP	H	R	ER	BB	SO
Martinez	7	8	5	5	6	5
Daal	1	0	0	0	0	1
Gott	2	0	0	0	0	2
Martinez	2	1	0	0	2	2
McDowell	3	0	0	0	1	0
Trlicek (L, 0–2)	4	2	2	2	2	2
Nichols	1/3	1	0	0	0	0

PHILLIES	IP	H	R	ER	BB	SO
Mulholland	7	8	3	2	1	3
Mason	1	0	0	0	1	1
Mt. Williams	0	1	2	2	3	0
Andersen	1	1	0	0	0	1
West	2	0	0	0	1	2
DeLeon	3	1	0	0	2	2
Mk. Williams (W, 1–0)	6	6	1	1	0	4

Mt. Williams pitched to 4 batters in the 9th. Trlicek pitched to 2 batters in the 20th. Time—6:10. Attendance—41,730.

OTHER '93 PHILLIES

Tyler Green

Tony Longmire

Tim Mauser

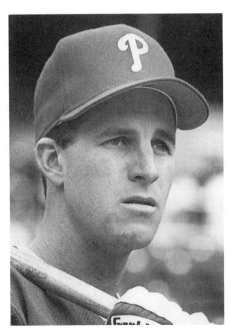

Joe Millette

GIANTS BELT 23 HITS TO ROUT PHILLIES

July 9—Giants 15, Phillies 8

San Francisco	AB	R	H	RBI
Lewis, cf	4	1	1	1
Benzinger, lf	2	0	0	0
Scarsone, 3b	7	2	4	3
Clark, 1b	3	3	3	1
Allanson, 1b	2	0	0	0
Bonds, lf	4	2	3	1
Carreon, rf	1	0	0	0
McGee, rf	2	3	2	1
Martinez, rf, cf	2	0	0	0
Clayton, ss	5	1	2	3
Manwaring, c	4	1	4	2
Brantley, p	0	0	0	0
Jackson, p	1	1	1	0
Righetti, p	0	0	0	0
Faries, 2b	5	1	1	2
Black, p	4	0	1	0
McNamara, ph, c	2	0	1	1
Totals	**48**	**15**	**23**	**15**

PHILLIES	AB	R	H	RBI
Dykstra, cf	2	0	0	0
Amaro, cf	3	1	1	0
Mt. Williams, p	0	0	0	0
Stocker, ss	5	1	3	1
Jordan, 1b	4	1	1	2
Hollins, 3b	4	1	1	0
Andersen, p	0	0	0	0
Thompson, cf	1	0	0	0
Incaviglia, lf	4	1	0	0
Chamberlain, rf	4	2	2	2
Pratt, c	4	1	2	2
Morandini, 2b	4	0	2	1
Rivera, p	0	0	0	0
Mason, p	2	0	1	0
West, p	0	0	0	0
Eisenreich, ph	1	0	0	0
Batiste, 3b	1	0	0	0
Totals	**39**	**8**	**13**	**8**

San Francisco	472	000	002 – 15
PHILLIES	000	202	211 – 8

DP—San Francisco 1. PHILLIES 1. LOB—San Francisco 15, PHILLIES 6. 2B—Scarsone (2), Bonds 2 (23), Manwaring (8), Jackson (2), Faries (1), Chamberlain (14). 3B—Stocker (1). HR—Jordan (4), Chamberlain (8), Pratt (2), Scarsone (1), Clark (7). SB—Hollins (1). SF—Faries.

San Francisco	IP	H	R	ER	BB	SO
Black (W, 8–1)	6	8	4	4	1	2
Brantley	1	2	2	2	0	1
Jackson	1	2	1	1	0	2
Righetti	1	1	1	1	0	2

PHILLIES	IP	H	R	ER	BB	SO
Rivera (L, 9–4)	1	8	9	9	3	1
Mason	4	10	4	4	1	1
West	2	1	0	0	3	4
Andersen	1	1	1	1	1	1
Williams	1	3	1	1	0	0

Rivera pitched to 5 batters in the 2nd. Andersen pitched to 1 batter in the 9th. HBP—Incaviglia by Jackson. Time—3:07. Attendance—38,695.

MORANDINI'S GRAND SLAM, FIVE RBI GIVE GREENE 11TH WIN

July 10—Phillies 8, Giants 3

San Francisco	AB	R	H	RBI
Lewis, cf	4	0	0	0
Scarsone, 3b	3	1	1	2
Clark, 1b	4	0	1	0
Bonds, lf	3	0	0	0
Martinez, rf	2	0	0	0
Carreon, rf	1	0	0	0
Clayton, ss	4	0	1	1
Manwaring, c	3	0	1	0
Faries, 2b	3	1	1	0
Rogers, p	0	0	0	0
Righetti, p	0	0	0	0
McGee, ph	1	0	0	0
Burkett, p	2	1	0	0
Johnson, 2b	2	0	2	0
Totals	**32**	**3**	**7**	**3**

PHILLIES	AB	R	H	RBI
Dykstra, cf	2	2	1	0
Morandini, 2b	5	1	2	5
Kruk, 1b	5	0	2	1
Hollins, 3b	5	0	0	0
Daulton, c	4	0	0	0
Eisenreich, rf	4	1	3	0
Thompson, lf	4	1	1	2
Stocker, ss	4	2	2	0
Greene, p	2	0	0	0
West, p	0	0	0	0
Andersen, p	0	0	0	0
Jordan, ph	1	1	1	0
Mt. Williams, p	0	0	0	0
Totals	**36**	**8**	**12**	**8**

```
San Francisco   120  000  000 – 3
PHILLIES        120  001  04x – 8
```

E—Scarsone (1). LOB—San Francisco 7, PHILLIES 9. 2B—Scarsone (3), Johnson 2 (2). 3B—Kruk (2). HR—Morandini (2), Thompson (3). SB—Dykstra (23). S—Lewis, Greene.

San Francisco	IP	H	R	ER	BB	SO
Burkett (L, 13–3)	5²/₃	8	4	4	3	3
Rogers	1¹/₃	3	3	3	1	0
Righetti	1	1	1	1	0	1

PHILLIES	IP	H	R	ER	BB	SO
Greene (W, 11–2)	6²/₃	6	3	3	4	4
West	²/₃	0	0	0	0	0
Andersen	²/₃	0	0	0	0	1
Mt. Williams	1	1	0	0	0	2

Rogers pitched to 3 batters in the 8th. WP—Greene 2.
Time—3:15. Attendance—41,869.

KRUK SLAMS FIVE HITS AS PHILS START SWEEP OF CARDINALS

July 27—Phillies 10, Cardinals 7

St. Louis	AB	R	H	RBI
Gilkey, lf	5	1	1	1
Murphy, p	0	0	0	0
O. Smith, ss	5	0	1	0
Jefferies, 1b	4	1	1	0
Olivares, p	0	0	0	0
B. Jordan, lf	1	0	0	0
Zeile, 3b	4	1	1	0
Lankford, cf	3	1	2	2
Whiten, rf	5	2	2	1
Alicea, 2b	3	1	1	1
Pagnozzi, c	2	0	0	0
Pappas, c	0	0	0	0
Magrane, p	0	0	0	0
Cormier, p	1	0	0	0
Perry, ph	1	0	0	0
Burns, p	1	0	0	0
Guetterman, p	0	0	0	0
Woodson, 1b	0	0	0	0
Brewer, 1b	1	0	0	1
Totals	**36**	**7**	**9**	**6**

PHILLIES	AB	R	H	RBI
Dykstra, cf	4	3	2	0
Duncan, ss	5	2	2	1
Kruk, 1b	5	3	5	3
Hollins, 3b	4	1	2	2
Mt. Williams, p	0	0	0	0
Daulton, c	5	0	1	1
Incaviglia, lf	5	0	2	0
Chamberlain, rf	4	0	2	0
Eisenreich, rf	0	0	0	0
Morandini, 2b	4	0	0	0
Greene, p	1	1	1	0
Mk. Williams, p	1	0	0	0
Mason, p	0	0	0	0
Thompson, ph	1	0	1	0
West, p	0	0	0	0
Andersen, p	0	0	0	0
R. Jordan, ph	1	0	0	0
Batiste, 3b	0	0	0	0
Totals	**40**	**10**	**18**	**7**

St. Louis	100	310	020 – 7
PHILLIES	430	100	02x – 10

E—Lankford (4), Whiten 2 (7). Hollins (17). DP—St. Louis 1, PHILLIES 1. LOB—St. Louis 8, PHILLIES 8. 2B—Zeile (25), Lankford (11), Alicea (8), Dykstra (27), Kruk (23). 3B—Whiten (4). HR—Gilkey (8), Hollins (11). SB—Jefferies (31). CS—Whiten (7), Incaviglia (1).

St. Louis	IP	H	R	ER	BB	SO
Magrane (L, 8–9)	1	5	5	5	1	1
Cormier	2	4	2	2	0	2
Burns	2⅔	3	1	1	0	0
Guetterman	⅓	1	0	0	1	0
Olivares	1	1	0	0	0	0
Murphy	1	4	2	2	0	2

PHILLIES	IP	H	R	ER	BB	SO
Greene	2⅔	2	1	1	1	5
Mk. Williams	⅔	4	3	3	0	0
Mason (W, 2–7)	2⅔	2	1	1	1	2
West	1⅓	1	2	1	2	1
Andersen	⅔	0	0	0	1	1
Mt. Williams (S, 27)	1	0	0	0	1	0

Magrane pitched to 1 batter in the 2nd. BK—Burns. Time—3:30. Attendance—45,383.

DOWN 4–0, PHILS RALLY TO TOP CARDS BEHIND DAULTON'S GRAND SLAM, SIX RBI

July 28—Phillies 14, Cardinals 6

St. Louis	AB	R	H	RBI
Alicea, 2b	3	1	1	0
O. Smith, ss	5	2	2	0
Gilkey, lf	4	2	2	2
Zeile, 3b	5	1	3	4
Whiten, rf	4	0	0	0
B. Jordan, cf	5	0	0	0
Pappas, c	4	0	1	0
Woodson, 1b	3	0	0	0
Perry, 1b	0	0	0	0
Tewksbury, p	2	0	0	0
Oquendo, ph	1	0	0	0
Guetterman, p	0	0	0	0
Lankford, ph	1	0	0	0
Cormier, p	0	0	0	0
Olivares, p	0	0	0	0
Totals	**36**	**6**	**9**	**6**

PHILLIES	AB	R	H	RBI
Dykstra, cf	5	3	3	0
Duncan, ss	4	3	3	2
Kruk, 1b	3	2	1	0
Hollins, 3b	3	2	2	3
Andersen, p	0	0	0	0
West, p	0	0	0	0
R. Jordan, ph	1	1	1	1
Mt. Williams, p	0	0	0	0
Daulton, c	3	1	2	6
Eisenreich, rf	5	1	2	0
Thompson, lf	4	0	1	1
Morandini, 2b	5	0	1	0
Mulholland, p	2	1	1	0
Batiste, 3b	1	0	0	0
Totals	**36**	**14**	**17**	**13**

```
St. Louis    400  000   200 – 6
PHILLIES     004  010   36x – 14
```

E—Mulholland (2). DP—St. Louis 2. LOB—St. Louis 9, PHILLIES 6. 2B—O. Smith (15), Zeile (26), Dykstra 2 (29), Thompson (11). 3B—Hollins (3), Daulton (3). HR—Gilkey (9), Zeile (8), Daulton (18). S—Duncan, Mulholland. SF—Hollins.

St. Louis	IP	H	R	ER	BB	SO
Tewksbury	6	8	5	5	3	0
Guetterman (L, 2–2)	1	3	3	3	1	0
Cormier	2/3	2	3	3	1	0
Olivares	1/3	4	3	3	0	0

PHILLIES	IP	H	R	ER	BB	SO
Mulholland (W, 10–8)	7	7	6	6	4	6
Andersen	1/3	1	0	0	1	0
West	2/3	0	0	0	0	1
Mt. Williams	1	1	0	0	1	1

Time—3:00. Attendance—46,346.

PHILS OVERCOME ANOTHER 4–0 DEFICIT TO BEAT BRAVES AND GREG MADDUX

August 5—Phillies 10, Braves 4

PHILLIES	AB	R	H	RBI
Dykstra, cf	3	3	1	0
Morandini, 2b	3	1	0	0
Kruk, 1b	5	0	0	0
Hollins, 3b	4	2	3	4
Daulton, c	3	1	0	0
Pratt, c	2	0	1	2
Eisenreich, rf	4	1	1	0
Thompson, lf	5	1	2	1
Stocker, ss	5	0	2	2
Rivera, p	4	1	0	0
Andersen, p	0	0	0	0
Totals	**38**	**10**	**10**	**9**

Atlanta	AB	R	H	RBI
Sanders, cf	5	1	1	0
Blauser, ss	4	1	0	0
Gant, lf	4	1	0	0
McGriff, 1b	4	1	2	1
Justice, rf	3	0	1	0
Pendleton, 3b	4	0	2	0
Berryhill, c	3	0	0	0
Lemke, 2b	3	0	2	2
Maddux, p	2	0	0	0
Bream, ph	1	0	0	0
Stanton, p	0	0	0	0
Borbon, p	0	0	0	0
Bedrosian, p	0	0	0	0
Cabrera, ph	1	0	0	0
Howell, p	0	0	0	0
Totals	**34**	**4**	**8**	**3**

```
PHILLIES    020  210  230 – 10
Atlanta     400  000  000 –  4
```

E—Blauser (14), McGriff (14), Lemke (11). DP—PHILLIES 1. LOB—PHILLIES 7, Atlanta 8. 2B—Dykstra (32), Hollins (20), Pratt (4), McGriff (18). 3B—Sanders (5). SB—Dykstra (27), Thompson (8). S—Morandini.

PHILLIES	IP	H	R	ER	BB	SO
Rivera (W, 10–6)	7²/₃	8	4	4	5	2
Andersen	1¹/₃	0	0	0	0	1

Atlanta	IP	H	R	ER	BB	SO
Maddux (L, 12–9)	6	7	5	1	0	6
Stanton	1	1	2	2	3	2
Borbon	¹/₃	1	3	3	2	0
Bedrosian	²/₃	1	0	0	0	1
Howell	1	0	0	0	0	0

WP—Rivera. PB—Berryhill. Time—3:14. Attendance—49,070.

GRAND SLAM BY BATISTE HELPS THIGPEN GET FIRST PHILS WIN

August 13—Phillies 9, Mets 5

New York	AB	R	H	RBI
R. Thompson, cf	4	0	2	0
O'Brien, c	4	0	0	0
Murray, 1b	4	0	2	0
Landrum, pr, lf	0	1	0	0
Bonilla, 3b	3	3	2	2
Gallagher, lf, 1b	4	1	1	1
Kent, 2b	3	0	0	0
Burnitz, rf	4	0	0	0
Baez, ss	4	0	1	0
Tanana, p	2	0	0	0
McKnight, ph	1	0	0	0
Maddux, p	0	0	0	0
Walker, ph	1	0	0	0
Schourek, p	0	0	0	0
Young, p	0	0	0	0
Totals	**34**	**5**	**8**	**3**

PHILLIES	AB	R	H	RBI
Dykstra, cf	4	0	0	1
Duncan, 2b	4	0	0	0
Kruk, 1b	3	1	0	0
Hollins, 3b	3	1	1	0
Thigpen, p	0	0	0	0
Morandini, ph	1	0	0	0
Daulton, c	4	1	2	0
Incaviglia, lf	3	1	0	0
Chamberlain, rf	4	1	2	3
Eisenreich, rf	1	1	0	0
Stocker, ss	3	2	1	0
Mulholland, p	2	0	0	0
M. Thompson, ph	1	0	0	0
Batiste, 3b	1	1	1	4
Totals	**33**	**9**	**7**	**8**

```
New York    010  100  030 – 5
PHILLIES    030  000  015 – 9
```

E—Baez (4), Kruk (6). DP—New York 1. LOB—New York 4, PHILLIES 1. 2B—R. Thompson (5), Stocker(5). HR—Chamberlain (10), Batiste (5), Bonilla 2 (26).

New York	IP	H	R	ER	BB	SO
Tanana	6	4	3	3	0	4
Maddux	2	2	1	1	0	2
Schourek	$^2/_3$	0	1	0	1	1
Young (L, 1–14)	0	1	4	0	2	0

PHILLIES	IP	H	R	ER	BB	SO
Mulholland	8	8	5	3	2	4
Thigpen (W, 1–0)	1	0	0	0	0	1

Time—2:41. Attendance—40,552.

STOCKER'S THREE-RUN TRIPLE SPARKS RALLY THAT DEFEATS ASTROS

August 20—Phillies 6, Astros 4

PHILLIES	AB	R	H	RBI
Dykstra, cf	4	1	1	0
Duncan, 2b	5	0	1	2
Kruk, 1b	5	1	1	0
Hollins, 3b	2	2	1	1
Daulton, c	4	0	1	0
Eisenreich, rf	3	0	0	0
Chamberlain, ph, rf	0	1	0	0
Thompson, lf	4	1	2	0
Stocker, ss	4	0	2	3
Schilling, p	3	0	0	0
West, p	1	0	0	0
Mt. Williams, p	0	0	0	0
Totals	**35**	**6**	**9**	**6**

Houston	AB	R	H	RBI
Biggio, 2b	4	0	2	1
Finley, cf	5	1	2	1
Bagwell, 1b	4	0	1	1
Anthony, rf	4	1	1	0
Caminiti, 3b	4	0	1	0
Gonzalez, lf	4	0	0	0
Taubensee, c	2	0	0	1
Servais, ph, c	1	0	0	0
Cedeno, ss	3	1	1	0
Harnisch, p	1	0	0	0
Candaele, ph	1	1	1	0
Jones, p	0	0	0	0
Osuna, p	0	0	0	0
Hernandez, p	0	0	0	0
Totals	**34**	**4**	**9**	**4**

```
PHILLIES    002  001  030 – 6
Houston     001  110  100 – 4
```

DP—Houston 1. LOB—PHILLIES 6, Houston 9. 2B—Duncan (17), Thompson (13), Bagwell (31). 3B—Stocker (3), Finley (8). HR—Hollins (14). SB—Caminiti (7). S—Harnisch, SF—Taubensee.

PHILLIES	IP	H	R	ER	BB	SO
Schilling	6⅓	8	4	4	3	8
West (W, 6–3)	1⅔	0	0	0	0	1
Mt. Williams (S, 35)	1	1	0	0	1	1

Houston	IP	H	R	ER	BB	SO
Harnisch	7	7	3	3	2	3
Jones (L, 0–1)	0	1	2	2	1	0
Osuna	⅓	0	0	0	0	0
Hernandez	1⅔	1	1	1	1	4

Jones pitched to 2 batters in the 8th. Time—3:06. Attendance—33,080.

RIVERA BLANKS CUBS WITH COMPLETE GAME, FOUR-HITTER

August 31—Phillies 7, Cubs 0

PHILLIES	AB	R	H	RBI
Dykstra, cf	3	2	1	0
Morandini, 2b	3	0	2	1
Duncan, 2b	1	1	1	2
Kruk, 1b	4	1	0	0
Hollins, 3b	5	0	1	0
Batiste, 3b	0	0	0	0
Daulton, c	5	0	2	1
Eisenreich, rf	5	0	1	1
Thompson, lf	5	1	1	0
Stocker, ss	4	2	2	0
Rivera, p	3	0	1	0
Totals	**38**	**7**	**12**	**5**

Chicago	AB	R	H	RBI
Smith, rf	3	0	0	0
Sandberg, 2b	4	0	2	0
Grace, 1b	3	0	1	0
Wilkins, c	4	0	1	0
Sosa, cf	3	0	0	0
Buechele, 3b	3	0	0	0
Roberson, lf	2	0	0	0
Vizcaino, ss	3	0	0	0
Morgan, p	2	0	0	0
Wilson, ph	1	0	0	0
McElroy, p	0	0	0	0
Plesac, p	0	0	0	0
Scanlan, p	0	0	0	0
Totals	**28**	**0**	**4**	**0**

```
PHILLIES    200  001  040 – 7
Chicago     000  000  000 – 0
```

E—Sosa (7), Buechele (7). DP—PHILLIES 2. LOB—PHILLIES 11, Chicago 6. 2B—Morandini (15), Daulton (28). 3B—Dykstra (4). SB—Smith (8), Sosa (25). CS—Sosa (7). S—Rivera 2.

PHILLIES	IP	H	R	ER	BB	SO
Rivera (W, 12–7)	9	4	0	0	4	9

Chicago	IP	H	R	ER	BB	SO
Morgan (L, 8–13)	7	9	3	3	3	5
McElroy	$1/3$	1	3	2	2	0
Plesac	$2/3$	1	1	0	0	2
Scanlan	1	1	0	0	0	2

HBP—Sosa by Rivera. Time—2:31. Attendance—19,951.

GREENE PITCHES 11-STRIKEOUT, THREE-HITTER, HITS HOME RUN TO BEAT REDS

September 3—Phillies 14, Reds 2

PHILLIES	AB	R	H	RBI
Dykstra, cf	3	2	1	1
Amaro, cf	1	0	0	0
Duncan, 2b	5	1	2	1
Morandini, 2b	0	0	0	0
Kruk, 1b	4	0	0	0
Jordan, 1b	0	0	0	0
Hollins, 3b	5	1	1	3
Batiste, 3b	0	0	0	0
Daulton, c	4	3	2	1
Eisenreich, rf	4	3	2	0
Incaviglia, lf	3	1	2	1
Longmire, lf	1	0	0	0
Stocker, ss	5	2	1	3
Greene, p	4	1	2	2
Totals	**39**	**14**	**13**	**12**

Cincinnati	AB	R	H	RBI
Howard, cf	3	0	1	0
Brumfield, 2b	4	0	0	0
Morris, 1b	4	0	0	0
Sabo, 3b	4	2	1	0
Costo, rf	4	0	1	0
Oliver, c	3	0	0	0
Branson, ss	3	0	0	0
Tubbs, lf	2	0	0	0
Ayala, p	1	0	0	0
Wickander, p	0	0	0	0
Koelling, ph	1	0	0	0
Bushing, p	0	0	0	0
Ruffin, p	0	0	0	0
Daugherty, ph	1	0	0	0
Spradlin, p	0	0	0	0
Totals	**30**	**2**	**3**	**0**

```
PHILLIES     001  283  000 – 14
Cincinnati   010  100  000 – 2
```

E—Hollins (23), Stocker (10), Brumfield 2 (5). DP—Cincinnati 1. LOB – PHILLIES 5, Cincinnati 3. 2B—Dykstra (38), Duncan (19), Eisenreich (15), Sabo (28). HR—Hollins (16), Daulton (23), Greene (2). CS—Howard (3). S—Greene.

PHILLIES	IP	H	R	ER	BB	SO
Greene (W, 13–3)	9	3	2	1	2	11

Cincinnati	IP	H	R	ER	BB	SO
Ayala (L, 5–7)	4⅓	8	9	9	4	5
Wicklander	⅔	2	2	2	2	1
Bushing	1	3	3	2	0	0
Ruffin	2	0	0	0	0	2
Spradlin	1	0	0	0	0	1

WP—Greene 2, Wickander, Bushing. Time—2:39. Attendance—26,157.

Phillies set NL record for most consecutive games (151) without being shut out

September 4—Reds 6, Phillies 5

PHILLIES	AB	R	H	RBI
Dykstra, cf	4	1	2	0
Duncan, 2b	5	1	1	0
Kruk, 1b	3	2	1	1
Hollins, 3b	5	0	0	1
Daulton, c	3	0	1	1
Eisenreich, rf	4	0	4	1
Thompson, lf	5	0	0	1
Stocker, ss	4	0	0	0
Jackson, p	0	0	0	0
Longmire, ph	1	0	1	0
Pall, p	0	0	0	0
Morandini, ph	0	0	0	0
Thigpen, p	0	0	0	0
Mt. Williams, p	0	0	0	0
Jordan, ph	0	1	0	0
Totals	**34**	**5**	**10**	**5**

Cincinnati	AB	R	H	RBI
Brumfield, cf	5	0	0	0
Morris, 1b	4	1	1	0
Sanders, rf	4	1	1	1
Sabo, 3b	4	0	2	0
Costo, lf	3	0	0	0
Reardon, p	0	0	0	0
Dibble, p	0	0	0	0
Service, p	0	0	0	0
Oliver, c	3	2	1	0
Samuel, 2b	4	2	4	1
Branson, ss	4	0	1	0
Rijo, p	3	0	2	4
Howard, lf	1	0	0	0
Totals	**35**	**6**	**12**	**6**

```
PHILLIES      000  100  004 – 5
Cincinnati    020  211  00x – 6
```

E—Hollins (24). DP—Cincinnati 1. LOB—PHILLIES 12. Cincinnati 9. 2B—Kruk (28), Eisenreich (16), Morris (13), Rijo (3). CS—Sanders (9). S—Jackson. SF—Daulton.

PHILLIES	IP	H	R	ER	BB	SO
Jackson (L, 11–10)	4	7	4	4	1	3
Pall	2	4	2	1	2	1
Thigpen	1	1	0	0	0	0
Mt. Williams	1	0	0	0	1	1

Cincinnati	IP	H	R	ER	BB	SO
Rijo (W, 13–7)	7	7	1	1	3	5
Reardon	1	1	0	0	1	3
Dibble	$1/3$	2	4	4	4	0
Service (S, 1)	$2/3$	0	0	0	0	0

PB—Daulton. Time—2:46. Attendance—31,166.

OTHER '93 PHILLIES

Bob Ayrault

Juan Bell

Paul Fletcher

Doug Lindsey

DYKSTRA'S TWO HOMERS, FIVE RBI LEAD WIN IN BRAWL-MARRED GAME WITH CUBS

September 9—Phillies 10, Cubs 8

Chicago	AB	R	H	RBI
Vizcaino, ss	4	2	1	0
Sandberg, 2b	5	3	3	0
Grace, 1b	5	0	1	0
Hill, lf	5	1	3	3
Sosa, cf	5	0	3	3
Buechele, 3b	4	1	1	0
Yelding, pr	0	0	0	0
Wilkins, c	4	1	1	0
Roberson, rf	5	0	2	1
Bautista, p	0	0	0	0
Castillo, p	0	0	0	0
McElroy, p	1	0	0	0
Dunston, ph	1	0	0	0
Scanlan, p	0	0	0	0
Smith, ph	1	0	0	1
Boskie, p	0	0	0	0
Totals	**40**	**8**	**15**	**8**

PHILLIES	AB	R	H	RBI
Dykstra, cf	5	3	3	5
Duncan, 2b	2	1	1	0
Morandini, 2b	3	0	1	0
Kruk, 1b	5	0	0	0
Hollins, 3b	3	3	2	1
Batiste, 3b	0	0	0	0
Daulton, c	5	0	4	3
Eisenreich, rf	5	0	2	1
Thompson, lf	4	0	1	0
Stocker, ss	2	1	0	0
Jackson, p	3	2	0	0
Thigpen, p	1	0	0	0
Mt. Williams, p	0	0	0	0
West, p	0	0	0	0
Totals	**38**	**10**	**14**	**10**

Chicago	200	100	212 – 8
PHILLIES	252	000	01x – 10

E—Hill (2), Roberson (3). DP—Chicago 1, Phillies 1. LOB—Chicago 9, PHILLIES 9. 2B—Buechele (24), Wilkins (21), Daulton (29). HR—Hill (6), Dykstra 2 (18), Hollins (17). SB—Sosa (2), Yelding (2), Hollins (2). S—Bautista.

Chicago	IP	H	R	ER	BB	SO
Bautista (L, 7–3)	1⅓	5	6	6	2	1
Castillo	1	4	3	3	0	0
McElroy	2⅔	0	0	0	1	1
Scanlan	2	2	0	0	1	0
Boskie	1	3	1	1	0	0

PHILLIES	IP	H	R	ER	BB	SO
Jackson (W, 12–10)	6⅔	11	5	5	2	5
Thigpen	1⅓	1	1	1	0	0
Mt. Williams	⅓	3	2	2	1	0
West (S, 3)	⅔	0	0	0	0	1

HBP—Stocker by Castillo. WP—Bautista 2, McElroy, Jackson 1. Time—3:13. Attendance—25,894.

Schilling wins seventh straight with seventh complete game

September 20—Phillies 7, Marlins 1

Florida	AB	R	H	RBI
Carr, cf	3	0	1	0
Barberie, 2b	3	0	1	1
Conine, lf	4	0	0	0
Destrade, 1b	4	0	0	0
Arias, 3b	4	0	2	0
Natal, c	4	0	0	0
Whitmore, rf	4	1	1	0
Weiss, ss	3	0	2	0
Hough, p	0	0	0	0
Wilson, ph	1	0	0	0
Lewis, p	0	0	0	0
Briley, ph	1	0	0	0
Nen, p	0	0	0	0
Carrillo, ph	1	0	0	0
Johnstone, p	0	0	0	0
Totals	**32**	**1**	**7**	**1**

PHILLIES	AB	R	H	RBI
Dykstra, cf	3	1	1	0
Morandini, 2b	5	2	3	0
Kruk, 1b	5	3	3	3
Hollins, 3b	2	0	1	2
Batiste, 3b	0	0	0	0
Daulton, c	4	0	0	0
Eisenreich, rf	4	0	1	2
Thompson, lf	4	0	2	0
Stocker, ss	4	1	1	0
Schilling, p	3	0	0	0
Totals	**34**	**7**	**12**	**7**

```
Florida      000  010  000 – 1
PHILLIES     240  000  10x – 7
```

E—Carr (6). DP—Florida 1, PHILLIES 1. LOB—Florida 6, PHILLIES 8. 2B—Morandini (17), Hollins (27). HR—Kruk (14). CS—Arias (1). S—Schilling.

Florida	IP	H	R	ER	BB	SO
Hough (L, 9–16)	2	7	6	6	2	0
Lewis	2	2	0	0	1	1
Nen	2	0	0	0	0	2
Johnstone	2	3	1	1	1	2

PHILLIES	IP	H	R	ER	BB	SO
Schilling (W, 15–6)	9	7	1	1	2	11

Time—2:28. Attendance—31,454.

GREENE STOPS BRAVES ON THREE HITS, AND WILLIAMS GETS RECORD SAVE

September 24—Phillies 3, Braves 0

Atlanta	AB	R	H	RBI	PHILLIES	AB	R	H	RBI
Nixon, cf	3	0	0	0	Dykstra, cf	3	0	1	0
Blauser, ss	4	0	0	0	Duncan, 2b	4	0	0	0
Gant, lf	4	0	0	0	Kruk, 1b	4	0	1	0
McGriff, 1b	2	0	0	0	Hollins, 3b	4	1	1	0
Justice, rf	2	0	1	0	Thompson, lf	0	0	0	0
Pendleton, 3b	3	0	0	0	Daulton, c	2	0	0	0
Berryhill, c	4	0	1	0	Incaviglia, lf	4	1	0	0
Jones, pr	0	0	0	0	Batiste, 3b	0	0	0	0
Lemke, 2b	3	0	1	0	Chamberlain, rf	3	1	1	1
Glavine, p	2	0	0	0	Eisenreich, rf	0	0	0	0
Bream, ph	1	0	0	0	Stocker, ss	2	0	1	0
Wohlers, p	0	0	0	0	Greene, p	3	0	2	2
Stanton, p	0	0	0	0	Mt. Williams, p	0	0	0	0
Klesko, ph	0	0	0	0					
Cabrera, ph	1	0	0	0					
Totals	**29**	**0**	**3**	**0**	**Totals**	**29**	**3**	**7**	**3**

```
Atlanta      000  000  000 – 0
PHILLIES     030  000  00x – 3
```

E—Daulton (8). DP—Atlanta 1, PHILLIES 2. LOB—Atlanta 10, PHILLIES 6. 2B—Greene (2). SB—Nixon (43).

Atlanta	IP	H	R	ER	BB	SO
Glavine (L, 20–6)	6	5	3	3	3	4
Wohlers	1	1	0	0	1	0
Stanton	1	1	0	0	0	0

PHILLIES	IP	H	R	ER	BB	SO
Greene (W, 16–3)	8^1⁄$_3$	3	0	0	8	6
Mt. Williams (S, 41)	^{2}⁄$_3$	0	0	0	0	2

PB—Daulton. Time—2:50. Attendance—57,792.

PHILLIES CLINCH NL EAST TITLE AS DUNCAN GETS SECOND GRAND SLAM OF SEASON

September 28—Phillies 10, Pirates 7

PHILLIES	AB	R	H	RBI
Dykstra, cf	5	2	4	3
Duncan, 2b	6	1	3	5
Kruk, 1b	5	0	2	1
Hollins, 3b	5	0	0	0
Pall, p	0	0	0	0
Daulton, c	4	1	3	0
Eisenreich, rf	5	1	1	0
Thompson, lf	3	2	2	0
Stocker, ss	5	2	2	1
Mk. Williams, p	2	1	1	0
Thigpen, p	0	0	0	0
Incaviglia, ph	1	0	0	0
Batiste, 3b	1	0	0	0
Totals	**42**	**10**	**18**	**10**

Pittsburgh	AB	R	H	RBI
Garcia, 2b	5	0	1	1
Bell, ss	4	2	2	1
VanSlyke, cf	5	2	3	1
King, 3b	5	0	1	1
Clark, rf	4	1	0	0
Young, 1b	4	0	0	0
Cummings, lf	3	1	0	0
Prince, c	3	1	2	2
Hope, p	1	0	0	0
Martin, ph	1	0	0	0
Ballard, p	0	0	0	0
Merced, ph	1	0	1	1
Robertson, p	0	0	0	0
Minor, p	0	0	0	0
Neagle, p	0	0	0	0
Miller, p	0	0	0	0
Womack, ph	1	0	0	0
Totals	**37**	**7**	**10**	**7**

```
PHILLIES      001  200  601 – 10
Pittsburgh    001  003  102 – 7
```

DP—Pittsburgh 1. LOB—PHILLIES 11, Pittsburgh 7. 2B—Dykstra (44), Kruk (33), Daulton (35), Van Slyke (13), Prince (14), Merced (26). HR—Duncan (11), Bell (9). SB—Garcia (18). S—Thompson, Mk. Williams.

PHILLIES	IP	H	R	ER	BB	SO
Mk. Williams	5²/₃	4	4	4	4	6
Thigpen (W, 3–1)	¹/₃	2	0	0	0	0
Pall	3	4	3	3	0	2

Pittsburgh	IP	H	R	ER	BB	SO
Hope	5	10	3	3	3	0
Ballard	1	1	0	0	0	0
Robertson (L, 0–1)	0	3	4	4	0	0
Minor	¹/₃	0	0	0	0	1
Neagle	²/₃	1	2	2	1	1
Miller	2	3	1	1	0	0

Robertson pitched to 4 batters in the 7th. WP—Mk. Williams. Time—2:54. Attendance—17,386.

SHUTOUT STREAK IS ENDED BY PIRATES' TIM WAKEFIELD

September 30—Pirates 5, Phillies 0

PHILLIES	AB	R	H	RBI
Dykstra, cf	5	0	0	0
Morandini, 2b	4	0	0	0
Kruk, 1b	2	0	1	0
Hollins, 3b	4	0	1	0
Incaviglia, lf	4	0	1	0
Eisenreich, rf	2	0	0	0
Pratt, c	3	0	0	0
Stocker, ss	2	0	1	0
Greene, p	2	0	0	0
West, p	0	0	0	0
Mulholland, p	0	0	0	0
Thompson, ph	1	0	0	0
Thigpen, p	0	0	0	0
Mason, p	0	0	0	0
Jordan, ph	1	0	0	0
Totals	**30**	**0**	**4**	**0**

Pittsburgh	AB	R	H	RBI
Womack, ss	4	1	1	0
Foley, 2b	4	1	3	0
Cummings, cf	2	0	0	1
King, 3b	2	1	1	1
Clark, rf	4	2	2	1
Martin, lf	4	0	1	1
Aude, 1b	3	0	0	0
Prince, c	4	0	0	0
Wakefield, p	4	0	1	0
Totals	**31**	**5**	**9**	**4**

PHILLIES	000	000	000 – 0	
Pittsburgh	301	010	00x – 5	

E—Pratt (1), Stocker (14), Foley (5). DP—PHILLIES 1, Pittsburgh 2. LOB—PHILLIES 10, Pittsburgh 8. 2B—Foley (11). 3B—Clark (2). HR—Clark (11). SB—King (8), Martin (16). SF—Cummings, King.

PHILLIES	IP	H	R	ER	BB	SO
Greene (L, 16–4)	4	6	4	4	3	5
West	1	0	1	0	1	3
Mulholland	1	1	0	0	0	0
Thigpen	1	1	0	0	0	0
Mason	1	1	0	0	0	1

Pittsburgh	IP	H	R	ER	BB	SO
Wakefield (W, 6–11)	9	4	0	0	6	1

HBP—Stocker by Wakefield. WP—Wakefield.
Time—2:22. Attendance—10,448.

PHILLIES FINAL 1993 RECORDS

Batting

	AVG	G	AB	R	H	TB	2B	3B	HR	RBI	HP	BB	IBB	SO	SB	CS	DP	E	SLG	OBP
Amaro	.333	25	48	7	16	25	2	2	1	6	0	6	0	5	0	0	1	1	.521	.400
Right	.500		28		14	23	2	2	1	5	0	4	0	1			0		.821	.563
Left	.100		20		2	2	0	0	0	1	0	2	0	4			1		.100	.174
Andersen	1.000	64	1	0	1	1	0	0	0	0	0	0	0	0	0	0	0	1	1.000	1.000
Ayrault	.000	10	2	0	0	0	0	0	0	0	0	0	0	2	0	0	0	0	.000	.000
Batiste	.282	79	156	14	44	68	7	1	5	29	1	3	2	29	0	1	3	10	.436	.298
Bell	.200	24	65	5	13	21	6	1	0	7	1	5	0	12	0	1	0	9	.323	.268
Right	.208		24		5	7	2	0	0	0	1	3	0	4			0		.292	.321
Left	.195		41		8	14	4	1	0	7	0	2	0	8			0		.341	.233
Brink	.000	2	1	0	0	0	0	0	0	0	0	0	0	0	0	0	0	1	.000	.000
Chamberlain	.282	96	284	34	80	140	20	2	12	45	1	17	3	51	2	1	8	1	.493	.320
Daulton	.257	147	510	90	131	246	35	4	24	105	2	117	12	111	5	0	2	9	.482	.392
Davis	.333	25	3	1	1	1	0	0	0	0	0	0	0	0	0	0	0	0	.333	.333
DeLeon	.000	24	6	0	0	0	0	0	0	0	0	0	0	5	0	0	1	0	.000	.000
Duncan	.282	124	496	68	140	207	26	4	11	73	4	12	0	88	6	5	13	21	.417	.304
Dykstra	.305	161	637	143	194	307	44	6	19	66	2	129	9	64	37	12	8	10	.482	.420
Eisenreich	.318	153	362	51	115	161	17	4	7	54	1	26	5	36	5	0	6	1	.445	.363
Foster	.000	2	2	0	0	0	0	0	0	0	0	0	0	0	0	0	0	0	.000	.000
Green	.000	3	2	0	0	0	0	0	0	0	0	0	0	2	0	0	0	1	.000	.000
Greene	.222	32	72	9	16	24	2	0	2	10	0	5	0	20	0	0	1	1	.333	.269
Hollins	.273	143	543	104	148	240	30	4	18	93	5	85	5	109	2	3	15	27	.442	.372
Right	.330		206		68	115	15	4	8	38	3	15	4	35			6		.558	.379
Left	.237		337		80	125	15	0	10	55	2	70	1	74			9		.371	.368
Incaviglia	.274	116	368	60	101	195	16	3	24	89	6	21	1	82	1	1	9	5	.530	.318
Jackson	.077	32	65	3	5	7	2	0	0	2	1	3	0	37	0	0	0	4	.108	.130
Jordan	.289	90	159	21	46	67	4	1	5	18	1	8	1	32	0	0	2	2	.421	.324
Kruk	.316	150	535	100	169	254	33	5	14	85	0	111	10	87	6	2	11	8	.475	.430
Lindsey	.500	2	2	0	1	1	0	0	0	0	0	0	0	1	0	0	0	0	.500	.500
Longmire	.231	11	13	1	3	3	0	0	0	1	0	0	0	1	0	0	0	0	.231	.231
Manto	.056	8	18	0	1	1	0	0	0	0	1	0	0	3	0	0	0	0	.056	.105
Mason	.333	34	3	0	1	1	0	0	0	0	0	0	0	1	0	0	0	0	.333	.333
Mauser	.000	8	4	0	0	0	0	0	0	0	0	1	0	2	0	0	0	0	.000	.200
Millette	.200	10	10	3	2	2	0	0	0	2	0	1	0	2	0	0	1	0	.200	.273
Morandini	.247	120	425	57	105	151	19	9	3	33	5	34	2	73	13	2	7	5	.355	.309
Mulholland	.065	29	62	3	4	4	0	0	0	0	0	1	0	27	0	0	0	2	.065	.079
Pratt	.287	33	87	8	25	46	6	0	5	13	1	5	0	19	0	0	2	2	.529	.330
Rivera	.098	30	51	3	5	5	0	0	0	0	0	3	0	24	0	0	0	1	.098	.148
Schilling	.147	34	75	3	11	12	1	0	0	2	0	2	0	19	0	0	0	0	.160	.169
Stocker	.324	70	259	46	84	108	12	3	2	31	8	30	11	43	5	0	8	14	.417	.409
Right	.381		84		32	37	5	0	0	7	0	13	5	9			3		.440	.464
Left	.297		175		52	71	7	3	2	24	8	17	6	34			5		.406	.383
Thigpen	.000	17	1	0	0	0	0	0	0	0	0	0	0	0	0	0	0	0	.000	.000
Thompson	.262	129	340	42	89	119	14	2	4	44	2	40	9	57	9	4	8	1	.350	.341
West	.400	76	5	0	2	3	1	0	0	2	0	0	0	2	0	0	0	2	.600	.400
Williams, Mt.	1.000	65	1	0	1	1	0	0	0	1	0	0	0	0	0	0	0	2	1.000	1.000
Williams, Mk.	.083	17	12	1	1	1	0	0	0	0	0	0	0	3	0	0	1	0	.083	.083
Pitchers	.130	162	368	23	48	60	6	0	2	17	1	15	0	144	0	0	3	15	.163	.166
Phillies	.274	162	5685	877	1555	2422	297	51	156	811	42	665	70	1049	91	32	107	141	.426	.351
Opponents	.252	162	5642	740	1419	2131	247	39	129	673	37	573	33	1117	101	49	93	138	.378	.322

Pitching

	W–L	ERA	G	GS	CG	GF	SV	IP	H	R	ER	HR	HB	BB	IBB	SO	WP	BK	AVG
Andersen	3–2	2.92	64	0	0	13	0	61.2	54	22	20	4	1	21	2	67	2	1	.233
Ayrault	2–0	9.58	10	0	0	3	0	10.1	18	11	11	1	1	10	1	8	1	0	.375
Brink	0–0	3.00	2	0	0	1	0	6.0	3	2	2	1	0	3	0	8	1	0	.143
Davis	1–2	5.17	25	0	0	4	0	31.1	35	22	18	4	1	24	1	28	1	0	.273
DeLeon	3–0	3.26	24	3	0	6	0	47.0	39	25	17	5	5	27	3	34	5	0	.231
Fletcher	0–0	0.00	1	0	0	0	0	0.1	0	0	0	0	0	0	0	0	1	0	.000
Foster	0–1	14.85	2	1	0	0	0	6.2	13	11	11	3	0	7	0	6	2	0	.394
Green	0–0	7.36	3	2	0	1	0	7.1	16	9	6	1	0	5	0	7	2	0	.444
Greene	16–4	3.42	31	30	7	0	0	200.0	175	84	76	12	3	62	3	167	15	0	.233
Jackson	12–11	3.77	32	32	2	0	0	210.1	214	105	88	12	4	80	2	120	4	0	.263
Mason	5–5	4.89	34	0	0	15	0	49.2	47	28	27	9	0	16	1	32	1	1	.246
Mauser	0–0	4.96	8	0	0	1	0	16.1	15	9	9	1	1	7	0	14	1	0	.238
Mulholland	12–9	3.25	29	28	7	0	0	191.0	177	80	69	20	3	40	2	116	5	0	.241
Pall	1–0	2.55	8	0	0	2	0	17.2	15	7	5	1	0	3	0	11	0	1	.231
Rivera	13–9	5.02	30	28	1	1	0	163.0	175	99	91	16	6	85	4	123	13	0	.273
Schilling	16–7	4.02	34	34	7	0	0	235.1	234	114	105	23	4	57	6	186	9	3	.259
Thigpen	3–1	6.05	17	0	0	5	0	19.1	23	13	13	2	1	9	1	10	0	1	.307
West	6–4	2.92	76	0	0	27	3	86.1	60	37	28	6	5	51	4	87	3	0	.194
Williams, Mt.	3–7	3.34	65	0	0	57	43	62.0	56	30	23	3	2	44	1	60	6	0	.245
Williams, Mk.	1–3	5.29	17	4	0	2	0	51.0	50	32	30	5	0	22	2	33	2	0	.253
Phillies	97–65	3.95	162	162	24	138	46	1472.2	1419	740	647	129	37	573	33	1117	74	7	.252
Opponents	65–97	4.79	162	162	2	160	42	1456.1	1555	877	775	156	42	665	70	1049	62	20	.274

Shutouts—Greene, Mulholland, Schilling 2, Jackson, Rivera 1.

DAY BY DAY IN 1993

Game	Date	Day	D/N	Club	W/L	Score	Winner (Record)	Loser (Record)	Crowd	Home Game	Total	Time	Pos.	G.A.	W–L
1	4/ 5	Mon	N	@ Houston	W	3-1	MULHOLLAND (1-0)	Drabek	44,560			2:10	1T	—	1-0
2	4/ 6	Tues	N	@ Houston	W	5-3	SCHILLING (1-0)	Swindell	18,686			2:38	1	1/2	2-0
3	4/ 7	Wed	N	@ Houston	W	6-3 (10)	DELEON (1-0)	Bell	16,471			3:17	1	1/2	3-0
4	4/ 9	Fri	D	Chicago	L	11-7	McElroy	RIVERA (0-1)	60,985	1	61,120	3:06	2	-1/2	3-1
5	4/10	Sat	N	Chicago	W	5-4	MULHOLLAND (2-0)	Morgan	21,081	2	82,201	2:16	1T	—	4-1
6	4/11	Sun	D	Chicago	W	3-0	SCHILLING (2-0)	Guzman	21,955	3	104,156	2:22	1	1	5-1
7	4/12	Mon	N	Cincinnati	W	5-4	DELEON (2-0)	Foster	20,107	4	124,263	2:37	1	1 1/2	6-1
8	4/13	Tues	N	Cincinnati	W	4-1	GREENE (1-0)	Belcher	20,482	5	144,745	2:26	1	1 1/2	7-1
9	4/14	Wed	N	Cincinnati	W	9-2	RIVERA (1-1)	Browning	21,111	6	165,856	2:43	1	1 1/2	8-1
10	4/16	Fri	D	@ Chicago	L	3-1	Morgan	MULHOLLAND (2-1)	16,255			2:21	1	1/2	8-2
11	4/17	Sat	D	@ Chicago	L	6-3	Guzman	SCHILLING (2-1)	32,680			2:58	1	1	8-3
12	4/18	Sun	D	@ Chicago	W	11-10 (11)	MtWILLIAMS (1-0)	Scanlan	28,758			3:36	1	2	9-3
13	4/20	Tues	N	San Diego	W	4-3 (14)	AYRAULT (1-0)	J.Hernandez	21,074	7	186,930	4:27	1	2	10-3
14	4/21	Wed	N	San Diego	PPD										
14	4/22	Thur	N	San Diego	L	2-1	Benes	MULHOLLAND (2-2)	15,826	8	202,756	2:36	1	1 1/2	10-4
15	4/23	Fri	N	Los Angeles	W	2-0	SCHILLING (3-1)	R.Martinez	21,702	9	224,458	2:22	1	1 1/2	11-4
16	4/24	Sat	N	Los Angeles	W	7-3	JACKSON (1-0)	Gross	37,457	10	261,915	2:59	1	1 1/2	12-4
17	4/25	Sun	D	Los Angeles	W	5-2	GREENE (2-0)	Candiotti	53,030	11	314,945	3:00	1	2 1/2	13-4
18	4/26	Mon	N	San Francisco	W	9-8 (10)	ANDERSEN (1-0)	Minutelli	17,170	12	332,115	4:33	1	3	14-4
19	4/27	Tues	D	San Francisco	L	6-3	Burkett	MULHOLLAND (2-3)	34,005	13	366,120	2:11	1	2	14-5
20	4/28	Wed	N	@ San Diego	W	5-3	SCHILLING (4-1)	Gr.Harris	10,905			2:34	1	3	15-5
21	4/29	Thur	D	@ San Diego	W	5-3	JACKSON (2-0)	Seminara	14,399			2:43	1	3 1/2	16-5
22	4/30	Fri	N	@ Los Angeles	W	7-6	AYRAULT (2-0)	Daal	43,679			3:34	1	4 1/2	17-5
23	5/ 1	Sat	N	@ Los Angeles	L	5-1	Candiotti	RIVERA (1-2)	44,023			2:55	1	3 1/2	17-6
24	5/ 2	Sun	D	@ Los Angeles	W	9-1	MULHOLLAND (3-3)	Hershiser	41,102			2:36	1	4 1/2	18-6
25	5/ 4	Tues	N	@ San Francisco	W	4-3 (12)	ANDERSEN (2-0)	Righetti	17,725			3:19	1	4 1/2	19-6
26	5/ 5	Wed	D	@ San Francisco	L	11-2	Swift	JACKSON (2-1)	20,289			2:42	1	4 1/2	19-7
27	5/ 7	Fri	N	St. Louis	W	4-3	GREENE (3-0)	Magrane	33,739	14	399,859	2:44	1	4 1/2	20-7
28	5/ 8	Sat	N	St. Louis	W	2-1 (10)	MULHOLLAND (4-3)	Perez	40,524	15	440,383	2:38	1	5 1/2	21-7
29	5/ 9	Sun	D	St. Louis	W	6-5	DAVIS (1-0)	L.Smith	43,648	16	484,031	2:33	1	6 1/2	22-7
30	5/10	Mon	N	Pittsburgh	W	5-1	JACKSON (3-1)	Walk	29,712	17	513,743	2:46	1	7	23-7
31	5/11	Tues	N	Pittsburgh	L	8-4	Wagner	DAVIS (1-1)	32,871	18	546,614	3:08	1	6	23-8
32	5/12	Wed	N	Pittsburgh	W	4-1	GREENE (4-0)	Tomlin	24,906	19	571,520	2:02	1	7	24-8
33	5/14	Fri	N	@ Atlanta	L	10-7	Glavine	MULHOLLAND (4-4)	48,449			2:47	1	6	24-9
34	5/15	Sat	N	@ Atlanta	L	5-3	G.Maddux	WEST (0-1)	48,425			2:41	1	4 1/2	24-10
35	5/16	Sun	D	@ Atlanta	W	5-4	JACKSON (4-1)	McMichael	48,890			3:01	1	4 1/2	25-10

Game	Date	Day	D/N	Club	W/L	Score	Winner (Record)	Loser (Record)	Crowd	Home Game	Total	Time	Pos.	G.A.	W–L
36	5/17	Mon	N	@ Florida	W	10-3	RIVERA (2-2)	Hough	38,519			3:24	1	5½	26-10
37	5/18	Tues	N	@ Florida	W	6-0	GREENE (5-0)	Armstrong	35,805			2:21	1	5½	27-10
38	5/19	Wed	N	@ Florida	L	5-3	R.Lewis	DAVIS (1-2)	33,970			2:36	1	5½	27-11
39	5/20	Thur	N	Montreal	W	9-3	SCHILLING (5-1)	Nabholz	28,123	20	599,643	2:51	1	6½	28-11
40	5/21	Fri	N	Montreal	L	6-2	K.Hill	JACKSON (4-2)	41,146	21	640,789	2:52	1	5½	28-12
41	5/22	Sat	N	Montreal	L	6-5	Fassero	MtWILLIAMS (1-1)	37,911	22	678,700	3:28	1	4½	28-13
42	5/23	Sun	D	Montreal	W	14-7	MULHOLLAND (5-4)	Heredia	52,911	23	731,611	3:23	1	5½	29-13
43	5/24	Mon	N	New York	W	6-3	GREENE (6-0)	Tanana	32,568	24	764,179	2:47	1	6½	30-13
44	5/25	Tues	N	New York	W	4-2	SCHILLING (6-1)	Schourek	34,578	25	798,757	2:55	1	6½	31-13
45	5/26	Wed	N	New York	L	5-4	Franco	MtWILLIAMS (1-2)	33,367	26	832,124	2:52	1	5½	31-14
46	5/28	Fri	N	@ Colorado	W	15-9	RIVERA (3-2)	B.Henry	58,312			3:17	1	6	32-14
47	5/29	Sat	D	@ Colorado	W	6-0	MULHOLLAND (6-4)	Blair	56,263			2:13	1	6	33-14
48	5/30	Sun	D	@ Colorado	W	18-1	GREENE (7-0)	Painter	56,710			2:38	1	7	34-14
49	5/31	Mon	N	@ Cincinnati	L	6-4	Reardon	ANDERSEN (2-1)	25,676			3:02	1	7	34-15
50	6/ 1	Tues	N	@ Cincinnati	W	6-3	ANDERSEN (3-1)	Cadaret	24,175			2:37	1	7	35-15
51	6/ 2	Wed	N	@ Cincinnati	W	5-2	RIVERA (4-2)	Smiley	25,904			2:29	1	8	36-15
52	6/ 4	Fri	N	Colorado	L	2-1	Blair	MULHOLLAND (6-5)	43,333	27	875,457	2:32	1	6½	36-16
53	6/ 5	Sat	N	Colorado	W	6-2	GREENE (8-0)	Reynoso	43,837	28	919,294	2:35	1	6½	37-16
54	6/ 6	Sun	D	Colorado	W	11-7	SCHILLING (7-1)	Ashby	55,714	29	975,008	3:24	1	7½	38-16
55	6/ 7	Mon	N	Houston	W	7-5	JACKSON (5-2)	Swindell	26,445	30	1,001,453	2:49	1	8½	39-16
56	6/ 8	Tues	N	Houston	L	6-3	Kile	RIVERA (4-3)	24,669	31	1,026,122	2:51	1	7½	39-17
57	6/ 9	Wed	N	Houston	W	8-0	MULHOLLAND (7-5)	Harnisch	25,389	32	1,051,511	2:22	1	8½	40-17
58	6/10	Thur	N	@ New York	W	7-6	WEST (1-1)	Gibson	22,377			3:11	1	9½	41-17
59	6/11	Fri	N	@ New York	W	5-2	SCHILLING (8-1)	Schourek	29,594			2:18	1	10½	42-17
60	6/12	Sat	N	@ New York	W	3-0	JACKSON (6-2)	Gooden	31,814			2:18	1	10½	43-17
61	6/13	Sun	D	@ New York	W	5-3	RIVERA (5-3)	A.Young	29,917			2:22	1	11½	44-17
62	6/14	Mon	N	@ Montreal	W	10-3	MULHOLLAND (8-5)	Shaw	13,235			2:46	1	11½	45-17
63	6/15	Tues	N	@ Montreal	L	8-4	Barnes	GREENE (8-1)	13,142			3:24	1	10½	45-18
64	6/16	Wed	N	@ Montreal	L	4-3 (10)	Rojas	WEST (1-2)	14,231			3:04	1	9½	45-19
65	6/17	Thur	N	Florida	L	4-1	Hammond	JACKSON (6-3)	38,855	33	1,090,366	2:29	1	8½	45-20
66	6/18	Fri	N	Florida	W	7-3	RIVERA (6-3)	Bowen	37,925	34	1,128,291	2:46	1	9½	46-20
67	6/19	Sat	N	Florida	W	5-2	MULHOLLAND (9-5)	Armstrong	50,391	35	1,178,682	2:45	1	9½	47-20
68	6/20	Sun	D	Florida	W	4-3	GREENE (9-1)	Hoffman	58,508	36	1,237,190	2:43	1	9½	48-20
69	6/21	Mon	N	Atlanta	L	8-1	G.Maddux	SCHILLING (8-2)	34,817	37	1,272,007	2:26	1	8½	48-21
70	6/22	Tues	N	Atlanta	W	5-3	JACKSON (7-3)	P.Smith	41,557	38	1,313,564	2:28	1	9½	49-21
71	6/23	Wed	D	Atlanta	W	8-3	RIVERA (7-3)	Smoltz	57,903	39	1,371,467	3:09	1	9½	50-21
72	6/25	Fri	N	@ Pittsburgh	W	8-6	DELEON (3-0)	Candelaria	21,173			3:21	1	9½	51-21
73	6/26	Sat	N	@ Pittsburgh	L	4-2	Cooke	SCHILLING (8-3)	39,439			2:15	1	8½	51-22

Game	Date	Day	D/N	Club	W/L	Score	Winner (Record)	Loser (Record)	Crowd	Home Game	Total	Time	Pos.	G.A.	W–L
74	6/27	Sun	D	@ Pittsburgh	L	4–3 (10)	Belinda	MtWILLIAMS (1–3)	27,824			2:47	1	7½	51–23
75	6/28	Mon	N	@ St. Louis	L	3–1	Cormier	JACKSON (7–4)	29,199			2:33	1	6½	51–24
76	6/29	Tues	N	@ St. Louis	W	13–10	RIVERA (8–3)	Urbani	39,344			3:21	1	7½	52–24
77	6/30	Wed	D	@ St. Louis	L	9–3	Osborne	GREENE (9–2)	32,022			2:52	1	6½	52–25
78	7/ 1	Thur	D	@ St. Louis	L	14–5	Tewksbury	SCHILLING (8–4)	39,610			2:25	1	5½	52–26
79	7/ 2	Fri	N	San Diego	L	5–2	Ettles	MULHOLLAND (9–6)	54,617	40	1,426,084	2:34	1		52–27
80				San Diego	W	6–5 (10)	MtWILLIAMS (2–3)	Hoffman				3:12	1	6	53–27
81	7/ 3	Sat	N	San Diego	L	6–4	Gr.Harris	JACKSON (7–5)	57,521	41	1,483,605	2:52	1	6	53–28
82	7/ 4	Sun	N	San Diego	W	8–4	RIVERA (9–3)	TiWorrell	33,379	42	1,516,984	2:57	1	7	54–28
83	7/ 5	Mon	N	Los Angeles	W	9–5	GREENE (10–2)	Hershiser	33,088	43	1,550,072	2:52	1	7	55–28
84	7/ 6	Tues	N	Los Angeles	L	7–5	Astacio	SCHILLING (8–5)	32,993	44	1,583,065	3:18	1	6	55–29
85	7/ 7	Wed	N	Los Angeles	W	7–6 (20)	MkWILLIAMS (1–0)	Trlicek	41,730	45	1,624,795	6:10	1	6	56–29
86	7/ 8	Thur	N	San Francisco	W	13–2	Swift	JACKSON (7–6)	37,745	46	1,662,540	2:58	1	5	56–30
87	7/ 9	Fri	N	San Francisco	L	15–8	Black	RIVERA (9–4)	38,695	47	1,701,235	3:07	1	5	56–31
88	7/10	Sat	D	San Francisco	W	8–3	GREENE (11–2)	Burkett	41,869	48	1,743,104	3:15	1	5	57–31
89	7/11	Sun	D	San Francisco	L	10–2	Hickerson	SCHILLING (8–6)	52,015	49	1,795,119	3:04	1	5	57–32
90	7/15	Thur	D	@ San Diego	L	5–2	Gr.Harris	JACKSON (7–7)	16,542			2:40	1	4	57–33
91	7/16	Fri	N	@ San Diego	L	5–3	P.A.Martinez	GREENE (11–3)	20,763			2:37	1	4	57–34
92	7/17	Sat	N	@ San Diego	L	4–2	Benes	MULHOLLAND (9–7)	32,505			2:34	1	3	57–35
93	7/18	Sun	D	@ San Diego	W	6–3	SCHILLING (9–6)	Brocail	12,569			2:41	1	3	58–35
94	7/19	Mon	N	@ Los Angeles	W	7–5	MASON (1–7)	Daal	33,615			3:12	1	3	59–35
95	7/20	Tues	N	@ Los Angeles	W	8–2	JACKSON (8–7)	R.Martinez	35,273			3:21	1	4	60–35
96	7/21	Wed	N	@ Los Angeles	W	7–0	GREENE (12–3)	Hershiser	47,819			2:46	1		61–35
97	7/22	Thur	D	@ San Francisco	L	4–1	Burkett	MULHOLLAND (9–8)	35,342			2:31	1	5	61–36
98	7/23	Fri	N	@ San Francisco	W	2–1 (14)	WEST (2–2)	M.Jackson	37,095			3:46	1	5	62–36
99	7/24	Sat	N	@ San Francisco	L	5–4	Burba	RIVERA (9–5)	51,557			2:57	1	4½	62–37
100	7/25	Sun	D	@ San Francisco	L	5–2	Swift	JACKSON (8–8)	49,935			2:34	1	4	62–38
101	7/27	Tues	N	St. Louis	W	10–7	MASON (2–7)	Magrane	45,383	50	1,840,502	3:30	1	5	63–38
102	7/28	Wed	N	St. Louis	W	14–6	MULHOLLAND (10–8)	Guetterman	46,346	51	1,886,848	3:00	1	6	64–38
103	7/29	Thur	D	St. Louis	W	6–4	WEST (3–2)	Murphy	55,861	52	1,942,709	3:12	1	7	65–38
104	7/30	Fri	N	Pittsburgh	L	4–2	Walk	RIVERA (9–6)	47,406	53	1,990,115	2:37	1	6	65–39
105	7/31	Sat	N	Pittsburgh	W	10–2	JACKSON (9–8)	Tomlin	48,171	54	2,038,286	2:40	1	6½	66–39
106	8/ 1	Sun	D	Pittsburgh	W	5–4	MASON (3–7)	Cooke	46,693	55	2,084,979	2:57	1	7	67–39
107	8/ 3	Tues	N	@ Atlanta	W	5–3	MULHOLLAND (11–8)	Avery	49,102			2:34	1	7½	68–39
108	8/ 4	Wed	N	@ Atlanta	L	9–8	Howell	WEST (3–3)	46,144			3:02	1	6½	68–40
109	8/ 5	Thur	N	@ Atlanta	W	10–4	RIVERA (10–6)	G.Maddux	49,070			3:14	1	6½	69–40
110	8/ 6	Fri	N	@ Florida	L	4–3	Aquino	MASON (3–8)	43,670			2:54	1	6½	69–41
111	8/ 7	Sat	N	@ Florida	W	8–7 (10)	MtWILLIAMS (3–3)	Turner	44,689			4:12	1	6½	70–41

Game	Date	Day	D/N	Club	W/L	Score	Winner (Record)	Loser (Record)	Crowd	Home Game	Total	Time	Pos.	G.A.	W–L
112	8/ 8	Sun	N	@ Florida	L	6–5	Hough	MULHOLLAND (11–9)	43,186			2:36	1	6½	70–42
113	8/10	Tues	N	Montreal	W	5–2	SCHILLING (10–6)	Nabholz	43,104	56	2,128,083	2:23	1	6	71–42
114	8/11	Wed	N	Montreal	W	6–5	WEST (4–3)	Wetteland	45,260	57	2,173,343	2:57	1	7	72–42
115	8/12	Thur	D	Montreal	W	7–4	MASON (4–8)	Scott	45,002	58	2,218,345	3:06	1	8	73–42
116	8/13	Fri	N	New York	W	9–5	THIGPEN (1–0)	A.Young	40,552	59	2,258,897	2:41	1	9	74–42
117	8/14	Sat	N	New York	L	9–5	B.Jones	JACKSON (9–9)	46,393	60	2,305,290	2:42	1	8	74–43
118	8/15	Sun	D	New York	W	5–4	WEST (5–3)	A.Young	58,103	61	2,363,393	2:37	1	9	75–43
119	8/17	Tues	N	@ Colorado	W	10–7	RIVERA (11–6)	Reynoso	63,193			3:21	1	9	76–43
120	8/18	Wed	N	@ Colorado	W	7–6	THIGPEN (2–0)	B.Ruffin	61,056			3:09	1	9	77–43
121	8/19	Thur	D	@ Colorado	L	6–5	M.Moore	MASON (4–9)	53,443			2:58	1	8	77–44
122	8/20	Fri	N	@ Houston	W	6–4	WEST (6–3)	T.Jones	33,080			3:06	1	9	78–44
123	8/21	Sat	N	@ Houston	L	3–2 (10)	D.Jones	ANDERSEN (3–2)	27,507			3:06	1	9	78–45
124	8/22	Sun	D	@ Houston	L	7–3	Kile	RIVERA (11–7)	28,940			2:25	1	9	78–46
125	8/23	Mon	N	Colorado	L	3–2 (13)	Wayne	MASON (4–10)	40,481	62	2,403,874	4:03	1	9	78–47
126	8/24	Tues	N	Colorado	W	4–2	JACKSON (10–9)	Blair	43,419	63	2,447,293	2:30	1	10	79–47
127	8/25	Wed	D	Colorado	W	8–5	SCHILLING (11–6)	Sanford	46,448	64	2,493,741	2:48	1	11	80–47
128	8/27	Fri	N	Cincinnati	L	8–5	Ruffin	MtWILLIAMS (3–4)	41,540	65	2,535,281	2:54	1	10	80–48
129	8/28	Sat	N	Cincinnati	W	9–5	Service	THIGPEN (2–1)	42,924	66	2,578,205	3:14	1	9	80–49
130	8/29	Sun	N	Cincinnati	W	12–0	JACKSON (11–9)	Pugh	58,363	67	2,636,568	2:47	1	10	81–49
131	8/30	Mon	N	@ Chicago	L	10–6 (11)	Pesac	MASON (4–11)	33,276			3:41	1	9½	81–50
132	8/31	Tues	D	@ Chicago	W	7–0	RIVERA (12–7)	Morgan	19,951			2:31	1	9½	82–50
133	9/ 1	Wed	D	@ Chicago	W	4–1	MULHOLLAND (12–9)	Harkey	23,519			2:25	1	9½	83–50
134	9/ 3	Fri	N	@ Cincinnati	W	14–2	GREENE (13–3)	Ayala	26,157			2:39	1	9½	84–50
135	9/ 4	Sat	N	@ Cincinnati	L	6–5	Rijo	JACKSON (11–10)	31,166			2:46	1	8½	84–51
136	9/ 5	Sun	D	@ Cincinnati	W	5–3	SCHILLING (12–6)	Pugh	28,741			3:01	1	9½	85–51
137	9/ 6	Mon	N	Chicago	L	7–6	Harkey	MKWILLIAMS (1–1)	30,765	68	2,667,333	2:53	1	8½	85–52
138	9/ 7	Tues	N	Chicago	L	5–4	Guzman	RIVERA (12–8)	27,041	69	2,694,374	2:48	1	7½	85–53
139	9/ 8	Wed	N	Chicago	L	8–5	Hibbard	WEST (6–4)	26,553	70	2,720,927	2:56	1	6½	85–54
140	9/ 9	Thur	D	Chicago	W	10–8	JACKSON (12–10)	Bautista	25,894	71	2,746,821	3:13	1	7	86–54
141	9/10	Fri	N	Houston	W	6–2	SCHILLING (13–6)	Swindell	31,146	72	2,777,967	2:38	1	7	87–54
142	9/11	Sat	N	Houston	L	4–1	Portugal	MKWILLIAMS (1–2)	45,738	73	2,823,705	2:49	1	6	87–55
143	9/12	Sun	D	Houston	L	9–2	Harnisch	RIVERA (12–9)	46,238	74	2,869,943	3:08	1	5	87–56
144	9/13	Mon	N	@ New York	W	5–0	GREENE (14–3)	B.Jones	17,497			2:49	1	5½	88–56
145	9/14	Tues	N	@ New York	L	5–4	Tanana	JACKSON (12–11)	18,292			2:37	1	4½	88–57
146	9/15	Wed	N	@ New York	W	6–3	SCHILLING (14–6)	Schourek	18,632			2:55	1	5½	89–57
147	9/17	Fri	N	@ Montreal	L	8–7 (12)	Scott	MtWILLIAMS (3–5)	45,757			4:30	1	4	89–58
148	9/18	Sat	N	@ Montreal	W	5–4	GREENE (15–3)	Boucher	50,438			2:49	1	5	89–58
149	9/19	Sun	D	@ Montreal	L	6–5	Scott	MtWILLIAMS (3–6)	40,047			3:27	1	4	90–59

Game	Date	Day	D/N	Club	W/L	Score	Winner (Record)	Loser (Record)	Crowd	Home Game Total	Time	Pos.	G.A.	W–L
150	9/20	Mon	N	Florida	W	7–1	SCHILLING (15–6)	Hough	31,454	75	2,901,397	2:28	1	4½	91–59
151	9/21	Tues	N	Florida	W	5–3	PALL (1–0)	Rodriguez	32,165	76	2,933,562	2:36	1	5½	92–59
152	9/22	Wed	N	Florida	W	2–1 (12)	MASON (5–11)	Harvey	31,556	77	2,965,118	3:55	1	5½	93–59
153	9/24	Fri	N	Atlanta	W	3–0	GREENE (16–3)	Glavine	57,792	78	3,022,910	2:50	1	6	94–59
154	9/25	Sat	D	Atlanta	L	9–7	Bedrosian	MASON (5–12)	57,176	79	3,080,086	3:43	1	5	94–60
155	9/26	Sun	D	Atlanta	L	7–2	Avery	SCHILLING (15–7)	57,588	80	3,137,674	3:13	1	5	94–61
156	9/27	Mon	N	@ Pittsburgh	W	6–4	RIVERA (13–9)	Cooke	15,847			3:04	1	6	95–61
157	9/28	Tues	N	@ Pittsburgh	W	10–7	THIGPEN (3–1)	Robertson	17,386			2:54	1	6	96–61
158	9/29	Wed	N	@ Pittsburgh	L	9–1	Walk	FOSTER (0–1)	21,159			2:32	1	5	96–62
159	9/30	Thur	N	@ Pittsburgh	L	5–0	Wakefield	GREENE (16–4)	10,448			2:22	1	4	96–63
160	10/1	Fri	N	@ St. Louis	W	4–2	SCHILLING (16–7)	Olivares	26,870			2:24	1	4	97–63
161	10/2	Sat	D	@ St. Louis	L	5–4 (10)	Murphy	MkWILLIAMS (1–3)	31,501			2:52	1	4	97–64
162	10/3	Sun	D	@ St. Louis	L	2–0	Guetterman	MtWILLIAMS (3–7)	40,247			2:11	1	3	97–65

About the Author

Rich Westcott is publisher and editor of *Phillies Report,* the oldest, continuous baseball team newspaper in the nation. He is co-author with Frank Bilovsky of both *The Phillies Encyclopedia* (originally published in 1984) and *The New Phillies Encyclopedia* (1993). Westcott is the author of *Diamond Greats,* a book of interviews and profiles of 65 former major league players, and a second book of interviews, *Masters of the Diamond,* being published in 1994. Westcott has served as a writer and editor on the staffs of a number of newspapers and magazines in the Philadelphia and Baltimore areas. A native of Philadelphia, he is a graduate of the William Penn Charter School and Drexel University, and holds a master's degree from Johns Hopkins University.

Acknowledgments

The author wishes to thank Alan Kravetz for taking the photographs for this book; Jack Carney, Jon Marks and Mike Schwager for their articles in *Phillies Report* that provided useful material; and Larry Shenk and the Phillies for statistical and other information.